VEGETABLES

VEGETABLES

ROGER PHILLIPS & MARTYN RIX

Assisted by James Compton and Alison Rix
Layout by Jill Bryan, Gillian Stokoe and Lucy Su

RANDOM HOUSE NEW YORK

Acknowledgements

We would like to thank Mike Day and the staff of the National Institute of Agricultural Botany Cambridge for their help with checking the text, and with many of the specimens; Colin Martin and The Royal Horticultural Society's Garden at Wisley for numerous specimens from the model vegetable garden. James Compton for help with the *Cucurbitaceae*; Anthony Rix for the many pictures and specimens from Malawai, and the Chinese Agricultural Mission; Sam Phillips for his photographs taken in Bolivia; Leslie Land for specimens and pictures from Cushing, Maine; Peter Maine for the specimens of old potatoes, and M. and Mme. Carvallo of Villandry for allowing us to photograph there.

The following also helped us by allowing us to take photographs in their gardens, and in other ways: Roger Holland, George Fuller, Bill Chowings, Alan and Carolyn Hardy, Harry Hay, Jacqui Hurst, Andrew Paterson, Ted Rix, Charles and Brigid Quest-Ritson, Gill Stokoe, Anne Thatcher, Rosemary Verey.

Published in the United States by
Random House, Inc., New York
First published in Great Britain in 1993 by
Pan Books Ltd,
a division of Pan Macmillan Publishers Limited, London

9 8 7 6 5 4 3 2 1

Text and illustrations copyright © 1993 by Roger Phillips and Martyn Rix

Library of Congress Cataloging-in-Publication Data

Rix, Martyn

  The Random House book of vegetables / by Martin Rix and Roger Phillips
    p.   cm.
  ISBN 0-679-75024-X
  1. Vegetable gardening.   2. Vegetables   I. Phillips, Roger
  1932– .   II. Title.
  SB321.R57 1994
  635—dc20   93-13857

Manufactured in Singapore by
Toppan Printing Co. (S) Pte. Ltd.

Contents

The Potager at Barnsley House

Introduction

In this book we illustrate over 650 different vegetables; we have concentrated on those suitable for temperate climates, but have also covered some which require greenhouse cultivation in areas with cool summers, such as the British Isles, northern Europe or the extreme northeast of North America. We have included a selection of Chinese vegetables, as their cultivation and cooking is becoming more and more popular in North America and Europe. We have not included edible grains such as wheat and barley, or oil seeds such as rape, which are nearly always grown by the field, rather than in the vegetable garden.

The Photographs

When shooting plants in the garden or in the wild, it is preferable to work with a tripod, so that you can take the opportunity to use a slow shutter speed and therefore a smaller aperture, giving a greater depth of vision. In practice the best speed to use is normally 1/15th sec., although if there is a wind you may have to go to 1/30th or even 1/60th. In very bright light conditions, the camera can be hand held with speed set at 1/60th sec.

The studio shots are taken on a Hassleblad 500 C/M, with a normal lens, with a flash as a light source. The field shots are taken in natural light with a Nikon FM. The film in both cases is Ektachrome 64, that used for the field shots being pushed one stop in development. Several different exposures are taken of each shot, one as indicated by the camera's exposure meter, the others half or one stop above and below that indicated. On an automatic camera the same effect may be had by changing the film speed indicator.

The Order

The vegetables are arranged in families and the families in a traditional botanical order, beginning with the *Cruciferae* (often called *Brassicaceae*), which includes cabbages, turnips and radishes, and ending with the monocotyledons, including onions and edible grasses such as sweetcorn. This is the same order that is used in our books on Perennials, though in that case the plants were also divided according to flowering time.

The Families

The plant families from which vegetables have been developed are listed below in alphabetical order, with notes on what parts of the plant are naturally or have been developed to be edible. As will be seen, the Chinese have been particularly innovative and clever in developing, by selection, different vegetables from the same plant. Europeans have been much less creative, only beet and the common cabbage having been developed into several distinct vegetables.

Important families

Alliaceae (p. 240)   Onions, garlic, leeks and chives belong to this family. In most cases it is their bulbs which are eaten, but in leeks and spring onions the elongated leaf bases are also edible, and the Chinese eat the blanched flowering stems of both garlic and Chinese chives. The characteristic onion and garlic smells are caused by alkyl sulphides which are found throughout the genus *Allium* and in other genera of the *Alliaceae* such as *Tulbaghia*.

Chenopodiaceae (p. 70)   Spinach and leaf beet are the most common green vegetables in this family. Beet has also been developed as sugar beet and beetroot, in which the edible part is the swollen base of the stem. In Swiss Chard the leaf-stalks are enlarged and succulent. Rarer vegetables include Good King Henry and orach. Many of these leaf vegetables, particularly spinach, are very high in vitamins and minerals such as iron, and should be cooked so that the water is absorbed, not thrown away.

Compositae (p. 202)   The daisy family contains such widely different vegetables as the Jerusalem artichoke, with its potato-like tubers, the Globe artichoke with its edible thistle-like flower heads, the chicory with its blanched leaves and the lettuce. The Chinese, ever ingenious, have developed celtuce or asparagus lettuce, with a thickened edible stem, and in France dandelions are grown for salad, looking not unlike the weed though leafier and tasting less bitter. Sunflowers are grown for their large, edible seeds. The tubers of Jerusalem artichoke (and those of the rare Andean vegetable yacon), contain inulin, rather than the commoner starch or sugar, and are suitable for diabetics, or as a substitute for potatoes.

Cruciferae (p. 18)   The cabbage family contains a great range of vegetables, developed in both Europe and China. In most it is the leaves (cabbage), flowering stems (cauliflower) or swollen roots (radish) which are eaten, but there is a radish with edible fruits in central Asia. In Europe, rape is grown for the oil in its seeds, and the same species has been developed into the turnip, but in China it has also been developed into different leafy vegetables.

Cucurbitaceae (p. 174)   Marrows, courgettes and cucumbers belong to this family. Most of the species are tropical American and it is the fruits that are eaten, often when immature and including the seeds. The large flowers of the marrows are edible though insubstantial. The starchy tuberous roots of the Mexican chayote are also eaten after boiling. In other tropical species such as the Oyster nut, *Telfairia pedata*, the seeds are the main edible portion of the plant, and some varieties of water melon are grown primarily for their huskless seeds.

Vegetable terraces in Madeira

An ancient vegetable, *Lathyrus sativus*

Graminae (p. 238)   The grass family contains the staple crops of all the advanced civilizations: wheat, maize and rice. Few, however, are eaten fresh as vegetables, except for the different varieties of sweetcorn. The swollen leaf bases of two other grasses are eaten in eastern Asia. Lemon grass, *Cymbopogon citratus*, is chopped finely and used as a flavouring, and *Zizania aquatica*, the wild rice, is eaten when its leaf bases are swollen due to infection by a fungus. The same species is collected as a grain by the North American Indians. Bamboo shoots are also commonly eaten in China, not only the young shoots of the giant tropical *Dendrocalamus latiflorus*, but also the thinner shoots of the temperate *Phyllostachys*.

Labiatae (p. 172)   Rich though it is in species of herbs used for flavouring, such as thyme, mint, sage and oregano, the family *Labiatae* has produced few vegetables. Edible tuberous roots are found in species of Woundwort i.e. *Stachys affinis*, the Chinese artichoke, and in the African genus *Plectranthus*.

Leguminosae (p. 82)   Most of the edible legumes produce pods of large seeds, which may be poisonous until cooked. In several species, such as snowpeas and French beans, the young pods are edible, and in China, peas and alfalfa are also grown for their young leafy shoots. A few species also produce edible root tubers – most common being the North American *Apios tuberosa* and the Mexican jicama, *Pachyrrhizus erosus*, which has a root like a turnip. The use of sprouting beans and peas is traditional in China, and the sprouts contain large quantities of vitamins not present in the dried seeds. Sprouts are edible both raw or quickly cooked, whereas many beans must be boiled until well cooked to break down poisonous alkaloids in the dry bean.

Solanaceae (p. 134)   The nightshade family produces a very valuable range of vegetables, almost all developed in Central and South America. Potatoes, tomatoes and peppers were all unknown in Europe and Asia until the Spaniards brought seeds back from Mexico and Columbia in the late fifteenth century. Even then many were at first viewed with considerable suspicion, as the European members of the family were mostly extremely poisonous. The only edible *Solanum* which originated outside America was the aubergine, thought to be a native of India. Potatoes, even when boiled, are very rich in vitamins, especially vitamin C and niacin.

Umbelliferae (p. 114)   The carrot family has been developed to produce edible roots, fleshy leaf stalks as in celery and Florence fennel and a swollen stem base in celeriac. Both parsley and a leaf variety of celery provide edible and aromatic leaves for salads. Carrots are a traditional and very rich source of vitamin A.

Lesser families   The following families have provided only one or two vegetables each, and most are grown in small quantities only. The most important are the *Araceae*, *Convolvulaceae* and *Dioscoriaceae* which produce Taro, Sweet potatoes and Yams, tubers which are widely grown in the tropics.
Aizoaceae – New Zealand spinach
Alismataceae – Arrowhead tubers
Amaranthaceae – Chinese spinach, Pigweed
Araceae – Taro, Dasheen, Elephant yam
Basellaceae – Ulluco, Ceylon spinach
Convolvulaceae – Sweet potato, Water spinach
Cyperaceae – Water chestnut
Dioscoriaceae – Yams
Liliaceae – Lily bulbs
Malvaceae – Okra, Mallow
Nymphaeaceae – Lotus root
Oxalidaceae – Oca
Tropaeolaceae – Anu
Valerianaceae – Lamb's lettuce
Zingiberaceae – Ginger, Turmeric

History of Vegetables

A modern vegetable garden contains plants originating from the different continents of the world, some cultivated for many thousands of years, others only recently developed. Primitive man was often very hungry and made use of any non-poisonous wild plants which he encountered in his wanderings in search of food. Only a few of these were ever taken into cultivation when man became settled, and even fewer have been developed into the

A giant aroid, *Amorphophallus*, in a garden on Mount Omei

economic vegetables, cultivated on a large scale today. Not only have vegetables been spread by man all over the world, but varieties have been developed which will grow in climates far removed from their natural range. Vegetables such as tomatoes which originated in the tropics can now be grown far north, and frost-hardy varieties of others such as potatoes are one of the goals of modern plant breeders.

Our knowledge of the food plants of early man comes from archaeology, ancient art and literature. Most vegetables, because of their soft and fleshy nature, do not survive longer than a few months when buried, but seeds, especially if they are charred, are often found on archaeological sites, and provide the major evidence for the antiquity of many of the vegetables now cultivated.

Northern Europe   Very few of the vegetables grown today originated in northwestern Europe. One can easily imagine the first inhabitants of Britain, who lived mainly on the coast anyway, varying their diet of shellfish and meat with sea beet, marsh samphire or the young shoots of seakale – and possibly a mouthful or two of wild celery and wild carrot leaves. While collecting the eggs of seabirds they would have come across the wild cabbage, and rock samphire with its fleshy, aromatic leaves. One of the most striking pieces of evidence we have of early vegetable eating in northern Europe is the stomach contents of the bodies found in peat bogs in Denmark, dating from the Iron Age, about the fourth century AD; two of the more famous are Tollund and Graubolle man. Shortly before being murdered, Tollund man had eaten a wide range of seeds, including six-row barley, *Polygonum*, *Camelina*, *Chenopodium* and *Spergula*. Graubolle man had eaten sixty-four species altogether, including emmer, spelt, oats, *Polygonum lapathifolium*, *Rumex acetosella*, *Chenopodium* and *Plantago*. One cannot help wondering whether such a varied diet was usual, or whether these were ritual murders in which the victims were carrying a good range of seeds down to the underworld, either as a sacrifice to obtain, or a thanksgiving after, a good harvest. *Spergula arvensis*, the corn spurry, now commonly found as a weed in cornfields, was grown as a crop in the Shetlands until this century, especially in its large-seeded form, var. *sativa*, called meal plant. *Camelina*, the Gold-of-Pleasure, was also grown until quite recently for its oil-rich edible seeds. *Spergula arvensis*, *Polygonum lapathifolium* and *Rumex acetosella* are all well known for their tolerance of acid soils and cool weather, so would have been particularly valuable in northwestern Europe in Iron Age times. Wheat, oats and barley, originating in western Asia, did not do as well in northern Europe then as they do today.

The Mediterranean, the Middle East, Egypt and Central Asia   The earliest archaeological evidence of crop cultivation has been found in the so-called Fertile Crescent, stretching from present-day Iraq and Syria to Egypt. Here the first cities were based on an agricultural economy which grew the primitive wheats Emmer and Einkorn, barley, flax, peas and lentils. The earliest remains of lentils date from about 8000 BC in Jericho; the earliest peas date from about a thousand years later, and were found at Jarmo in Iraq. A common vegetable at that time was *Lathyrus sativus*, the blue vetchling, which was valuable in dry areas both as a fodder crop and as a pea substitute in times of drought; the seeds are slightly toxic, however, if eaten in quantity.

All these seeds were preserved by being carbonized. They are smaller than present-day cultivated varieties, though they are thought to have been cultivated rather than collected wild.

Onions and carrots are thought to have originated further east in Afghanistan or central Asia. Evidence for the cultivation of onions, garlic and black radishes in Egypt dates back to about 3200 BC. Cucumbers and melons, leeks, onions and garlic are mentioned among the good things the Israelites regretted leaving behind in Egypt after the Exodus in around 1500 BC, when they were fed up with a diet of manna. By Greek and Roman times there is ample literary evidence of the range of vegetables which were grown. The Romans grew and appreciated such delicacies as asparagus and globe artichokes, and appear to have developed

A greengrocer in Kashmir

cabbages, cauliflower and thick-stemmed kale or broccoli.

The cultivated carrot was brought from the east by the Arabs in about the tenth century AD, probably from Afghanistan. It was originally white or deep red in colour with the pigment anthocyanin, as it is at present in parts of Pakistan. Orange-coloured carrots, containing the pigment carotene, first appeared in Holland in the sixteenth century.

North America   Few cultivated vegetables originated in North America; those that did were overshadowed by the great variety already domesticated in Mexico and the Andes when Europeans arrived. Jerusalem artichokes were possibly cultivated by the Indians, and were first recorded by Samuel Chaplin at Nausett Harbour, Massachusetts in 1605. The tuberous bean, *Apios americana*, was never developed as a vegetable and neither was wild rice, in spite of its hardiness and the large size and good food value of its grains. Other bulbs such as *Camassia*, *Calochortus* and *Fritillaria camschatcensis* were commonly eaten by the Indians in different areas, but never grown for food. More details of wild food plants in North America can be found in Roger Phillips' *Wild Food* (Little, Brown 1986).

Mexico and South America   Although the Fertile Crescent is generally considered to be the cradle of civilization, there is even earlier evidence for the cultivation of vegetables in Central and South America. In the Guitarrero cave deposits in Peru there is evidence for the use, if not the cultivation, of beans and squashes from about 10,000 BC onwards and remains of cultivated potatoes found near Lake Titicaca and the Chilca canyon in the dry coastal area date from around 8000 BC.

In Mexico, also, cucurbits were probably cultivated about 8500 BC, as remains of *Cucurbita pepo*, the summer squash, have been found in caves in the Oaxaca valley dating from this time. Maize originated in Mexico, and the early civilizations of the Mayas, the Aztecs and the Incas were based on the cultivation of maize, squashes and beans.

9

Planting out peppers in Sichuan

Evidence for the early domestication of maize and common beans is found in caves in the Tehuacan area south of Mexico City, and dates from about 5000 BC, and Tepary beans are found at slightly higher levels dated at about 3000 BC. Seeds of peppers appear in the earliest deposits, dated about 7000 BC, but these may have been gathered in the wild rather than cultivated. Weedy annuals such as peppers and tomatoes would be likely inhabitants of waste ground or dung deposits around early cave sites, and therefore among the earliest plants cultivated, perhaps unintentionally, by man, since their seeds pass through the stomach with their viability unimpaired. Large-scale agriculture based on maize is generally considered to have begun in Mexico in around 5000 BC, and spread southwards. Potatoes remained especially important in the high Andes where the growing season was too short for maize to be a worthwhile crop.

China and eastern Asia Vegetables were first cultivated by man in tropical Asia, perhaps as early as 8000 BC. Yams and taro were probably the first plants to be grown, as they are easily propagated and thrive in rich wet soil along rivers in areas which are flooded in the monsoon. They will also thrive in areas of forest newly cleared by burning, and this shifting cultivation is still widely practised in the tropics. As they are grown for their tubers and leaves, their remains have not been preserved.

Rice is often thought to be a native of India, but probably originated in the warm, wet parts of southwestern China, Thailand or Malaya in about 7000 BC. An ingenious theory correlates the beginnings of rice culture with the rise in sea level at the end of the last ice age, which flooded large areas of southeast Asia. The resulting increase in the concentration of the human population forced the people to rely on agriculture rather than hunting and gathering wild food. The earliest known archaeological records of rice are from about 5000 BC in northern Thailand, but records from further north in China date from about 4000 BC, while the oldest definite record from India is from 2500 BC.

The soybean is the most important present-day food plant that is a native of China. Its use is recorded from about 1000 BC, and it is considered to have originated in northeastern China, spreading throughout southeast Asia by the third century BC. Most of the very diverse range of vegetables now grown in temperate China are of relatively recent origin, many having been developed since regular trade with Europe began in the fifteenth century. The hot food of Sichuan, based as it is on the liberal use of chili peppers,

must have developed since the sixteenth century, though other spices such as the true pepper (*Piper nigrum*) were used before this time.

One grain which probably did originate in China is the foxtail millet, *Setaria italica*, which was cultivated in the loess areas of the northwest about 5000 BC. Common Millet, *Panicum miliaceum*, is also recorded from deposits in China dating from around this time, and may have originated here. There are, however, even earlier records of its use in Greece.

Africa Of the common vegetables which originated in Africa, the cowpea is today the most important. Wild cowpeas are found across the southern Saharan area, and they were probably domesticated first in West Africa or in Ethiopia. From here they spread to India about two thousand years ago, and to China, where the yard-long bean was developed.

Early agriculture in Africa was based on millets, notably sorghum and pearl or bulrush millet, and their cultivation dates from about 4000 to 3000 BC. There is doubt whether African agriculture began in Ethiopia with people who had migrated from the Middle East, or whether it originated independently in West Africa, the likely origin of pearl millet. These millets also spread by sea to India about 1000 BC. African yams, *Dioscorea rotundata* and *D. cayensis*, are also of great antiquity as cultivated plants. They spread to central America and the Caribbean with the slave

Bamboos round a Sichuan farmhouse

trade, and there became important crops alongside the native American species.

The Kalahari desert and other dry areas of southern Africa are the native habitat of the Water melon, which was a valuable source of food and water for the bushmen.

Cultivation

This book does not set out to be a manual for the cultivation of vegetables. That job is admirably done by other books, notably *The Vegetable Garden Displayed* first published by the Royal Horticultural Society in 1941 as part of the wartime efforts to grow more food. The most recent edition, by Joy Larkcom, was published in 1991. A similar guide for North America is *The Home Vegetable Garden Handbook no. 69* from the Brooklyn Botanic Garden. We have, however, provided brief notes on cultivation, enough for reasonable crops to be grown by an amateur, and mostly based on our own experience.

Number of days to maturity

American vegetable books and seed catalogues often cite the number of days a particular variety takes to reach maturity. This is based on results obtained in the eastern part of the United States, and can vary with growing conditions, temperature and so on. A variety of sweetcorn which matures in seventy days in eastern America may take a week or more longer in cooler parts of the United States or Canada, and fifty to sixty days longer to mature in southern England, or on cool parts of the west coast, in an average summer. Similar information for England is found in the Wisley Handbook, *Vegetable Varieties for the Gardener*.

Fertilizers and plant nutrients

Most chemical fertilizers, and many based on natural materials, give a breakdown of the plant nutrients they contain. The main nutrients are nitrogen (N), phosphate (P) and potassium (K). Minor amounts of other nutrients, especially magnesium, calcium and iron, are required by plants but they are present in most soils, and are often added to commercial fertilizers. On some soils they may be present but not available to the plant. Other nutrients required in minute amounts only are called trace elements, and are also often added to commercial fertilizers, though they are amply present in most soils.

'Organic' versus 'Inorganic'

The current vogue for so-called organic gardening should really be called 'gardening without chemicals', or possibly 'natural gardening'. In chemistry, the term *organic* means that the

South facing raised beds at Trengwainton, Cornwall

Tagetes as a biological control

substance referred to contains carbon and hydrogen atoms, while the term *inorganic* indicates that the substance referred to does not contain carbon and hydrogen atoms.

Two distinct topics, manuring and pest control, have become confused in this context. Those who prefer not to use chemicals are of the opinion that plants grow and taste better when fertilized with farmyard manure, compost or some similar substance ('organic'), than with purer chemicals which also contain the required nutrients (inorganic). The humus content of bulky manures is certainly beneficial to soil structure on many soils, and so to plant growth, and encourages the bacterial and fungal soil organisms. Concentrated chemical fertilizers are also more likely to leach quickly into the groundwater, and so are not only wasted, but positively harmful when, as has happened in many areas, nitrates in the water are concentrated enough to affect human health.

In this context it is worth mentioning that rock phosphate, one of the major sources of phosphate in chemical fertilizers, is an entirely natural substance. Before this was imported in quantity, much phosphate fertilizer was made from animal and even human bones. Similarly natural origins can be found for nitrogen, derived from Chilean nitrate, and for potash, which comes from saltpetre (potassium nitrate) and potassium chloride from the Dead Sea, and from Kainite, mined in Germany, which is a mixture of sodium chloride (salt), potassium and magnesium chloride. Although these substances are of natural origin, they are relatively pure and easily leached. A longer-lasting potash source is rock potash, derived from Adularian shale, mined in Scotland. Other fertilizers, such as sulphate of ammonia, are produced by purely artificial means.

Further details of natural fertilizers and composts can be found in *Month by Month Organic Gardening* by Lawrence D. Hills, published by the Henry Doubleday Research Association.

Nitrogen-loving and phosphate-potash-loving crops

Different vegetables require and use up different nutrients. Leaf vegetables such as spinach or lettuce generally need ample nitrogen to form lush leaves, and similar amounts are needed by gross feeders such as marrows and pumpkins which produce large fruit. This can be supplied either by farmyard or other manure, or by chemical nitrogen such as sulphate of ammonia, which is best on alkaline soils, or nitro-chalk (calcium carbonate combined with ammonium nitrate), which is best on acid soils.

Peas and beans not only need less nitrogen to produce their seeds, but also have the capacity to obtain nitrogen from the atmosphere by means of bacteria-filled nodules on their roots. Their main fertilizer requirements are for phosphate, and to a lesser extent for potash. Potash is supplied either by applying bonfire ash to the soil, in which case it is the highly soluble

Joy Larkcom's Potager in Suffolk

potassium carbonate which is available to the plant, or by using high-potash fertilizer.

Root crops such as carrots and parsnips will make too much leaf growth if given too much nitrogen; they need a balanced fertilizer with sufficient potash to encourage good root production and assist in the formation of sugars. Starchy roots such as potatoes also benefit from extra potash.

Fruit crops such as tomatoes also store sugar; here nitrogen is needed in sufficient quantity to build up a good plant, and then, after the onset of flowering, high potash and phosphate are needed to benefit fruit production and ripening.

Farmyard Manure and Compost

The use of ample organic manure is fundamental to the success of most vegetable gardens, and especially to those newly created on sandy or clay soils. Organic matter provides food for plants, especially nitrogen and phosphate; sandy and light chalky soils are improved because the humus holds more water, and clay soils are made more easily workable.

Organic matter for vegetable gardens is traditionally provided by using farmyard manure, generally from cows or horses, mixed with straw, or more rarely with peat. Ideally the manure should be heaped up in a pile at least 1.5 m high and across and allowed to heat up so that the straw is rotted by the bacteria. After a few weeks the pile is turned so that the unrotted straw around the edge is put into the middle of the heap to rot down. The finished manure is very dark brown throughout, and crumbly rather than soggy, often containing bright pink, banded worms, called by fishermen, brandlings. It can be put on the garden, either on the surface or well dug in so that the most vigorous roots of the plants reach it. Only really greedy plants such as marrows, summer squashes and leaf beet thrive in newly manured ground, where the ample nitrogen makes them put on lush, leafy growth. For most vegetables it is better to spread manure before the winter frost and

dig it well in so that the frost can get to the surface of the soil and make it easier to produce a good surface for planting in spring, and worms can work the manure into the soil beneath.

A traditional open manure heap is expected to take about four months to rot down ready for use. In *Month-by-Month Organic Gardening*, Lawrence Hills described how this period can be reduced to four to six weeks by building the heap on a sheet of heavy polythene to catch the drainings, making it firm with the spade, and then covering it with polythene and weighing it down with stones, planks or old tyres. This keeps the heat in and the humidity high, speeds up rotting and means that the straw on the edges rots as quickly as the middle.

Household and garden compost heaps are another good source of valuable humus and plant food. They can be made of all the remains of vegetables from the kitchen, and of a certain amount of newspaper, provided that it is torn up. All green garden waste can also be composted, though the coarser and tougher it is, the longer it takes to rot. Lawn mowings rot down very well when mixed with coarser rubbish, but tend to get soggy if left in a mass. Garden weeds compost well, but should have as little soil as possible left on the roots.

Dead leaves from trees should be kept separate and used to make leafmould. Compost heaps of green refuse need air to rot, so trenches, pipes or spaced out bricks must be placed underneath the heap and brushwood laid on top of the bricks. The rubbish is then placed in layers about 30 cm deep, and on this is sprinkled a nitrogen-rich activator to help feed the bacteria. The next 30 cm layer of rubbish has a generous sprinkling of garden lime placed on it, and the heap is built up in these alternating layers until it reaches about 1.5 m high, making sure that the air has a free passage to the underside of the heap. As with the manure heap, the compost heap will need turning once the first burst of heating has ceased. If the heap is covered with an old carpet or piece of plastic it will rot more quickly and not need turning. If heating is slow to start, it may be helpful to make holes through the heap with an iron rod, to let air in. Again the presence of the small red

Comfrey growing in Yunnan

Mustard as a green manure

Lupins as a green manure

Phacelia tanacetifolia attracts hoverflies

worms is an indication that the heap is ready for use.

Excellent compost may be made using a chipper. This grinds up sticks, prunings, coarse leaves and tough stems so that they rot down more quickly. The pieces of stick help to keep the whole well aerated and good compost is made in a few months. Activator and lime speed rotting, but make the compost less useful for lime-hating shrubs in the garden.

It is often very easy to obtain horse manure from stables where the horses are bedded on wood shavings. Reports on the usefulness of this are very mixed. I have used it for some years and found that it is good for improving the texture of heavy soil, though I have often used liquid feed as a nitrogen supplement. There are two main theories against using wood shavings: first that the bacteria which rot wood take nitrogen from the soil and so impoverish it, and second that they encourage the growth of woodrotting fungi which are harmful to vegetables. I have not encountered either problem, but it is important that the shavings be well rotted before use, and a lookout be kept for any sign of lack of nitrogen in the crop. These rotted wood shavings are excellent for growing woodland lilies and other garden plants from similar habitats. Even those who do not advocate the use of woodshaving manure in the vegetable garden acknowledge that it is useful as a mulch to keep down weeds and keep moisture in.

Leafmould is a very valuable source of garden humus, for vegetables as well as shrubs and flowers. The leaves are collected in autumn and piled in heaps with wire netting sides. They rot slowly, usually taking more than a year. This rotting may be speeded up either by adding urine so the leaves are just wetted, which increases the nitrogen available, or by adding and mixing in fresh lawn mowings in the spring. For use on vegetables it may be necessary to add extra lime, as leafmould tends to be acid.

For those who have neither the time nor the space to make their own compost, there are many concentrated organic manures on the market which can be used instead. As a halfway stage, a variety of small compost-making bins is available, which enable the gardener to make smaller amounts of compost in a short time.

Black polythene as a mulch

Green Manures

These are plants which are sown thickly and then, when growing well, are dug in, providing nitrogen and other nutrients as they rot. They are used to increase the fertility and humus content of the soil. Many species can be used, but the most useful are those which grow through the winter and can be dug in in spring prior to planting out the vegetables. The warmer the temperature, the sooner the green manure will rot and its nutrients be available to the crop.

Several species, and especially members of the pea family, add nitrogen to the soil by means of nodules in their roots. Other nutrients are taken up and held by the plants instead of being washed away by rain. Green manures may also be grown for

Vegetables growing well in large tubs at Wisley

Vegetables in blocks at Wisley

adding to the compost heap and deep-rooted perennials such as comfrey and alfalfa are especially suitable for this purpose.

The usual species grown are various rapes and mustards, vetches and clovers, notably the robust *Trifolium incarnatum*, buckwheat, and annual grasses such as Italian rye.

The first stages of decomposition take nitrogen from the soil, and so, if crops are planted very soon after digging, it is beneficial to water the young plants with a high nitrogen fertilizer to ensure they get a good start.

Pest and disease control

Organic vs inorganic   As with manure, the use of chemical pesticides has also become caught up in the organic versus inorganic debate. Since the publication of *The Silent Spring* by Rachel Carson in 1962, the public has realized the dangers of using pesticides such as DDT, dieldrin, 2,4,5–T and similar compounds. These were developed by the chemical industry and are complex organic compounds, i.e. they contain carbon, and often chlorides or phosphates as well. The initial benefits of these compounds were very great; they were lethal to insects or weeds at very low concentrations, and less toxic to crop plants. They enabled large areas of the world to be cleared of malaria, and resulted in huge increases in crop production. Unfortunately they had serious long-term and insidious side-effects, both harming wildlife and increasing the incidence of cancers in the human population. Many, such as aldrin and dieldrin, were very persistent in the food chain, and became concentrated in predators such as falcons and hawks, reducing their populations drastically. In other cases such chemicals have been widely used in treating food for years, before being withdrawn on suspicion of causing human cancers. It is for these reasons that the 'organic' lobby is rightly against using these synthetic though technically organic compounds. Other simple inorganic compounds such as the fungicide Bordeaux mixture, a combination of copper sulphate and lime, or organic compounds such as soft soap and nicotine, used as insecticides, have been around for many years and have not, as far as I am aware, been shown to have any adverse, long-term effect on human health.

A more recent development has been the commercial production of natural pest controls, especially for use in glasshouses. These are insects, mites or bacteria which kill particular pests and work very well if they are given the right conditions. By keeping down pest populations they make spraying with insecticides unnecessary. Addresses of suppliers are given below.

Sensible but unfanatic vegetable gardeners will use any available cultural methods which keep pests or diseases away, but will make day-to-day decisions as to which chemicals it is safe to use. They will also use physical barriers to pests such as putting rings around the base of cabbage transplants to prevent root flies

from laying their eggs, or interplant carrots and onions so the carrot flies cannot find the carrots by smell.

The Henry Doubleday Research Association   Advice on 'Organic' gardening in Europe can be had from the Henry Doubleday Research Association, Ryton-on-Dunsmore, Coventry CV8 3LG. They have a demonstration garden at Ryton, and publish numerous leaflets. They have also been very active in saving old varieties of vegetables, whose survival was threatened by new varieties more suitable for the commercial grower, and by unnecessary legislation from the EEC in Brussels. Their Heritage Seed Programme aims to preserve old varieties of vegetable, and make seed of them available to its members. The use of more natural methods of pest control and the preservation of diversity in vegetable varieties were both the objects of long campaigns by the HDRA's remarkable founder Lawrence D. Hills. Lawrence Hills named the association after Henry Doubleday of Coggeshall (1813–1902), a Quaker and connection of the founder of the American publishing house. Henry Doubleday had a gum factory which supplied the postage stamp printers, de la Rue; he imported a hybrid comfrey from Russia to produce a substitute for gum arabic; the gum project failed, but he continued to experiment with comfrey as a fodder plant. Lawrence Hills also worked on and promoted comfrey as a source of natural fertilizer and organic bulk material, as its powerful root system can exploit minerals from deep in the ground. In North America the interest in old varieties, so-called Heritage vegetables, is well established and several nurseries specialize in selling their seed.

'Seed Savers Exchange', set up by Kent and Diane Whealy, aims to locate and preserve old varieties in North America.

It is unfortunate, though understandable, that modern vegetable breeding is aimed at the large-scale commercial grower; the grower is in turn dominated by the demands of his major market, the supermarket chains. Fortunately, although there is a demand for a greater uniformity of size and presentation, there is also an increasing demand for diversity of variety, so there is some incentive for breeders to produce a range of varieties.

Modern vegetable varieties aim to be uniform in size, shape and maturity time. This uniformity is a necessity to the commercial grower, but a disadvantage to the amateur who is faced with a glut of one vegetable when a whole row is ready at once. A range of sizes and maturity dates is useful and is available in many vegetables, so that they can be picked over a longer period. These characteristics, together with pest and disease resistance and an ability to produce a crop in less than optimum conditions, are often found in old traditional varieties.

List of vegetable seed Suppliers

The Vegetable Finder published by The Henry Doubleday Research Association lists all the vegetable varieties available in Britain, and the names and addresses of all the seedmen who stock them. This list includes some we have encountered ourselves:

A seaside garden at Inverewe, N.W. Scotland

INTRODUCTION

Villandry: looking down from the Château

Bakker Holland, P.O. Box 111, Spalding, Lincs PE12 6EL
Thomas Butcher, 60 Wickham Road, Shirley, Croydon, Surrey CR9 8AG
Carters Tested Seeds Ltd, Herle Road, Torquay, Devon TQ2 7QJ
Chiltern Seeds, Bortree Stile, Ulverston, Cumbria LA12 7PB
Mr Fothergill's Seeds Ltd, Gazeley Road, Kentford, Newmarket, Suffolk CB8 7QB
S. E. Marshall & Co, Wisbech, Cambs PE13 2RF
Suttons Seeds Ltd, Hele Road, Torquay, Devon TQ2 7QJ
Scotston Garden Potatoes, Laurencekirk, Grampian AB3 1ND
Suffolk Herbs Ltd, Sawyers Farm, Little Conard, Sudbury, Suffolk CO10 0NY
Thompson and Morgan (Ipswich) Ltd, London Road, Ipswich, Suffolk IP2 0BA
A. L. Tozer, Pyports, Downside Bridge Road, Cobham, Surrey
Unwins Seeds Ltd, Histon, Cambridge CB4 4ZZ

In America, *The Complete Vegetable Gardener's Sourcebook* by Duane Newcomb and Karen Newcomb (Prentice Hall Press, New York, 1989) lists all available vegetable varieties and their sources, as well as suppliers of insect predators, and contains excellent chapters on cultivation and pest control. The list below includes some of the vegetable seed sources we have used ourselves.

Seeds Blum, Idaho City Stage, Boise, Idaho, 83706
W. Atlee Burpee Co., 300 Park Av., Warminster, PA 18991–0001
The Cooks Garden, Box 65, Londonderry, VT 05148
Harris Moran Seed Co., 3670 Buffalo Road, Rochester, NY 14624 and 1155 Harkins Road, Salinas, CA 93901
Nichols Garden Nursery, Albany, OR 97321
Park Seed Co., Cokesbury Road, Greenwood, SC 29647
The Pepper Gal, 10536 119th Ave.N., Largo, FL 34643
Thompson & Morgan, P.O. Box 1308, Jackson, NY 08527
Vermont Bean Seed Co., Fairhaven, VT 05743–0250
Willhite Seed Co., Poolville, Texas 76487
Wilton's Organic Potatoes, P.O. Box 28, Aspen, CO 81611

Sources of natural pest control

Natural Pest Control Ltd, Yapton Road, Barnham, Bognor Regis, West Sussex, PO22 0BQ
W. Atlee Burpee Co., Warminster PA 18974
Natural Pest Controls, 8864 Little Creek Dr., Orangeville, CA 95662
Unique Insect Controls, PO Box 15376, Sacramento CA 95851

Sacred Lotus

Nelumbo nucifera Gaertn. (*Nymphaeaceae*)
Lin Ngau (rhizome), Lin Tze (seed) Chinese

No plant is more beautiful than the lotus, with its leaves of pure waxy green emerging from stinking black mud, and its huge pale pink flowers on gently curving stalks. It has been cultivated in China for at least 14,000 years, and is now associated with Kuan Yin, the goddess of mercy, and with Buddha and is regarded as a sacred symbol of eternal life. It is a native of still water from the Volga delta, and the Caspian coast in Iran, eastwards to China, Japan and northeastern Australia. As well as being cultivated for its exceptional beauty, it is also commonly eaten in China and Japan.

The rhizomes, which consist of a short chain of oval segments, are sliced across to show a pretty pattern of circular air channels, and are pickled in vinegar or syrup, or cooked with other vegetables. The young leaves can be eaten raw or cooked, and are used to wrap small parcels of food before cooking. The seeds, which are carried in a pepper-pot-like head with round holes in the top, can be roasted and eaten, or used in cooking like nuts. They have a bitter, green embryo (usually called a plumule) inside, which must be removed before they are cooked. This embryo consists of one or two young leaves enclosed in a delicate sheath, hidden between the thick and fleshy cotyledons.

Cultivation is easy, provided the plants are given sufficient heat and light. They need temperatures of 20–30°C to grow properly, and a growing season of about five months. I have seen good plants grown in Chinese pickled egg jars which can be bought in Europe. The young rhizomes should be planted in nitrogen-rich mud in water 10–20 cm deep. The mature rhizomes are best harvested after the leaves have died down in autumn; they should be stored in a frost-free place, either in the tub or in moist sand. Joy Larkcom reports that in China the pink-flowered varieties are preferred for seed, the white-flowered for their rhizomes. There are several beautiful ornamental cultivars grown in Japan and the warm parts of North America.

There is a second species, *Nelumbo lutea* (Willd.) Pers., a native of North America. It has pale yellow flowers and is found growing in ponds and slow rivers, and in estuaries from Florida and Texas north to New York, southern Ontario, Minnesota and Iowa. Its seeds and tubers are edible.

Lotus roots for sale in Chengdu

Lotus: the young leaves emerge rolled towards the middle

Lotus flower

LOTUS

Lotus on the Dal Lake in Kashmir

Wild cabbages on the cliffs at Dover

Cabbage and related vegetables

Brassica oleracea L. (*Cruciferae*)

In the three thousand or so years during which it has been cultivated, the wild cabbage has been developed into several distinct vegetables. The commonest are the cabbage, in its many forms, the cauliflower, the broccoli, the Brussels sprout and the kohlrabi. Related species of *Brassica* have produced the turnip and the swede, the different forms of Chinese cabbages, and the oil-seed rape.

Wild cabbage, *Brassica oleracea* L. subsp. *oleracea* is found growing along the coast from southern England and western France to northwest Spain. A closely related species, *Brassica montana* Pourret (syn. *B. oleracea* subsp. *robertiana* (Gay) Rouy & Foucaud), is found along the Mediterranean coast from northeast Spain to northern Italy. Other related species are found on the coasts of Corsica, Sardinia and North Africa (*Brassica insularis*), in southern Italy and Sicily (*Brassica rupestris*, *B. incana*, *B. villosa* and *B. macrocarpa*), in the eastern Mediterranean (*Brassica cretica* and *B. hilarionis*) and on the Canary Islands (*Brassica bourgeaui*). Some authorities have suggested that *Brassica cretica* may have been the ancestor of the cauliflower, but the most recent account of the wild brassicas by Snogerup, Gustafsson & von Bothmer considers that all the modern cultivars were derived from *Brassica oleracea* subsp. *oleracea*.

Most species have yellow flowers, but in *B. insularis* flowers are white, and in *B. cretica*, *B. bourgeaui* and *B. hilarionis* often white. Cultivated var. *alboglabra* and Couve Tronchuda often have white flowers.

In England wild cabbages always grow on chalk and limestone sea cliffs, where they form low, many-branched plants, like small purple-sprouting broccoli. There has been some discussion about whether the species is truly native in England, or whether it was introduced by the Romans or by the Saxons, both of whom were great lovers of cabbage and kale. It is now found wild in about twenty sites from east Kent near Broadstairs and on the White Cliffs of Dover, westwards around the coast to the Great Orme's Head in North Wales. It grows both on isolated cliffs and near towns and villages and is usually associated with breeding colonies of gulls. The oldest definite account of the plant as wild is recorded in William Turner's *A New Herbal*, dating from 1551. It does, however, grow on the ramparts of Dover Castle, which has been inhabited since Roman times.

Wild plants on the southeast coast of Scotland and northeast England are generally considered to be more recent introductions, having been recorded only from the early nineteenth century. Similar doubts exist about the history of the wild cabbages on the Atlantic coast of France, but Snogerup and his co-authors writing in 1990 consider most of these populations are truly wild.

The earliest records of cultivated cabbages date from around 600 BC when kale is mentioned in early Greek literature; the word used indicated that the stems were eaten, so the plant was probably a primitive cauliflower or broccoli. Leaf cabbages with heads 30 cm across, and a type close to kohlrabi were described by Pliny, writing in about AD 77. These ancient cultivars were presumably derived from Mediterranean species, and there are records of *Brassica cretica* being cultivated in recent years on Samos. Populations of the Italian species *Brassica incana* in the Crimea, and the Cretan *Brassica cretica* in the Lebanon are considered by Snogerup *et al.* to be ancient introductions.

The direct history of the various modern cultivated groups can be traced from the Middle Ages onwards, and are discussed below.

The **Couve Tronchuda**, also called Braganza, Portugal or Seakale cabbage is a distinct plant, characterized by the white, fleshy ribs of its leaves, and its white or sometimes yellow flowers.

Wild cabbage is close to sprouting broccoli

Young mixed brassicas at Wisley

Wild cabbage in flower at Dover

Both outer leaves and the rather small heart are tender. It withstands frost well, and can be cut from autumn through the winter – particularly valuable when winter vegetables are scarce. In Madeira, where it is widely grown, the outer leaves are used in spring, finely shredded, to make soup.

Cabbage

Brassica oleracea L. var. *capitata* (L.) Alef

Modern cabbages are thought to have originated in Germany, where both red and white cabbages were grown by 1150. Savoy cabbages, with crinkled leaves, were recognized in Germany by 1543, and probably originated in Italy.

At present cabbages are divided into eight main types:

Spring cabbage are made up of two main sorts: spring greens grown for their fresh loose leafy heads, and spring hearting cabbage, which are hardy, growing slowly through the winter, and maturing in early spring. Both are planted out in late September and are ready in April and May. 'Durham Early' is suitable both as spring greens, and later as a small hearting cabbage.

Summer cabbage are all hearting cabbages, with either pointed or round hearts. These are planted out in April or May, having been raised indoors, and are ready for harvest from June to August, with some varieties such as 'Minicole' remaining in good condition into the autumn. 'Hispi' and 'Greyhound' are early, pointed varieties in this group; 'Stonehead' is a late, long-keeping variety. Early-maturing red cabbages are planted out and harvested at the same times.

Autumn cabbage are planted out in late June and mature quickly, by September and October. 'Shamrock' is a recommended variety in this section.

The white-flowered Tronchuda cabbage in Madeira

'Midway' (text see p. 23)

'Castello' (text see p. 23)

Winter white (Capitata group) are large cabbages grown for storage; they are planted out in early June, and mature in November and December. Many varieties will store through the winter as solid white heads.

Savoy cabbage (Subanda group) are recognized by their very crinkly and often bluish leaves. They are planted out in early July, and harvested from October to March, according to variety. Most are very hardy.

Savoy hybrids are crosses between savoy and white cabbages, and are denser than savoys. They are very hardy and will often stand in good condition until March.

January King cultivars are generally planted out in early June, and are mature by November and December, often standing through the winter; they generally have slightly crinkly and purplish leaves, and exceptionally good flavour.

Red cabbage (Rubra group); these cultivars are not ready for harvest until October or November, and can be stored into the winter. 'Autoro' is a well-known hybrid variety of this type. Another old group now seldom seen are the **cow cabbages**, grown for cattle fodder, which are like giant coarse, rather blue, winter cabbages.

Cultivation

Cabbages and other brassicas grow best in well-drained soil, with a high degree of fertility and an open position with full light. Cabbage seed is generally sown in a seedbed, or singly in pots or soil blocks and the young plants are planted out when 1–2 months old. They should be grown as sturdily as possible, without much fertilizer. They can be planted at their final spacing into holes made with a trowel or dibber and pressed in well. It is important that the soil be firm, and it should be cleared but not dug over before planting. The surrounding soil can be worked with a hoe. It is better to apply fertilizer round each plant when it is already established, and from then until maturity the plants should have ample supplies of water. Faster-growing crops such as French beans or lettuces can be sown between slow-maturing varieties of cabbage.

On light soils the plants can be placed in a shallow drill, and earthed up through the growing season, and especially at the onset of winter. Tall varieties may need staking, especially in windy sites, and this applies especially to other tall brassicas such as Brussels sprouts and broccoli which stand through the winter.

Diseases

The worst disease of Brassicas is clubroot, a small soilborne fungus which invades the root system, causing the roots to swell and become sometimes grotesquely deformed. The plants live, but fail to thrive and wilt in hot weather. The fungus rests in the soil between crops, ready to reinfect any brassicas or related *Cruciferae* that may be planted nearby. Total eradication of clubroot from infected soil is not easy, but it is less serious on alkaline and well-drained soils. On soils where clubroot is known, the young transplants can be treated on planting by dipping the roots in calomel or benomyl, or another recommended fungicide. Downy mildew can infect the leaves, but is seldom serious except in humid and overcrowded conditions.

Pests

Brassicas are attacked by numerous pests. The worst is cabbage root fly, which lays its eggs on the soil at the base of the plant. The small white maggots which hatch from them attack the base of the stem at ground level and eat away the surface layer. The first signs of infection are the yellowing of the outer leaves and the wilting of the plants in hot weather. The main time of attack by the adult root flies is April and May, and good control may be had by placing a barrier around the stem after planting; a round piece of roofing felt is usually recommended, as shown here, but any barrier which covers the soil for about 10 cm round the base of the plant will do.

The caterpillars of the Large and Small White butterflies, sometimes called cabbage worms in America, are common pests of all brassicas. In his classic work *Butterflies*, E. B. Ford contrasts the habits and taste of these two species. Large White caterpillars are hairy and conspicuous, with yellow and black markings, and feed on the upper side of the leaves, whereas those of the Small White are green and inconspicuous and burrow into the heart of the plants. 'To me the flavour (of the Small White) is bland, while that of the Large White is slight, but rather unpleasant'! Both these pests can be killed with a suitable insecticide, or by a prolonged and heavy spraying with water. Ordinary salt in water is also an effective control, and will kill slugs too.

Cabbages can also be affected by mealy aphids which form greyish fluffy patches on the underside of the leaves, and will in the end stunt and spoil the plants. It is important to treat an infestation early, by spraying with insecticidal soap, or by picking off the young colonies as soon as they appear.

Cabbage White fly can be a serious pest for all brassicas in gardens. They are similar to the glasshouse whitefly in general appearance. The pests overwinter on old brassica plants and reinfest the young plants in the spring. Therefore it is important to remove old plants or ensure they are clean, before new plants are put out nearby. The eggs are laid on the lower leaves on the plant, so it is a help to remove these if they show any sign of whitefly pupae, which look like small brown scales. Control of adults is more difficult. They can be drowned by spraying with insecticidal soap; make sure you wet the underside of the leaves and repeat several times at weekly intervals. The Henry Doubleday Research Association recommends growing flowering umbellifers such as fennel and lovage, or *Phacelia tanacetifolia*, which attract the parasitic wasps *Aphelinus*.

A young pointed-heart cabbage

Summer cabbage, 'Greyhound' (text see p. 23)

Savoy cabbages at Sandling Park

The effects of club root

A collar of black roofing felt protects against cabbage root fly

'January King' Asmer Special

'Comet'

'Wintessa'

'January King
Hardy Late Stock 3'

'Winterton'

Specimens from NIAB, Cambridge, photographed 15 February

Savoy hybrid, 'Santana'

Savoy hybrid, 'Saga'

'January King' in autumn sunlight

Savoy, 'Wivoy'

Early Savoy hybrid, 'Julius'

'January King'

'Castello' (illustrated on p. 20) An F1 hybrid early midseason autumn cabbage, with good standing ability. Heads dense, round, grey-green. 80 days from transplanting to maturity.

'Comet' A January King × white hybrid raised by Asmer Seeds.

'Greyhound' (illustrated on p. 20) An early maturing summer cabbage, for planting in early spring from the greenhouse, to mature in 62 days from transplanting.

'January King' (syn. 'Pontoise', 'Blaugrüner' 'Winter', 'Chou Milan de l'Hermitage') An old French variety, now a group of varieties, listed by Vilmorin in 1883. Very hardy when planted in early July.

'January King Hardy Late Stock 3' A particularly hardy late-maturing stock from Tozers, with medium sized heads, lasting into March and April.

'Julius' A savoy raised by Sluis & Groot BV. Head around 17 cm across, 19 cm deep, with short internal stalks. A very early maturing, F1 variety.

'Midway' (illustrated on p. 20) A savoy.

'Saga' A savoy F1 hybrid, raised by Royal Sluis Ltd. Early mid-season; small and very dense.

'Santana' A savoy F1 hybrid, raised by Royal Sluis Ltd. An early-mid season variety.

'Winterton' A cross between a white cabbage and a January King, becoming reddish in cold weather, raised by Bejo Zaden BV.

'Wintessa' A late savoy raised by Bejo Zaden BV. The latest-maturing variety, 200 days to maturity. Fairly loose head.

'Wivoy' Raised by Nickerson Zwaan: a cold-resistant and lightly savoyed variety, with small heads which can stand through the winter until March or April. One of the hardiest of the savoys.

23

CABBAGES

'Kissendrup'

'Red Dutch'

'Red Dutch'

Specimens from NIAB, Cambridge, photographed 1 November

'Kissendrup'

Red Cabbages are generally very hardy, with thick leaves, and are suitable for storage in areas with very cold winters. On cooking the red colour can become bluish in alkaline water; a little vinegar added keeps the colour red. Cultivation is the same as for other cabbages.

'Kissendrup'   An old German variety, known since 1889. Leaves greyish-red.

'Late Purple Flat Poll'   A very large fodder cabbage, grown in the past for cattle feed in winter; slow to mature; photographed on 1 November.

'Mohrenkopf' (syn. 'Negrohead')   Plant 50 cm tall, 80 cm across, head 20 cm across, spherical. An old variety, known since before 1911.

'Red Drumhead'   Suitable for pickling. Resistant to yellow virus. An old open pollinated red cultivar.

'Red Dutch'   Forming solid large heads; late maturing and suitable for pickling. Probably the same as 'Mohrenkopf'.

'Vesta'   A red cabbage. Suitable for storage.

CABBAGES

A good range of winter cabbages at Sandling Park

'Late Purple Flat Poll'

'Mohrenkopf' (*left*), 'Vesta' (*right*)

'Red Drumhead'

Cabbages and spinach beet at Joy Larkcom's

'First of June'

Specimens from NIAB, Cambridge, photographed 10 July

'Delphi' Raised by Royal Sluis Ltd. An F1 hybrid. An early Primo-type slightly later than 'Golden Cross'.

'Derby Day' Raised by Dr C. D. R. Dawson and introduced by A. L. Tozer Ltd. Heads around 15 cm in diameter, 15 cm high, maturing June to August.

'First of June' Raised by Dr C. D. R. Dawson and introduced by A. L. Tozer Ltd; 27 cm high, 63 cm across; head 22 cm across, 11 cm high.

'Golden Cross' An F1 hybrid, for early or late-summer use. Quick-maturing.

'Green Express' An F1 hybrid. Head 20 cm in diameter, 20 cm high; for summer maturity.

'Hispi' Raised and introduced by Bejo Zaden BV. Heads around 18 cm in diameter, 25 cm high, pointed. An F1 hybrid. Quick maturing, in late May from an early sowing indoors.

'Hornspi' Raised by Nickerson Zwaan BV. Head pointed. Early maturing and suitable for growing in frames.

'Jersey Wakefield' An ancient variety, introduced in 1788, and probably the oldest variety still going. Summer maturing with pointed heads.

'Myatt's Offenham Compacta' Raised by Dr C. D. R. Dawson and introduced by A. L. Tozer Ltd; 30 cm high, 43 cm across. Heads small, but plants suitable also for spring greens, in April–May. Sow in early August.

'Pixie' Raised by Dr C. D. R. Dawson and introduced by A. L. Tozer Ltd. For autumn sowing, to mature in May. 23 cm tall; head small and solid, 14 cm across, 22 cm high. Very early maturing, for both spring greens and hearts. Suitable for those with small gardens.

'Quickstep' Suitable for summer or autumn maturity; 23 cm across, 21 cm deep; head 17 cm in diameter. A Drumhead type raised by Nickerson Zwaan BV for an autumn crop.

'Spitfire' An F1 hybrid with pointed heads, later than Hispi. Long-standing with dark green colour.

'Spring Hero' An F1 hybrid. Unusual for a spring cabbage, this has a round head, weighing about 1 kg, tender and with good flavour.

Summer cabbage ready for harvest

'Jersey Wakefield'

'Pixie'

'Myatt's Offenham Compacta'

'Hispi'

'Spring Hero'

'Spring Hero'

'Quickstep'

'Early Half Tall'

'Bedford Fillbasket'

'Rubine'

Specimens from NIAB, Cambridge, photographed 1 November

A row of young 'Rubine'

Brussels Sprouts

Brassica oleracea L. Gemmifera group, syn. var. *gemmifera* DC

Brussels sprouts were first recorded in Belgium in about 1750, and
reached England and France in about 1800. There had been an
earlier rather similar cabbage, called *Brassica capitata polycephalos*,
which was illustrated in 1587 in D'Alechamps's *Historia Generalis
Plantarum*.

Modern Brussels sprouts are grown for evenness of sprout size,
with as many as possible maturing at one time. These are often F1
hybrids, giving both vigour and uniformity. A traditional variety
suitable for the amateur gardener is 'Noisette'; it is hardy with a
long cropping season from October to February. The modern
varieties 'Peer Gynt' and 'Widgeon' also have a long season. Other
variations are the traditional purple-leaved sprouts, such as
'Rubine Red', and the new cabbage sprout 'Ormavon', in which
the top forms a cabbage-like head.

Do not be in a hurry to throw out sprout plants with loose or
unpicked sprouts. They will begin to grow in early spring and
produce a sweet and excellent-tasting flowering shoot like a
sprouting broccoli.

General cultivation of sprouts is the same as for winter cabbage.
Seed should be sown between February and April, to give strong
young plants to be put out in May and June about 60–90 cm apart.
Wider spacing will give larger plants which can be picked over a
longer period. Tall plants may need supporting in windy sites. By
using different varieties it should be possible to get a crop from
September to April.

Cabbage mealy aphid can be very damaging, and should be
looked out for in late summer, and again in early spring, so that
any overwintering colonies can be removed before they infect new
crops.

'Bedford Fillbasket'   A traditional variety, with large sprouts
and high yields. October to December cropping. Sutton's variety
of this type was first offered in 1925. The sprouts are exceptionally
large but still firm and of good quality.
'Early Half Tall'   Raised by Messrs A. Hansen in Denmark.
Plant short, 45–50 cm tall, 75 cm across, dark bluish-green.
October cropping, continuing until December.
'Mallard'   An F1 hybrid available from Unwins, raised by
Tozer's of Cobham before 1984.
'Montgomery'   An F1 hybrid available from Marshalls, raised
by Tozer's of Cobham. Sprouts smooth and dark green, ready
from December onwards.
'Oliver'   An F1 hybrid: the earliest of the modern varieties, for
September harvest.
'Rubine'   A red-leaved variety. Late maturing, usually not
before November. Good flavour.

'Oliver'

'Mallard'

'Montgomery'

Curly kale 'Frosty'   Palm-tree cabbage

Kale

Brassica oleracea L. var. *acephala* DC
Borecole, Collards, Colewort

Kale is the name given to various forms of non-heading brassicas.
Most have a tall, thick stem and are very hardy, overwintering and
being harvested in spring when the young leaves and shoots
develop. Marrow-stem kale, called also Chou moellier, has
particularly thick stems. Many of the kales grown as vegetables
have very crisped and curled leaves, and large coarse kales are also
commonly grown for winter cattle and sheep feed.

Kales were probably the earliest type of cultivated brassicas,
being similar in many ways to the wild forms of *Brassica oleracea*.

There are two main groups of cultivars:

Scotch kale or **Borecole** (Sabellica group) has very curly, usually
dark green or bluish-green leaves.

Siberian kale is more variable and generally has broader leaves,
which are sometimes curled or frilled. There is a red-leaved
variety, 'Russian Red'. 'Laciniato', an Italian variety, has deeply
cut flat leaves. An ancient perennial variety, 'Ragged Jack', has
wavy, red leaves, and another old one, 'Thousand-headed',
produces young shoots in early spring; it is exceptionally hardy.

Ornamental kales, with white or pink markings on the leaves, are
often cultivated as curiosities, and were popular in Victorian times
in exotic bedding schemes, and as table decorations.

Collards are very similar to plain-leaved kales and are especially
popular in the Southern States of America; they are harvested
during the summer and autumn after spring sowing in cool areas,
or in hot areas are sown in late summer for harvesting in winter.
Kale and collards are easier to grow than other brassicas, being
tolerant of poor soils. Kale is exceptionally hardy, and said to be
less attractive to pigeons, which can strip other brassicas during a
hard winter.

Tree cabbage, Walking-stick cabbage, Chou Cavalier or Giant
Jersey kale, has normal non-curly leaves on top of a tall straight
stem.

Palm tree cabbage or Chou Palmier is an old variety, known since
the nineteenth century, with narrow, recurved, savoyed leaves in a
rosette on top of the stem.

Cultivation

Kale seed is sown in May, and the plants set out in July or early
August, the dwarf varieties 45 cm apart, the large ones 75 cm
apart. Soil should not be too rich or the plants will be less hardy. A
top dressing of high nitrogen fertilizer in late winter will
encourage lush young shoots. An early crop of young greens may
be had by planting seed thickly under glass in January or
February, cutting the young plants like spinach when 15 cm high.
The roots will re-sprout. Thompson & Morgan sell a variety
'Spurt' especially for this purpose.

Collards are sown in May in areas with cool summers, in late
summer in hot areas with a mild winter. The variety 'Florida' is
quickest to mature, being ready in forty-five days. The
commonest variety, 'Georgia', is ready in seventy to eighty days.
Plants should be spaced about 60 cm apart.

Chinese Broccoli

Brassica oleracea L. var. *alboglabra* (Bailey) Sun
Chinese Kale, Gai Lohn

An annual Chinese variety, closely allied to European broccoli,
and the Portuguese 'Couve Tronchuda' cabbage, still grown in
Portugal and Madeira. An early Portuguese introduction to China
is the likely origin for this variety, as the first Portuguese contacts
with Canton were in 1517.

Chinese broccoli looks rather like a slender, leafy calabrese or a
short kale with a small head of flowers but a good, fleshy stem.
The flowers are usually white, but may be yellow in some
varieties. Dr Herklots mentions a red-flowered variety. Some
varieties grow best in hot weather; others are winter vegetables in
tropical areas such as Thailand, and are better in a cool climate. In
suitable climates harvesting may be continued for six months, new
shoots being produced throughout this period. In cooler climates
it is wise to delay sowing until midsummer, so the plants have a
chance to build up to a good size before they begin to flower. The
F1 hybrid 'Green Lance' is one of the quicker growing, heat-
resistant varieties, being ready in about fifty days. Another
variety, sold as 'Gai Lohn', 'Gai Choi', 'Kaai Laan', or 'Chinese
Kale' is better in cool weather, maturing in about seventy days. It
is illustrated on p. 49 (top right).

A cabbage close to Couve Tronchuda in China

A vegetable garden in Chengdu, Sichuan

Ornamental kale, 'Coral Queen'

A blue curly kale

Mustards and cabbages interplanted in China

Curly kale going to seed in spring

Ornamental kale, 'Russian Red'

'White Sprouting Late'

Cape broccoli, 'Oasis'

'Purple Sprouting'

'White Sprouting Early'

Specimens from NIAB, Cambridge, photographed 29 March

Romanesco growing in a frame in November

'Mercedes' in flower

Calabrese and romanesco are often sown where they are to grow, the seeds being planted in threes, 20 cm apart in the rows. The seedlings are thinned to a single plant, and the plants are grown on as fast as possible, being given ample water in dry weather. Romanesco can be used throughout the winter if the plants are protected from frost and rain by a frame. Once picked the plants can be thrown away, as they seem unable to make side shoots, or break from the leaf axils. Some varieties of Calabrese do make side shoots, others do not.

Perennial broccoli is grown in the same way as overwintering broccoli. All the flowering shoots, which are white in 'Nine Star', should be picked each year, and the plants looked after carefully when not in production. A top dressing of fertilizer is needed after cropping has finished, so the plant makes good growth for the following season.

'Mercedes'   F1 hybrid. A quick-maturing, calabrese type, green broccoli, with wide stems and rather flat heads about 15 cm across. For a quick summer crop, the plants should be planted out in June, and will mature in about fifty days.

'Oasis'   A purple Cape broccoli, strictly a purple cauliflower, for planting in summer and harvesting the following spring. These are generally hardier than white cauliflowers and have more flavour.

'Early Purple Sprouting'   In this very traditional variety cropping begins around March according to the season, and continues into May, with smaller and smaller shoots.

'Late Purple Sprouting' (p. 35) extends the season, coming into production about a fortnight later.

'Early White Sprouting'   This is a white equivalent of 'Purple Sprouting', and again the 'Early' is about two weeks earlier than the 'Late'.

Broccoli

Brassica oleracea L. Cymosa group, syn. var. *italica* Plenck
Calabrese

Broccoli is said to have come to Italy from Crete, Cyprus or the eastern Mediterranean area in the seventeenth century. From Italy it spread to northern Europe, being called 'Italian asparagus' in Miller's *Gardener's Dictionary* in 1724.

There are three main types of broccoli grown today. Annual green or, more rarely, purple broccoli, maturing in summer, generally known as calabrese; romanesco, maturing in late summer and autumn, with numerous yellowish-green conical groups of buds arranged in spirals; sprouting broccoli, an overwintering annual or perennial, ready in early spring, usually either white or purple. Perennial broccoli is an old variety, still available, generally called 'Nine Star'. All these types have been grown since the early nineteenth century. In the past overwintering cauliflowers were known as broccoli, but they are now classed as winter cauliflower.

Cultivation

Overwintering sprouting broccoli is sown in a seed bed in April or early May and the young plants are set out in June and July, 60 cm apart in the rows. The aim should be to get the toughest and hardiest plants, so they are not killed by a cold winter. Very large plants may benefit from staking. Soil should be well drained and not too rich in nitrogen, which makes the plants soft and sappy, with very leafy growth.

A blue-green calabrese in Malawi

'White Sprouting'

'Emperor'

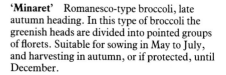

'Green Comet'

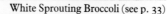
White Sprouting Broccoli (see p. 33)

'White Sprouting'

'Minaret'

'Citation' (Calabrese)   Early mid-season, with narrow stems and large sometimes bluish buds. Resistant to downy mildew. An F1 hybrid.

'Cruiser' (Calabrese)   Mid-season, with medium-sized buds. 58 days to harvest in USA. Good for hot, dry conditions; produces secondary shoots.

'Emperor' (Calabrese)   Tolerant of black rot and downy mildew. Suitable for spring or outdoor crop maturing in c. 70 days in summer, 83 days in spring. An F1 hybrid, producing high yields. Buds uneven.

'Green Comet' (Calabrese)   Fast maturing in about 80 days from sowing. Produces a central head with numerous side branches, 23 cm diameter on a short plant.

'Lancelot' (Calabrese)   Early mid-season. Plant very short, buds slightly uneven. An F1 hybrid.

'Minaret'   Romanesco-type broccoli, late autumn heading. In this type of broccoli the greenish heads are divided into pointed groups of florets. Suitable for sowing in May to July, and harvesting in autumn, or if protected, until December.

'Shogun' (Calabrese)   Raised by T. Sakata & Co. of Yokohama. Plants tall, with central head 10.5 cm across on narrow stems; bluish-grey heads, large but irregular in shape. Tolerant of wet weather. Suitable for sowing indoors in October, and keeping under cover for an early crop in May–June, and for late crops.

'White Sprouting'   A selection from the Institute of Horticultural Research at Wellesbourne (87500).

'Purple Sprouting Late' (see p. 33)

'Purple Sprouting Late' (see p. 33)

'Purple Sprouting' (see p. 33)

'Purple Sprouting' (see p. 33)

'Lancelot'

'Citation'

'Cruiser'

'Shogun'

'Markanta' in the trial fields at the National Institute of Agricultural Botany, Cambridge

Purple Cape broccoli

Cauliflower

Brassica oleracea L. Botrytis group, syn. var. *botrytis* L.

Summer and autumn cauliflowers mature during the summer in which they are sown, while winter cauliflowers mature during the winter in mild areas such as Brittany or Cornwall, or overwinter and mature in spring in less mild areas. The quickest-maturing summer varieties such as 'Early Snowball' are ready in about fifty to sixty days; the winter kinds may take nearly a year to mature. There are also several purple varieties, sometimes called 'Cape broccoli' (see page 32), a few bright yellowish-green ones, an orange, and 'floccoli', a broccoli/cauliflower hybrid, with pale green heads.

A recent development has been the mini-cauliflowers which produce heads about 8 cm across. They are quick maturing and are grown at close spacing. Two varieties available at present are 'Garant' and 'Predominant', the first maturing more quickly. Those who do not have large families find the mini-cauliflowers a more suitable size for a single meal.

Mini-cauliflowers

Cauliflowers are thought to have originated in Crete, Cyprus or the eastern Mediterranean, and arrived in Italy in about 1490 – though a similar vegetable was grown by the Romans. They are first recorded in England by Gerard in the late sixteenth century, but did not become really popular until the end of the eighteenth century.

'Garant' and **'Predominant'** Two varieties of mini-cauliflower, similar except in time of maturing. 'Garant' is about a week earlier. Both are harvested when 4–11 cm across, in around 90 days in warm weather.
'Limelight' An open pollinated, early to mid-season variety, cropping in late September from a sowing in late May. Curds medium-green.
'Markanta' (Walcheren-Winter type) An overwintering cauliflower, cropping in late-April from a sowing in mid-May.
'Purple Cape' Cropping in spring from a sowing in mid-May.

'Limelight', a lime-green cauliflower

Cultivation

Cauliflowers need a higher pH than most brassicas, so the soil should be well limed before planting. Nitrogen content should not be too high, but the soil should be moisture retentive, so that the plants grow unchecked through the growing season. Lack of water can cause the plant to produce deformed or abnormally small heads.

Seed can either be planted indoors, in a seed bed, or sown directly in the row or block. Early cauliflowers are generally sown in October and overwintered indoors before being planted out in March at 50 cm apart. Those for late summer and autumn use are sown in March to May and planted out when about six weeks old. The quickest maturing varieties mature in around fifty days ('Abuntia' and 'Snow King' are said to mature in forty-five days); the slower ones in a hundred days or more. Mini-cauliflowers can be sown in succession, at about 15 cm each way. They mature in about eighty-five days. A group of cultivars such as 'Angers No 1', 'Penzance' or 'Veitch's Self-Protecting' are suitable for climates with little winter frost and mature in mid-winter. They should be sown in May and transplanted in late July, about 70 cm apart.

Winter cauliflower are hardy and should be grown as tough as possible (i.e. without too much nitrogen when they become weak and flabby) so that they survive winter better. They are ready from March to May, and benefit from a nitrogen-rich top dressing in late winter which will increase the size of the heads. Purple Cape cauliflowers are also suitable for overwintering, and are particularly hardy. Early varieties grow well through the winter in subtropical climates.

A cauliflower gone pink!

Autumn Purple Cape broccoli, 'Violet Queen'

'Alverda', a lime-green cauliflower

Summer cauliflower, 'Andes'

Purple Cape is variously described as cauliflower or broccoli, though in size and structure it is generally closer to cauliflower. It is also commonly associated with Sicily as well as the Cape. This suggests that the early varieties needed mild winters for a good crop, although nowadays varieties are available which mature in autumn as well as hardier ones which mature in spring. The curds turn green on cooking.

'Alverda'   An early mid-season green cauliflower, with dark green curds, cropping in late September from a sowing in mid-May. From Suffolk Herbs.

'Andes'   A heat and cold tolerant variety, usually sown in mid-March for cropping in July and August. Heads c. 16 cm across, knobbly, self-wrapping.

'Arcade'   An F1 hybrid, overwintering cauliflower, for early spring heading, from a sowing in mid-May.

'Armado April' (Walcheren-Winter type)   An overwintering cauliflower, cropping in April from a sowing in mid-May.

'Markanta' (Walcheren-Winter type)   An overwintering cauliflower, cropping in late April from a sowing in mid-May.

'Purple Cape'   An overwintering cauliflower, cropping in spring from a sowing in May or June.

'Violet Queen'   An autumn Cape cauliflower F1 hybrid, quick maturing and ready in about 2 months in ideal conditions, from a sowing in early summer.

Purple Cape broccoli

Early spring cauliflower, 'Arcade'

Early spring cauliflower, 'Armado April'

Early spring cauliflower, 'Markanta'

Kohlrabi in China

Kohlrabi

Brassica oleracea Gongylodes group, syn. var. *gongylodes* L.

In this form of cabbage the stem remains very short, and swells forming an edible corm.

Kohlrabi originated in northern Europe in the fifteenth century, though a similar vegetable was described by Pliny in about AD 70. It is found in two colours, white or pale green and purple. Kohlrabi is fast growing and more tolerant of drought than most brassicas, and matures in forty to seventy days, according to variety; the corms are best eaten young, up to the size of a tennis ball. They should be peeled before cooking, especially if rather old, as most of the fibres are in the outer part of the corm.

Cultivation

Kohlrabi are generally sown where they are to grow, a few seeds sown at a time from February in warm gardens, until September. The plants should be about 25 cm apart, and seedlings can be transplanted carefully before they are 5 cm tall. The purple varieties are hardier, and tend to be sown late to be harvested during late autumn and winter.

Pests and diseases are the same as for cabbages; notably cabbage root fly and, on acid soils, clubroot.

Varieties
Traditional cultivars are 'White Vienna' and 'Purple Vienna', and it is these two which are still commonly grown. Modern selection aims at getting faster-maturing varieties, and recently F1 hybrid varieties have become available. Seed of old or heirloom varieties such as 'Purple Delicacy' and 'Rolano' can be found through the vegetable seed source lists.

Young kohlrabi at the best eating size in Malawi

KOHLRABI

Kohlrabi for sale in the early morning vegetable market on Dal Lake, Kashmir

Kohlrabi, 'White Vienna'

Kohlrabi, 'Purple Vienna'

Kohlrabi, 'White Vienna'

Chinese mustard

Turnip

Brassica rapa L. syn. *Brassica campestris* L. (*Cruciferae*)

Brassica rapa is the plant from which turnips, oil-seed turnip-rape and many varieties of Chinese cabbage (see page 47) have been developed. It is related to ordinary cabbage, with which it has combined to form the swede, *Brassica napus*. Other related vegetables are the Chinese mustard, *Brassica juncea*, and the radish. *Brassica rapa* is usually divided into several subspecies as follows: (The European subspecies are relatively straightforward, the Chinese and Japanese very complex and confused. One variety can produce several different vegetables.)

Subspecies *sylvestris* is the wild type, still found commonly all over Europe and much of Asia, generally growing as a weed in open ground, or by streams. It is either annual or biennial forming a leafy rosette the first autumn, and flowering the following spring. Its native range is uncertain, but central Europe has been suggested as a likely area. It is also a common weed in North America.

Subspecies *rapa* is the cultivated turnip. The fleshy taproot is usually almost round in present-day European varieties, but the Japanese also have long narrow carrot-shaped varieties, called 'Hinona Kabu'. Joy Larkcom reckons this was probably derived from the old European variety 'Long Red Tankard', grown in the nineteenth century. Present day varieties are grown with both white and yellow flesh, and their skins may be yellow, white, green or purple topped. Turnip greens are used for spring greens in Europe, either by sowing late and overwintering or by sowing in very early spring and harvesting the plants when about 15 cm high.

Cultivation

Turnips are easily grown, provided they grow quickly when young and are not allowed to dry out. A good crop will be ready about seventy days after sowing. An early summer crop may be had by sowing in February under cover, or in March and April outside. Turnips for storage and overwintering are generally sown in July and August, and watered well if the weather is dry. A final distance of 15 cm between the plants will give large enough turnips for eating, and the spring varieties can be sown closer and harvested small, when they can be delicious. The fast-growing 'Tokyo Cross F1' is better sown in July or August, and can be ready for harvest in thirty-five days. 'Snowball' is suitable for spring sowing, and 'Manchester Market' and the yellow 'Golden Ball' are recommended for late sowing and overwintering. Dry weather and attacks by cabbage root fly are the commonest causes of failure.

'Purple Top Milan'   Flattish white roots with purple markings; early-maturing and good for overwintering.
'Purple Top White Globe'   This is now considered the same as 'Veitch's Red Globe'. An old variety, with round or slightly flattened roots, reddish-purple above ground, white below.
'Tokyo Cross'   An F1 hybrid, raised by Takii & Co., in Japan. Roots round and white, quick-maturing and heat-tolerant, suitable for sowing in mid-summer for an early autumn crop, and will also stand into winter.
'Snowball' syn. 'Early Six Weeks', a fast-maturing white, and **'Golden Ball'** are popular varieties. 'Golden Ball' has yellow flesh and is good for use in winter from an early autumn sowing.

Swede

Brassica napus L.
Rutabaga, Swedish Turnip

This is grown mainly in two forms, swede and oil-seed rape, which is now such a common feature of spring in Europe. There is also a leafy rape grown for animal fodder, particularly for sheep, in northern Europe and New Zealand.

Brassica napus is known to have originated from crosses between *B. rapa*, the turnip, and *B. oleracea*, the cabbage, although the cross is very difficult to make artificially. It is likely that swedes first appeared in medieval gardens where turnips and kale were growing together, and oil-seed rape occurred from crosses between kale and a non-tuberous *Brassica rapa*.

The oriental equivalent of *Brassica napus*, *B. napella*, does not appear to have been grown as a vegetable.

Swedes were first mentioned in European botanical literature by Caspar Bauhin in 1620, but they are probably considerably older than this. They arrived in England from Sweden about 1775, and that is how the common name originated, but they are traditionally eaten in midwinter in Scotland as an accompaniment to haggis. Swedes are hardier than turnips, and their usually yellow-fleshed roots are less watery, particularly in the variety 'Marian'. A few varieties, such as 'Merrick', have white-fleshed and more watery turnip-like roots.

Cultivation

Swedes do best in light but rich soils and an open site. They mature in autumn, and are generally sown in May or June, earlier in the north to give a longer growing season. Seed should be sown direct, and the plants thinned to 20–30 cm apart. Watering will be needed in dry weather. The roots can be left in the ground until used, or lifted and stored in a clamp or covered with straw in a cold shed. Most swedes are relatively disease resistant, but Flea Beetles are a common trouble. They damage and weaken the seedlings by eating round holes in the young leaves. Late sowings and healthy fast-growing plants are least likely to be damaged.

'Purple Top White Globe'

'Purple Top Milan'

'Tokyo Cross'

Swede 'Marian'

Rugose-leaved Chinese mustard in Lijiang, 'Yunnan'

Chinese Mustard

Brassica juncea (L.) Czern.
Mustard Greens, Brown Mustard, Kai Tsoi

This species is now commonly grown in Europe for mustard seed, having replaced the traditional black mustard *Brassica nigra*. It has long been grown in India as an oil-seed, and is also grown for oil in China and Japan. In China, however, it has also been developed into a remarkable variety of different vegetables.

Brassica juncea is known to have originated by hybridization between *Brassica rapa* and black mustard (*B. nigra*), followed by doubling of the chromosomes to form a new species. This has been proved experimentally, though there is doubt about exactly which subspecies of *B. rapa* was involved, and whether the species was formed once, or on several different occasions.

Brassica juncea is most diverse in four areas: central Asia and the Himalayas, thought to be the most ancient area of domestication; the Caucasus; India; and China, especially in the warm central province of Sichuan.

Herklots divides the varieties he recognized in Hong Kong into four groups:

Var. sareptana Sinskaja has thickened leaf stalks and a slightly swollen shoot. The leaves are lyrate, with three pairs of separate basal lobes. The plant is usually grown as a winter crop and the tips of the young shoots are eaten, often salted.

Var. integrifolia (Rupr.) Sinskaja, including var. *rugosa* (Roxb.) Tsen & Lee and var. *foliosa* Bailey, called 'Swatow Mustard', forms a leafy, lettuce-like plant, often producing a round, dense

heart. Some Japanese varieties such as 'Osaka Purple' and 'Red Chirimen' have red or purple leaves, and others puckered leaves like a savoy cabbage. 'Big Stem Mustard' has thickened stems like a celtuce, and simple, oval leaves; 'Wrapped Heart' has small hearts on a rather tall plant; in 'Bamboo Mustard' the stems are elongated and cylindrical, and the plant is generally eaten fresh, as it is more delicate in flavour and less hot than the others.

Var. japonica (Thunb.) Bailey includes several different varieties with jaggedly lobed or finely cut leaves. Some are exceptionally hardy, and are called 'Green-in-the-Snow', 'Luxuriant-in-the-Snow', or literally 'Red-in-the-Snow' (var. *multiceps* Tsen & Lee). These seem to be used salted and pickled in China, but they can also be eaten fresh in salads or cooked. The variety grown as 'Green-in-the-Snow' in England is still fresh and growing as I write this in mid-January and continues undamaged in spite of frosts of −6°C. The taste is good but decidedly peppery, like a strong radish.

Var. crispifolia Bailey   In this the leaves are curled and finely cut like a curly kale. The leaves are picked when young and fresh and eaten cooked or, sparingly, raw. This variety can be valuable for overwintering and providing young greens in early spring.

Herklots records three other varieties which were grown in Sichuan and exported to Hong Kong preserved in salt; var. *tumida* Tsen & Lee, called 'Cha tsoi', had a swollen stem with about eight bulges representing rudimentary lower petioles and is used to make 'Zhacai' pickle; var. *strumata* Tsen & Lee, called 'Parcel-and-Pocket mustard', had small knobs developing on the upper surface of the flattened petioles, and the third, var. *megarrhiza* Tsen & Lee, had a roughly swollen tuberous root.

Cultivation

Mustards are best grown in a similar way to Chinese cabbage (see page 47), which is not surprising as they are adapted to a similar climate. The climate in Sichuan, where many varieties seem to grow best, is very warm, humid and cloudy with ample rain from June to the end of August, and cooler and drier thereafter. Winter is cool, but there is little frost. In Europe and temperate North America mustards need warm, fertile soil with ample water when young, and can tolerate cooler or cold temperatures when mature. If the plants are cold or dry when young, they are likely to run to seed early. In cold areas sowing is best in July; in warmer areas in August or September, so that the plants can grow on through the winter. The small, quick-growing varieties are often ready in as little as a month from sowing. Pests and diseases are similar to those of cabbage, but the mustards are generally tough and trouble-free.

Komatsuna

Although very similar in appearance and taste to the leafy forms of the mustard *Brassica juncea*, these are actually forms of turnip (*Brassica rapa*) developed for their leaves and leaf-stalks. They are described in great detail by Joy Larkcom in *Oriental Vegetables*. The varieties shown here are

'Big Top' F1, syn. 'All Top', which also produces turnip-like roots;

'Tendergreen' F1 is very similar to the original komatsuna and can be ready for its first picking in as little as twenty days (see also pp. 48–9).

Chrysanthemum   for text see p. 231.

Ipomoea aquatica   for text see p. 132.

'Mei Quing Pak Choi'   for text see p. 48.

'Mizuna Early'   for text see p. 48

Pak Choi   for text see p. 48.

CHINESE GREENS

Chinese cabbage, 'Eskimo'

Pak choi

'Mizuna Early'

Komatsuna

'Tendergreen'

'Big Top'

Chrysanthemum

'Mei Quing Pak Choi'

Malaysian pak choi

Ipomoea aquatica (land form) (text page 132)

'Green-in-the-Snow' at Sellindge, Kent, in January

'Kasumi'

'Jade Pagoda'

'Eskimo'

'Comanche'

Specimens from NIAB, Cambridge, photographed 28 September

Broad-leaved Chinese mustard, *Brassica juncea* var. *rugosa*, in Malawi

Chinese Leaves

Brassica rapa L. subspecies *pekinensis* (Lour.)
Celery Cabbage, Pe Tsai, or Peking cabbage

This is the plant generally grown as Chinese cabbage. The plants are like large cos lettuces or cabbages, but with a crisp watery texture and mustard-like taste. There are both round and elongated varieties with solid hearts, open leafy varieties with broad stalks, and the self-blanching variety 'Eskimo' which looks like a large endive with a white heart. Celery cabbage may be eaten raw or cooked.

Cultivation

Those varieties grown as young greens or small flowering plants, such as pak choi, are of easy cultivation, requiring only ample water, rich soil and warm temperatures. They are best sown in mid-summer for cropping in late summer and autumn, and do well at high temperatures.

The large-heading Chinese cabbage with a dense, white, crunchy heart (subsp. *pekinensis*) is more difficult to grow well. They are best sown late, from July to mid-August, and grow best in cooler temperatures or in winter in the tropics. Ample water and rich soil are the key to successful cultivation, allowing the plants to grow quickly. Seeds are best sown singly in pots or sown *in situ* and thinned to 30 cm apart, as they resent root disturbance and are now nearly as tough and drought-resistant as ordinary cabbage. Harvest may be from forty-five days onwards, according to the variety and temperature. Other varieties, such as 'Spring A-1', are bolt-resistant and suitable for spring sowing in cool climates.

These are much the same as for the ordinary cabbages, but Chinese cabbage seems to attract both pests and diseases such as cabbage root fly, aphids and mildew, so an extra keen watch should be kept for their arrival. The thin leaves are especially easily damaged by slugs.

'Early Jade Pagoda'   Michichili group. A quick-maturing form of 'Jade Pagoda'.

'Eskimo'   F1 hybrid. An unusual variety with a self-blanching heart of creamy-white leaves.

'Jade Pagoda'   Michichili group. F1 hybrid, up to 35 cm tall, and 15 cm across; dark green loose heads with a long internal stalk, but good resistance to bolting.

'Kasumi'   Dense heavy heads with a short internal stalk and good resistance to bolting.

Chinese cabbage (barrel-type), in Malawi

Michichili or 'Early Jade Pagoda'

Pak choi

A large specimen of 'Joi Choi', photographed 27 September

Pak Choi

Brassica rapa L. subspecies *chinensis*
Bok Choi (Cantonese), Qing Cai

Var. *chinensis*
Pak choi is a small plant with a rosette of upright leaves with thickened and flattened usually white petioles and smooth, rounded blades. It has been grown in China since the fifth century AD. This is a fast-growing annual; some varieties do well in a hot, wet summer climate, and can be ready in as little as five weeks; others are better in autumn and in cooler climates, and grow more slowly. Pak choi is usually chopped before being cooked, but small specimens may be cooked whole. The flowering shoots may also be eaten if the plants bolt prematurely, or have been left to flower. 'Joi Choi' is an F1 hybrid in this group, with very white leaf stalks; 'Mei Quing Pak Choi' is another F1, with a green leaf stalk. It has good resistance to bolting at 65–70°C.

Var. *parachinensis* Flowering white cabbage or pak choi sum. This has white leaf stems but yellow flowers, and is grown for the young flowering shoots which are eaten just as the flowers begin to open, usually with about four leaves of varying width.
Var. *rosularis* or **var. *atrovirens*** (possibly the same as subsp. *narinosa*), Rosette pak choi or 'tat soi'. This has very dark green, spoon-shaped leaves in a perfect rosette, the blades usually pressed flat on the ground, but sometimes with more upright leaves. The Chinese name means 'very ancient cabbage', so it may be an old variety. The rosettes are very hardy and the plant can survive both frost and snow.
Subspecies *oleifera* Turnip-rape, Flowering rape. This is closest of the varieties to wild *Brassica rapa*, and is grown mainly for its oil, but the young flowering shoots are sometimes eaten in China.

Mizuna

Brassica rapa L.
Subspecies *nipposinica* var. *laciniata* (syn. var. *japonica*)

Mizuna greens are commonly grown in Japan. They are very quick growing and easy, forming clumps of finely dissected leaves which stand for a long time without getting tough. They can be harvested at any time and will soon grow again, and can either be eaten in a salad or cooked. They are also reasonably hardy, standing several degrees of frost without damage, and so are useful during the winter.
'Tokyo Beau' is a hybrid variety with broader dark green leaves.
Mibuna greens, grown in the Mibu area near Kyoto, are described in Joy Larkcom's *Oriental Vegetables*. The plants are clump forming with long petioles and narrow smooth blades, not dissected like Mizuna.
Subspecies *perviridis* Bailey (syn. var. *komatsuna* Hara) is generally called 'Spinach Mustard', 'Mustard Spinach' or 'Komatsuna Na', and is a Japanese vegetable, almost unknown in China. It is a large, fast-growing annual, overwintering if sown late, and often planted in rice fields in late September after the rice has been harvested. The leaves are eaten like spinach or young kale, and are valuable, being hardy to about minus 10°C. In Japan, Komatsuna have been hybridized with both the turnip and with pak choi.
Subspecies *dichotoma* Toria, or Indian rape, is usually grown for the oil in its seeds, as is subspecies *trilocularis* Yellow-seeded Sarson. Both these are constituents of Indian mustard oil.

Left to right, 'Shanghai Pak Choi', 'Bok Choi', 'Gai Choi'

Tat Soi (var. *rosularis*)

'Mei Quing' pak choi in Malawi

'Mizuna Early' in Kent

Large, old seakale plants in bud at Dungeness, Kent

Summer leaves of seakale

Detail of leaves

Seakale

Crambe maritima L.
Chou Marin (French)

Seakale is blanched in early spring, when the young leaf stalks and flowering shoots have a mild and subtle flavour. They are cooked rather like asparagus, and eaten with melted butter or a mild sauce. The young flowering shoots may also be eaten, like purple-sprouting broccoli.

Seakale is a particularly English vegetable, as its cultivation has never been popular elesewhere in Europe, although Jane Grigson records that the great French chef Carème learnt of its use when cooking for the Prince Regent at Brighton in 1816, approved of it and coined the name 'sickell' for it.

The plant is a long-lived perennial, growing wild on shingle beaches on the shores of the Atlantic, Baltic and Black Seas. It is common along the southern coast of England on suitable beaches, but rather rare elsewhere. In summer the leaves form conspicuous mounds of greyish-green, but in winter they die away completely to the ground, in contrast to the leaves of wild cabbage which remain green all winter on a stem of variable height. Other species of *Crambe*, found in the steppe regions of eastern Europe and Central Asia, are also said to be eaten, but as far as I know none are cultivated on any scale. The giant inflorescences of *Crambe cordifolia* would make a fine perennial vegetable if blanched and tender, and would be suitable for growing in cold continental climates.

Named varieties include:

'Lily White' which we have not seen, but it is a very pale selection with little of the purple colouring often found in wild plants. Other old varieties were called 'Ordinary Pink-tipped' and 'Ivory White'.

Cultivation

Seakale is easily grown. Seed can be sown in spring in well-drained, very deep, sandy soil and the young plants grown on through their first year. Any that are forced after the first year are likely to be rather small, but by the end of their second year the plants should have reached full size.

There are two main methods of cultivation. The plants can be grown in a permanent bed and blanched *in situ* with seakale forcing pots, a frame covered in heavy black polythene, or about 30 cm of peat, leafmould or sand. The bed, which can be 1.5 m or more wide, should be raised if the soil is at all heavy and be very stony with rich soil. The top 15 cm or so could be composed of sand and gravel. Young plants, which can also be grown from root cuttings (see below), are planted out in spring, at least 75 cm apart, and grown throughout the summer. Seaweed fertilizer would be appropriate for a summer feed, and old books recommend applications of salt, which probably controls any slugs.

The plants are blanched in early spring, February and March in southern England, and two or three cuts can be taken off each plant. The ideal shoot is about 20 cm long. Later the plants are allowed to grow in full light, and fertilized well to encourage good growth for the next season. The beds should be replanted with young plants after about five years.

Alternatively, plants may be grown as annuals in a row in the garden and forced indoors from December onwards. The young plants are dug up in autumn after the leaves have died down, and the roots are carefully trimmed to 10–15 cm long. The pieces cut off, and any side roots, are kept for next year's cuttings, being careful to ensure that the upper ends of all the roots point in the same direction, as it is from here that the new shoot arises. These cuttings are then put in a large pot of damp sand or planted in bundles in a warm corner of the garden, ready to be lined out 30 cm apart in early spring. The main thick part of the root, with the pointed bud on top, is then blanched as needed in a warm cellar or cupboard, in a pot of damp sand or peat, and kept quite dark. In the past the roots were often retarded in icehouses to prolong the season into May.

Pests and diseases

Seakale is generally free from troubles, though young shoots in the open garden may be killed by late frosts and hungry rabbits can find and eat the dormant buds. Slugs and other pests which eat the young crowns can be kept off with sand or ash placed over the plants in autumn. The fleshy growths are liable to get a slimy rot or botrytis if they are wet and shaded, or if the leaves are too crowded during humid weather. They do not suffer these problems on an open, windy seashore.

A blanched flowering shoot

A seakale forcing pot

Seakale forced in a frame covered with black polythene

Horseradish

Armoracia rusticana P. Gaertner, B. Meyer & Scherb. (*Cruciferae*)

Horseradish is widely grown for its pungent root, which is usually grated and combined with oil and vinegar or with cream to make sauce for beef, smoked fish or asparagus. The plant forms a clump of large leaves, and has a deeply penetrating, fleshy, forked root. The flowers are small and white, on a tall branching inflorescence.

Horseradish is thought to be native to southern Russia and the eastern Ukraine, but is now found wild on roadsides throughout Europe and North America. It has been cultivated at least since Classical times, and was probably spread around Europe by the Romans for medicinal as well as gastronomic reasons. A second species, *A. macrocarpa* (Waldst. & Kit.) Kit. ex Baumg. from marshes in the Danube basin in Hungary and Yugoslavia, has untoothed leaves and larger seed pods with about twenty seeds.

Horseradish is easily cultivated, and is grown from root cuttings; indeed, any live piece of root will eventually make a new plant. Present-day garden clones are almost sterile, and seldom produce good seed. Root cuttings or young plants should be set out in spring, allowing at least 60 cm between the plants, and roots should be worth digging by the following autumn. Once established horseradish will tolerate any amount of neglect, but will not thrive in the shade of trees. The usual plant has dark green leaves, but there is an attractive variegated form which is rare in cultivation, though available from a few nurseries.

Rocket

Eruca sativa Miller, syn. *Eruca vesicaria* (L.) Cav. subsp. *sativa* (Mill.) (*Cruciferae*)
Arugula, Roquette, Rucola

Rocket is a salad vegetable, which has recently become very popular in America. It has a long history of cultivation in Europe both as a salad and as a medicinal plant; the oil extracted from the seeds was said to act as an aphrodisiac. Seed is generally sown in the open ground in spring, or in early autumn in mild areas where the plants can survive overwinter. After about forty days the rocket is ready to eat.

Plants form a rosette of deeply lobed leaves, with a large terminal lobe and two to five narrow lobes on each side. The flowers are up to 2 cm long, pale yellow or cream-coloured, with purple veins. The leaves are picked when young, at about 7.5 cm long, and can either be cooked like spinach or used raw in salads, to which they give an added peppery flavour. They go best with bland salads such as lettuce, rather than mixed with other strong flavours.

Shepherd's Purse

Capsella bursa-pastoris (L.) Medik. var. *auriculata* Makino (*Cruciferae*)

This common and very variable weed is found throughout the world. It is reported by both G. H. Herklots and Joy Larkcom to be grown and sold in both Taiwan and Shanghai. It can be eaten raw in salads and cooked like spinach, or in the Chinese style, floating around in a clear soup. The plants are annuals, forming rosettes of jagged leaves which may be 20 cm across in good soil. The flower stems, which are also edible when young, appear in spring if the rosettes have overwintered, but otherwise can be produced at any time of year.

Turkish Rocket *Bunias orientalis* L. and *Bunias erucago* L. (*Cruciferae*) (not illustrated) are both yellow-flowered weedy plants, native to the Mediterranean area. The former is a perennial or biennial, with deeply cut leaves, sometimes eaten as a salad. The young shoots are eaten, like sprouting broccoli. The latter is usually a biennial, and the young stems and roots are eaten.

A row of horseradish in a Scottish garden

Variegated form of horseradish

Mustard and Cress

Sinapis alba L. and *Lepidium sativum* L. (*Cruciferae*)

These two are often grown together to provide quick-growing spicy greenery for salads and sandwiches. Packs bought in shops commonly contain only mustard, as this is the quicker grower, being ready in about ten days, two to four days sooner than cress.

Sinapis alba, white mustard, is a common wild plant in most of Europe, but is probably not a native of the British Isles, although grown here by the Romans. It is common in other areas of the world, being a particular pest in parts of California, where it invades the native grassland, shading out the annual wildflowers. It is easily recognized when in fruit by the flattened hairy end to the seedpod. The dark green, rounded cotyledons are eaten, with the white stalk below them, so they are better grown in a warm dark place, where they become etiolated. *Sinapis alba* seeds give the hot taste to English mustard and most is cultivated around Norwich; it is also grown for use as table mustard. When grown for salad, the round pale brown or yellowish seeds are sown on wet tissue paper or peat, and should not be allowed to dry out.

Cress *Lepidium sativum* is recognized by its narrow reddish-brown seeds and deeply three-lobed cotyledons. The mature plant is about 40 cm tall, with deeply cut leaves, small white flowers and seed pods 5–6 mm long. It is found as a relic of cultivation in many places, but is probably native in the eastern Mediterranean area and Egypt. It should be sown about three days before mustard, so that the two are ready together.

Horseradish on a roadside

Rocket

Shepherd's Purse, *Capsella bursa-pastoris*

Mustard and cress

Winter-cress (*Barbarea* sp.)

American Land Cress (*Barbarea* sp.)

Watercress

Nasturtium officinale R.Br. (*Cruciferae*)

Watercress is a popular and important vegetable, but because it requires very specialized conditions for proper growth, it is seldom grown by amateurs. Only those whose gardens contain a chalk or limestone spring or pure stream are able to produce a safe crop, as any pollution in the water will endanger the eater.

There are two species of watercress found wild throughout Europe, *N. officinale*, a diploid, and *N. microphyllum* (Boenn.) Reichenb., a tetraploid. The sterile triploid hybrid between them is common in the wild and was often cultivated, called 'brown cress' because it often has a brownish tinge in cold weather. Its cultivation has now declined because of a virus infection in vegetatively propagated stocks. Watercress is now found wild as an escape from cultivation in North America and New Zealand, and may even become a pest.

Watercress has been recognized as a valuable salad plant since Roman times, primarily as a source of vitamins to protect against scurvy. Commercial cultivation of watercress was first recorded in Germany around Erfurt in about 1750, and in England near Gravesend in 1808. The main areas of cultivation in England today are in Hampshire, associated with the chalk springs in the Test and Itchen valleys. The water emerges at about 10°C, so the crop continues to grow through the winter.

Fertilization is by nitrates already in the water, and by superphosphate applied to new beds. Watercress is now generally raised from seed, so as to produce healthy, virus-free plants, and the aim is to get plants which flower as late as possible, to give a longer cutting season.

Winter-cress

Barbarea vulgaris R. Br. (*Cruciferae*)
American or Land Cress, Upland Broad Leaf Cress, Herbe de Sainte Barbe

This is an easily grown biennial or perennial, with rosettes of pinnately-lobed, dark green leaves which stand well through the winter. They are powerfully flavoured, and generally eaten in salads, though they might be better for soup. The plants flower in early spring, with attractive heads of yellow flowers. There are about fourteen species, native in Europe and Asia, with one species, *B. orthoceras* Ledeb., native throughout North America in the far north and the mountains, and in northern Japan and eastern Siberia. All the species grow in rather damp waste places, on river banks and in marshes.

Winter-cress has been grown as a salad crop at least since the seventeenth century, and is used as a substitute for watercress when flowing water is not available. By the eighteenth century its cultivation had died out in England, though it is still a common wild plant. In America, however, it remained popular, being very hardy.

Seed is generally sown in July and August in rich, moist soil, and the plant will tolerate some shade. These late-summer-sown plants should stand well through the winter and may be harvested from late autumn until the plants flower in late spring.

Watercress beds in Hampshire

Wasabi

Wasabia japonica (Miq.) Matsum. syn. *Eutrema japonica* (Miq.)
Koidz. (*Cruciferae*) (not illustrated)

This is the plant from which is made the sap-green pungent paste
which forms the sauce for Sushi when mixed with soy. It is native
of Japan and Sakhalin and is found throughout the islands,
growing by streams in the mountains. It is often collected from the
wild but in Japan it is also cultivated in running water, with the
rhizomes held down by stones.

Wasabi is a perennial, closely related to *Cardamine* and true
watercress. It has a thick creeping rhizome, 1–2 cm across, with
long-stalked, kidney-shaped, toothed leaves, and few-leafed
flowering stems to 40 cm tall. The flowers are white, in a loose
head. It is very similar in appearance to *Pachyphragma*, from the
Caucasus, but has cylindrical, not flattened, fruits. It is the
rhizome which is used to make the paste, which tastes rather
similar to horseradish. It must be both very finely and freshly
grated, and goes well with raw fish such as tuna.

Young plants of watercress

55

Radishes in the market in Ili, Chinese Central Asia

Radish

Raphanus sativus L. (*Cruciferae*)

In Europe the radish is only a minor salad plant, but in China and Japan it is an important root vegetable, eaten both raw, preserved and cooked, and often carved to make a decorative garnish. In parts of Asia, a special variety, the Mougri radish, is grown for its long edible seed pods.

Wild radishes, *Raphanus raphanistrum* L., are common on wasteland by the sea and in sandy areas inland throughout the British Isles and much of Europe. Subspecies *rhaphanistrum*, which is an annual weed of wasteland and fields, has white flowers in southern Europe, yellow in the north. Subspecies *maritimus* (Sm.) Thell. is found on cliffs and sandy seashores in western Europe and the northern Black Sea coast; it is a perennial with a thick root and sulphur-yellow flowers. Another subspecies, subsp. *rostratus* (DC) Thell., confined to the Aegean region, has pale lilac flowers with darker veins. Two other subspecies, both usually found as weeds, occur in southwest Europe. A wild radish, var. *raphanistroides*, is found in Japan, but it is not clear whether this is a native variety or the cultivated radish gone wild.

History

Cultivated radishes are known to have been grown by the Egyptians in about 2780 BC, when they were included in the rations given to the workers on the Great Pyramid. The origin of the cultivated radish is not clear, though presumably it is descended from the wild species, and was first domesticated in the eastern Mediterranean area. By 500 BC it was grown in China, and by AD 700 in Japan.

Black radishes were the earliest to be cultivated. White radishes are first mentioned in Europe in the late sixteenth century when they were long and tapering. The round radish first appeared in the eighteenth century, and the red skins at about the same time. Soon every known shape, and green- and yellow-skinned varieties, were grown.

Modern cultivated radishes are usually divided into four groups: white or red radishes, black radishes, Mougri radish, and oil-seed radish. In Europe red and white radishes are grown as very quick-maturing salad plants, always eaten young and raw. Recent developments have aimed to reduce bolting in summer temperatures, speed up maturity and reduce a tendency to pithiness in the root. 'Cherry Belle' was one of the earliest extra crisp varieties, ready for harvest in around twenty-three days. Round red varieties are the most popular, but there are also long red varieties, and a light golden one is still available. The varieties 'Easter Egg' and 'Rainbow Mix' produce purple-skinned radishes as well as red and white.

In Japan and China radishes are generally eaten cooked and sliced, often boiled in soups. There, most varieties are long and white, slow to mature, and many of them will stand through the winter. Some, which originated in northern China, have white or green skin and green, purple, red, pink or veined flesh, and Joy

'China Rose'

Sea radish

Larkcom describes how these are carved into beautiful flowers and butterflies by chefs in Beijing. In Japan different shapes and growth habits have been developed to suit different soils. In the 1930s the Russian botanist N. I. Vavilov was most excited to find a variety (now called 'Sakurajima') reaching a weight of 16 kg on the volcanic peninsula of Sakurajima opposite Kagoshima in southern Japan; specimens up to 45 kg are reported nowadays. Long-rooted varieties, adapted for deep sandy soils, can reach a length of 120 cm. Radish leaves and seedlings are often eaten cooked.

Black radishes are the most ancient group. They are now seldom seen, but were popular in the seventeenth century as they were long-lasting, standing through the winter. Both long and round varieties were grown, with either black or dark brown and rather rough skins. The modern varieties come from Spain or Italy.

Mougri or rat-tailed radish

This is grown for its seed pods which are elongated and many become 20–100 cm long(!) according to Banga, writing in Simmonds' *The Evolution of Crop Plants*. The upper measurement of 100 cm does seem immensely long, and the 60 cm mentioned by Dr Herklots is a more likely length. These exceptional varieties have been developed in India. I bought the seed of one of these varieties in a market in Bokhara, but the longest seed pods produced were about 5 cm long. This is similar to the variety 'München Bier' which also has an edible white root.

Cultivation

Small salad radishes are among the quickest and easiest vegetables to grow. They need an open position and a light, fine soil with adequate moisture so they grow rapidly. They can be sown through the summer at one- or two-week intervals, aiming to get the seeds about 2.5 cm apart. The quickest varieties can be mature in twenty days.

Oriental radishes need more care, and different varieties are adapted for sowing at different seasons. 'April Cross' is a very easy variety which can be sown either in spring or in late summer to overwinter. 'Tokinaski' can be sown at any season, except winter. Other varieties are best for sowing in late spring, and are heat tolerant. Most varieties are best sown after mid-summer, and will be ready in autumn, winter and the following spring. They need fifty-five days growing, or more, to reach a good size, and benefit by having cool weather at the end of their growing season.

The black radishes should be sown in July and August, and thinned to 15 cm apart. They should not be allowed to become dry, or the roots will crack when it rains and their growth makes a

spurt. Too much water will make them produce leaf growth at the expense of the roots.

Radish seed pods are usually plentiful if any plants have been left to flower. They should be picked when young and crisp.

Pests and diseases

Radishes are very closely related to cabbages, and prone to most of the pests and diseases which affect Brassicas. Nevertheless, the large oriental radishes are remarkably free from disease. Slugs are the commonest pests, and cabbage root flies can spoil the roots in dry weather. White mildew on the leaves can also be a problem in dry weather; resistant varieties are available. Flea beetle commonly attacks the seedlings, eating small round holes in the leaves, but the plants soon get past the susceptible stage.

Wild radish in Brittany

'Black Spanish Long'   'Black Spanish Round'

Specimens from NIAB, Cambridge, photographed 1 November

'Pfitzer's Maindreieek'

Specimens from NIAB, Cambridge, photographed 1 November

'Black Spanish Long'   Another old variety, dating from 1882, but similar varieties were grown much earlier. For eating both raw and cooked like a Japanese radish.

'Black Spanish Round'   An old variety with white flesh. They are sown in July, for use in winter and are lifted as needed. Chinese radishes are usually large and grown over the winter. This green-topped variety is common in Hunnan.

'Pfitzers Maindreieek'   A winter radish, with brown skin but white flesh.

'Violet de Gournay' (not shown) has a large blackish-purple root and white flesh. An old French variety, best used in autumn.

Chinese radishes in Yunnan

'Prinz Rotin'

'French Breakfast'

'Saxa Short Top'

'Cherry Belle'

'Pontvil'

Specimens grown at Sellindge, Kent, photographed 3 July

RADISH

'April Cross' An F1 hybrid. An easy variety, standing well through the winter and remaining crisp. Roots to 38 cm long. Can also be planted in early spring to harvest in about 63 days.

'Beacon' Round-rooted; claimed to be resistant to pithiness.

'Cherry Belle' Root round, scarlet. A very popular variety. 22–24 days.

'French Breakfast' 1.6 cm diameter. Cylindrical. Scarlet with white tip. 23 days; best harvested very young.

'Minowasi Summer No. 2' A Japanese radish with long tapering roots, for sowing in late spring or summer and harvesting in autumn.

'Pontvil' 24 days; oblong; stands well.

'Prinz Rotin' syn. 'Red Prince' 25 days; a globe variety, which stands well.

'Saxa Short Top' 18 days. Scarlet; mild flavour. Good for forcing.

'Scarlet Globe' 24 days; suitable for forcing.

'Sparkler' Syn. 'Early Scarlet' 25 days: scarlet with white tip.

'Tsukushi Spring Cross' A Japanese radish for sowing in spring or early summer and harvesting in summer and early autumn.

Specimens from NIAB, Cambridge, photographed 5 July

'Tsukushi Spring Cross' (*left*)
'Minowasi Summer No 2' (*right*)

'April Cross'

'Burgundy'

'Dwarf Green Longpod'

Okra

Hibiscus esculentus L. syn. *Abelmoschus esculentus* (L.) Moench. (*Malvaceae*)
Gombo, Gumbo, Bindi or Lady's Fingers

Okra is a tropical vegetable, requiring considerable heat to grow successfully. The flowers are like those of a hollyhock, and the fruits, which are eaten in the young state, are long and green, tapering to a blunt point, and often five-sided in cross-section. They have a delicate flavour and a mucilaginous texture inside.

Okra has long been cultivated in west Africa, Ethiopia and Sudan and in India. Its origin is not known, but the majority of cultivated forms seem to be complex polyploid hybrids between some of the thirty species of *Hibiscus* section *Abelmoschus*. It is not clear whether it originated in Africa or India, and hybrids between traditional Indian and African okra are partially sterile, suggesting they are not closely related.

Most okra breeding is now carried out in India or the southern States of North America, to which the gumbo arrived from west Africa with the slave trade. Nowadays in the United States around thirty varieties are available. The plants vary from dwarfs, around 1 m tall, to full sized varieties, up to 4 m in 'Perkin's Mammoth'. Most modern varieties have spineless fruits and the fruits may be 7.5 cm long at the edible stage in the short varieties like the dwarf 'Blondy' to 25 cm in the popular variety 'Clemson Spineless', though even these are better eaten when smaller. Most fruits are green, but both leaf stalks and fruits are red in 'Burgundy' and 'Red Okra'. In 'White Velvet' the fruits are velvety and white. 'Vining Green' is almost a climber, and needs support.

'Clemson's Spineless' was raised in 1939 by the South Carolina Agricultural Experimental Station at Clemson. It was a selection from 'Perkin's Spineless': plant 120–180 cm tall; pods c. 25 cm, cropping in about fifty-six days in warm climates.

Okra thrives in the same conditions as sweetcorn, but requires more heat. Soil should be fertile, with a high potash content, so a dressing of bonfire soil before planting is beneficial. Most varieties need about four months of good heat, but in the hot season in the subtropics fruits may be ready in as little as fifty days. Soak the seeds in warm water for twenty-four hours before planting, and keep the seed pots and young plants at a temperature of 75°F or above. Below this temperature the plants grow very slowly. In the greenhouse, plants may be grown in pots or in peat-filled growing bags, and a watch kept for botrytis if conditions are cold and damp.

Shown here are:
'Dwarf Green Longpod'   Plant 75–90 cm tall; pods 18–20 cm long, cropping in about fifty days.
'Burgundy'   Plant c. 100 cm tall. Pods 15–20 cm. Tolerates cool weather.

Mallow

Malva verticillata L. including *Malva crispa* (L.) L. (*Malvaceae*)

Mallow plants were formerly grown in vegetable gardens in Europe, and are still common in China today. They are easily grown annuals, forming rosettes of long-stemmed leaves before sending up a tall, branching flowering stem. All parts of the plant are edible when young, and have a mucilaginous texture.

Malva verticillata, which is the plant generally grown as a vegetable, is a native of eastern Asia. *Malva crispa* is a variety of it, which comes true from seed, and has leaves with a particularly wavy or crinkly edge. It has small, pale pinkish flowers with petals about 7 mm long. Both have a long history of cultivation in Europe, and are naturalized in North America.

Seed is sown in spring and the plants thinned or spaced to about 20 cm apart. Young leaves and shoots may be picked as required and eaten in soups or lightly boiled like spinach. *Malva neglecta* Wallr. is said to be have been much grown in Egypt as a pot herb.

A tall tropical okra in Malawai

Malva verticillata in Sichuan, China

Flower of okra 'Dwarf Green Longpod'

Malva crispa

Sacks of potatoes and Okra in a market in La Paz, Bolivia, photographed by Sam Phillips

Anu

Tropaeolum tuberosum Ruiz & Pavon (*Tropaeolaceae*)
Tuberous Nasturtium. Other local names: anyu (Quecha, in S.
Peru); apina-mama (Titicaca basin and Peru); mashua (C. Andes,
C. Peru to Ecuador and S. Colombia); isanu, cubio (Bogota).

Anu is grown in the High Andes in the same areas and often in the
same fields as potatoes. The plant is originally a climber, as are
most of the members of the genus *Tropaeolum*, which includes the
familiar garden nasturtium and the Canary creeper.

Like the primitive potatoes, most of the clones are short-day
plants – that is, they only flower and make tubers in northern
latitudes after the middle of September when the day length
reaches twelve hours or less. The clone shown here, however, is
one which regularly flowers from July onwards, and appears to be
day-neutral. It is named 'Ken Aslet' after the former
superintendent of the rock garden at Wisley, who was
instrumental in its distribution and cultivation in England. Like
most of the large-tubered cultivated clones, it belongs to var.
lineamaculatum Cardenas, describing the stipples and spots of red
on the yellowish tuber.

A second variety is var. *pilifera*, which is confined to Columbia,
and has slender white tubers with a purplish apex. This is possibly
synonymous with subsp. *sylvestre Sparre*, which is thought to be a
wild form, and has slender, white tubers. It also differs from
subsp. *tuberosum* in its bright orange-red flowers and smaller,
more deeply cut leaves.

Anu is easily cultivated by planting tubers in loose, leafy soil in
a warm position, after all danger of frost has passed. The shoots
grow up very quickly, and the plants need water throughout the
growing season; they will die down if they become dry. The tubers
should be harvested as soon as the vines have been cut down by
frost. All the tubers should be brought in or protected from frost
in the same way as potatoes.

They are generally eaten after having been boiled for about ten
minutes, and have a slight but pleasant, not acid flavour. In Peru
they are eaten half dried, or boiled and then frozen.

The leaves of the annual species of *Tropaeolum*, *T. majus* L. and
T. minus L., may be eaten in salad, and have a slightly peppery
flavour. This is the origin of their common name 'Nasturtium',
which was originally, and still is in botanical Latin, applied to
watercress. *Tropaeolum minus* was the first to be introduced to
Europe from Peru in about 1576, under the name 'Indian cress',
and was given the Latin name *Nasturtium indicum* by John
Tradescant in 1656. The larger-flowered *T. majus* did not appear
until about 1680.

Oca

Oxalis tuberosa Molina (*Oxalidaceae*)
Other local names: iribia (Bogota); cuiba (Venuzuela); New
Zealand yams (NZ)

This is a common crop in the Andes, second only to the potato in
popularity. It is grown in the same fields as potatoes, along with the
fourth common Andean tuber crop, the ulluco (see pages 80–81),
or in warmer areas with maize. Its cultivation ranges from
Venezuela to northern Argentina, and is the staple diet in the
Titicaca area of Bolivia. It is also popular in parts of New Zealand,
to which it was said to have been introduced from Chile in 1869.

Oxalis tuberosa is unknown as a wild plant, but it is presumed to
have originated in Peru. Numerous cultivars are grown, varying in
skin colour, size, shape and oxalic acid content. The variety grown
in New Zealand has an elongated shape, about 10 cm long, and a
red skin, similar to the form shown here from Peru. It has a flavour
like a potato, with slightly sour overtones caused by the oxalic acid.
The acidity can be reduced by leaving the tubers in the sun for a few
days, and this is commonly done to the more sour varieties. They
then become floury and sweet. Our large photograph shows sacks of
oca for sale in a market in Peru.

The form shown opposite, top left, is a clone which has been
grown for many years outdoors in the Royal Botanic Gardens, Kew.
These tubers were very small, perhaps because the roots had only a
short time to develop in the late autumn; like the primitive potatoes
and anu, the tubers begin to form only after the days are shorter
than nine hours. Before this the plants produce ample top growth
with rather fleshy stems and leaves. The flowers are orange-yellow.
Other tuber colours are white, yellow, piebald or black, and they
are commonly elongated, but also round.

The tubers should be planted in spring, in large pots, and
plunged or planted outside when all danger of air frost is past. In
autumn the plants should be brought under cover, with a frame, so
that they can continue to grow for as long as possible. This would
have been our advice for growing the first potatoes introduced to
Europe in the sixteenth century, and with intensive breeding oca
could become as easy a vegetable to cultivate in northern latitudes.

Leaves of *Oxalis tuberosa*

Tropaeolum tuberosum, 'Ken Aslet'

Tropaeolum minus

Small tubers of *Oxalis tuberosa*

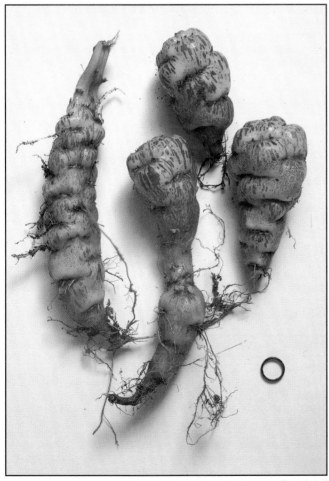

Tubers of *Tropaeolum tuberosum*, 'Ken Aslet'

Tropaeolum tuberosum subsp. *sylvestre*

Rhubarb 'Royal Red'

Rhubarb 'Brown's Crimson'

Rhubarb

Rheum rhabarbarum L. (*Polygonaceae*)

Rhubarb is unusual among vegetables, since it is generally eaten with sugar. Only the leaf-stalks of the young leaves are edible; when mature the leaf blades are poisonous because of the calcium oxalate they contain, though the young leaves of some varieties can be eaten like sorrel. Rhubarb is a popular crop in cool areas of Europe and North America, but the plants will not survive the summer in hot climates.

History

The history of rhubarb cultivation is closely connected with its use as a medicinal plant. Rhubarb root is a powerful laxative, an effect that seems to have been especially valued by ancient cultures, and its use is recorded in China about 2700 BC, in the Pen-King herbal. The root was dried before use and in this state was a valuable export, brought to Europe first by Marco Polo, and later imported through Smyrna (today Izmir). By the sixteenth century this trade had become especially valuable, as rhubarb had become known as a cure for venereal diseases. The Chinese drug was obtained from *Rheum officinale* and *Rheum palmatum*, now often grown as an ornamental. A less efficacious drug was imported to western Europe from east of the Volga; this was *Rheum rhabarbarum*, which is native in Mongolia. It was first cultivated in England in 1573, again as a medicinal plant for its root, rather than as a vegetable. It was only in the eighteenth century that rhubarb stalks became popular for eating (this discovery is said to have been made in France), and their forcing and blanching is said to have been discovered by chance at the Chelsea Physic Garden only around 1817. By 1830 the forced stalks were a common winter vegetable in markets around London, produced by the methods already used for seakale.

In eastern Turkey the leaf-stalks of the prickly-leaved *Rheum ribes* are gathered for eating and sold by the roadside. They have been considered a delicacy since the thirteenth century, and taste much like ordinary rhubarb.

Rheum rhaponticum L., the name often used for cultivated rhubarb, is a rare species, native only on mountain rocks in the Rila Planina in Bulgaria. It was grown by Prosper Alpinus in the Botanic Garden in Padua in 1603. There are numerous cultivars of modern rhubarb, some of which may be derived from hybrids with other species such as *R. palmatum* and *R. undulatum*. They vary mainly in colour (the red varieties being the more popular) in acidity and in the degree of 'winey' taste, as indicated by names like 'Hawkes' Champagne'.

Cultivation

Rhubarb plants are long-lived and almost indestructible perennials. They can be raised from seed sown in the spring, but the best crops are said to come from named clones of which there are many. Bare-rooted young plants are best planted when dormant, but potted ones can be planted at any time. When dividing established plants, each piece should be left with a bud on a piece of root. Soil should be rich and moist though not waterlogged, and the site should be open and not shaded by the branches of trees. Liberal applications of old manure and compost should be mixed in the soil before planting. Both watering and mulching will help young plants, but on all but the driest soils, established plants should not need water. Purists cut off the flowering stems as they appear; most of us enjoy the tall branching spikes of creamy flowers, but there is no point in letting the plants set seed. Plants can be forced by bringing them inside in winter, and rhubarb pots are used to blanch young stems in the spring. If fresh, warm manure is piled around the pots, an even earlier crop may be had. Pests and diseases are few, but old plants can be killed by honey fungus and other rots.

'Appleton's Forcing'   Raised at Winnington's Nurseries, Norwich, in the nineteenth century. It was raised from 'Prince Albert' and, probably, 'Hawkes' Champagne'.
'Brown's Crimson'
'Brown's Red'
'Cawood Castle'   Raised at the Stockbridge House Experimental Horticulture Station, Cawood, near Selby, Yorkshire, around 1960.
'Early Cherry'
'Early Victoria'   This is an early form of 'Victoria', a popular nineteenth-century variety raised by Joseph Myatt, at Manor Farm, Deptford, in 1837.
'Hawkes' Champagne'   Raised by Mr Hawkes of Loampit Hill, Lewisham. A popular early nineteenth-century variety, still suitable for forcing, but not now one of the earliest in the open. Stems red.
'Royal Red'
'Stockbridge Cropper'   Raised at the Stockbridge House Experimental Horticulture Station.
'The Sutton'   Raised by Mr Daw at Kew, and introduced by Messrs Suttons in 1893. Forces well; almost sterile.
'Timperley Early'   Raised by H. Marshland before 1945; early growing; red-skinned, but green-fleshed. Leaves c. 45 cm long.

Rhubarb plants and forcing pots at Hope End House

'Appleton's Forcing'

'Brown's Red'

'Stockbridge Cropper'

'Early Victoria'

'Timperley Early'

'Stockbridge Cropper'

'Hawkes' Champagne'

'The Sutton'

'Early Cherry'

'Cawood Castle'

Young leaves of Houttuynia at edible stage

Houttuynia cordata in flower

Chinese spinach in the market

Houttuynia

Houttuynia cordata Thunb. (*Saururaceae*)

Houttuynia is a creeping perennial, which is common in damp woodland in most of temperate eastern Asia, from the Himalayas and China to Japan and Java. The leaves and young shoots are picked in early spring, when they are about 8 cm long, and eaten either raw in salads or cooked like spinach. They were collected avidly by the Chinese botanists with whom I was travelling in Sichuan, and were also on sale in the market in Chengdu. The flowers are minute, in dense spikes, surrounded at the base by petal-like bracts.

Houttuynia belongs to the small and primitive family *Saururaceae*, which contains only three genera and about four species. The most conspicuous is the Yerba Mansa, *Anemopsis californica* Hook., which was formerly used medicinally for diseases of the skin and blood. It grows in wet, open alkaline meadows from eastern California to Texas and Mexico.

Three forms of *Houttuynia* are grown in gardens in Europe as ornamentals: the wild, single form; a form with double flowers, i.e. with several rows of bracts; and a form with beautifully marked leaves, variegated with red and white, called 'Chameleon' or 'Variegata'. All are easily grown in moist soil in partial shade, and will creep to form loose mats of heart-shaped leaves.

Chinese Spinach

Amaranthus gangeticus L. syn. *A. tricolor* L. (*Amaranthaceae*)
Tampala Spinach, Yin Tsoi (Chinese), Bayam (Malay)

This substitute for spinach is commonly grown in India, southeast Asia, China and Japan. The whole plant is edible, but the parts usually eaten are the young shoots and leaves. Older side shoots from the main stem may be peeled and eaten like the stalks of Good King Henry.

The plant is easily grown, but needs much heat and moisture combined with very fertile soil to do well. Liquid feed with a high nitrogen content is valuable during growth. When grown as a substitute for spinach the plants can be spaced or thinned to 8–10 cm apart, and harvested after six to eight weeks, when about 20 cm tall. Joy Larkcom gives further detailed instructions on growing these plants. Lack of warmth is the main threat to this tropical crop in temperate climates.

Other species such as *A. hypochondriachus* and *A. cruentus* from Mexico were grown primarily as grain crops, and may be eaten as sprouted seedlings. These two, and *A. caudatus* from the Andes, were important food crops among the Aztecs and earlier cultures in Central and South America. *A. hypochondriachus* has become much grown as a grain in the mountains of South India, though its cultivation has almost died out in Mexico, and dark red forms of

Chinese spinach growing with lemon grass

A. cruentus are still used as dye plants in India and other parts of the world. *A. gangeticus* is also grown in Europe and North America as an ornamental, often under the name *A. tricolor*. The leaves are usually narrower than vegetable varieties, and very colourful. *A. caudatus* is grown under the name 'Love-Lies-Bleeding'; there are red and green forms with long hanging or shorter erect tassels. It is also now being grown experimentally in New Zealand as a particularly nutritious, gluten-free and high-protein grain crop.

New Zealand Spinach

Tetragonia tetragonioides (Pallas) O. Kuntze, syn. *T. expansa* Murr. (*Aizoaceae*)
Tetragone cornu (French)

This substitute for spinach is readily available from most seedsmen, but seldom grown. It has the advantage over true spinach in that it is perennial and grows well in dry soils and hot weather.

Tetragonia is a native of New Zealand, Tasmania and southern Australia, of many of the Pacific islands, China, Japan and southern South America, growing wild on sandy and stony beaches along the coast. It is also found along the Pacific coast of California, northwards to Oregon, where it is said not to be native, and is considered to be naturalized in the Azores and Portugal.

With this wide distribution, it is surprising that it was from New Zealand that it was first brought to Europe, at the time of Captain Cook's visit in 1770, when it was collected by Sir Joseph Banks at Queen Charlotte Sound. It was not eaten on that voyage, but on a later visit to New Zealand Cook found it to be a valuable source of the vitamin C needed to combat scurvy among the crew, and ordered a whole boatload to be collected. Seeds from Sir Joseph Banks' collection were being grown at Kew as a botanical curiosity in 1772, but it was not used as a vegetable in Europe until 1819.

The plants are usually grown as annuals; the seeds are planted in late spring, when there is no danger of frost, or may be started indoors and planted out, at least 45 cm apart. They do best in deep sandy soil, and will soon cover a considerable area. Once established the plants are tolerant of drought, but will produce a better crop if watered well in dry weather. The tips of the shoots are pinched out and used when about 8 cm long. They then produce ample side shoots. The tenderest shoots and leaves may also be eaten raw. In the tropics it will grow well through the dry winter season, but does not do well in hot, wet conditions.

Ice Plant

Mesembryanthemum cristallinum L. (*Mesembryanthemaceae*)
Brakslaai (Africaans)

This creeping annual or overwintering biennial can be eaten as a substitute for spinach. The name 'Ice plant' refers to the crystal-like cells on the surface of the leaf, which make the plant look as if it is covered by hoar-frost. Similar though less well-developed cells may be seen on the leaves of New Zealand spinach. The flowers are small and white, like daisies.

Ice plant is a native of the southwestern Cape area of South Africa, northwards into Namibia. It is also found wild in the Mediterranean area and Arabia, usually growing near the coast, on sand dunes and in salt marshes. It is naturalized in California.

Other members of the Mesembryanthemum family are also edible, notably both the fleshy leaves and the large, juicy fruits of the hottentot figs, *Carpobrotus acinaciformis*, and *C. edulis*, and the yellow-flowered *Conicosia pugioniformis* from the western Cape.

In frost-free climates the seeds of Ice Plant are sown in late summer, and the young shoots and leaves picked through the winter and spring; in cold climates the plants are grown as summer annuals, being raised indoors and planted out when all danger of frost is past. They are harvested through the summer, and often do best in early autumn with the onset of cooler weather.

New Zealand spinach

Ice Plant (whole plant in flower)

Ice Plant (detail of young leaves)

'Rhubarb Chard' or Red Stemmed Beet at Villandry

Beet

Beta vulgaris L. (*Chenopodiaceae*).)
Beetroot; Chard, Seakale Beet or Swiss Chard; Perpetual Spinach

Beet has provided a range of vegetables nearly as diverse as those provided by the cabbage. Sugar beet (subsp. *vulgaris*) is a very widely grown source of sugar, second only to that produced by sugar cane. Other swollen-rooted beets include beetroot, and mangolds, used as winter feed for stock. In chard (subsp. *cicla* (L.) Arcangeli), the swollen and flattened leaf-stalks are eaten, and perpetual spinach produces edible leaves over a long period.

Wild beet, *Beta vulgaris* subsp. *maritima* (L.) Arcangeli, is a common seaside plant with fleshy leaf blades, found around the coasts of south and west Europe, North Africa and Asia. It is generally perennial, and is commonest on shingle beaches, often only just above high tide mark. Leaves and stems are usually green, though some plants show traces of the red colour characteristic of garden beetroot.

It was already cultivated by the Greeks, red chards being mentioned by Aristotle, and red beetroots were later developed by the Romans. Indeed, in the late Middle Ages beetroot was still referred to as 'Roman beet'. Swiss chards with broad stalks are recorded by Bauhin in 1596, and Gerard grew a red-stemmed variety in England at the same time. Chard was also grown in China in the seventh century, and remains popular there today, grown mainly during the winter in the south.

The cultivation of beet for sugar production began in Silesia in 1801, and was greatly stimulated by the Napoleonic War during which the English blockaded France and cut off the supply of sugar from the West Indies. Napoleon set up schools for the study of sugar beet and encouraged the industry, protecting it from foreign competition after the end of hostilities.

Chard or Seakale Beet   Several varieties have white leaf-stalks, and the leaves of some are savoyed, others smooth. 'Rhubarb Chard' has crimson stalks and green leaves, and 'Burgundy Chard' has reddish-purple leaves as well. 'Rainbow Chard', available from Thompson and Morgan, has leaf-stalks of many colours but mainly red, orange and yellow.

Perpetual Spinach Beet   These have smaller stems than the Swiss chard, and resistance to bolting is of paramount importance to give a long standing crop. There are only a few varieties, 'Erbette' is one, from Italy.

Beetroots   Red, round, usually called 'globe' beets are the most popular, with a large number of very similar cultivars. Semi-globe is a longer shape, with more tapering roots. Many varieties when densely planted quickly produce very small beets, to be eaten at golfball size. There are also long cylindrical beets, suitable for slicing. Other colours are rare, but there is a golden variety, and a white and one with concentric rings of pink and white; these alternative colours, especially the yellow, have excellent flavour.

'Barbietola di Chioggia' syn. 'Chioggia'   An old Italian variety, with alternating red and white rings when sliced raw, pale pink when cooked. Variously described as delicious or horrible! Probably therefore best eaten young.

Beetroot 'Barbietola di Chioggia' in Maine

Wild beet in the Scilly islands

'Rhubarb Chard'

Red coloured plants are also found among wild beet populations

Leaves of wild beet, close to and as good as Perpetual Spinach Beet

Swiss chard in the foothills of Mount Omei

'Conrad'

Cultivation

Chards are among the easiest and most productive of vegetables, provided they have sufficient water and nitrogen. Soil should be rich and moist with ample manure. Seed can either be sown indoors in March and the young plants put out in April, or sown in April *in situ* and thinned to 30 cm apart. In dry areas and well-drained soils it is useful to plant in a shallow trench to make watering easier and more efficient. A second sowing may be made in August to harvest the following summer, and watering with soluble fertilizer will improve the crop in its second year. Both perpetual spinach and chard can be harvested as required, by pulling or cutting off single leaves at ground level. In climates with a very hot, wet summer, chard grows better in the cooler, drier winter months. All beet responds well to salt, which is not surprising as it is originally a seaside plant. The rate recommended is 30 gm per square metre, worked into the soil a week before planting, preferably with potash in some form.

'Conrad'   A beetroot with green leaves, photographed in the trial at Wisley, September 1990.

'Lucullus'   An improved variety of seakale beet with broad, light green savoyed blades and wide midribs. 'Fordhook Giant' syn. 'Dark Green Lucullus' from Marshalls and widely available in the USA is very similar.

'Perpetual Spinach beet'   A tough variety producing wide leaf blades with narrower ribs, for use as a spinach substitute throughout the summer.

CHARD

Swiss chard at the HDRA garden at Ryton

Villandry

Perpetual Spinach Beet at Sellindge

Swiss chard 'Lucullus'

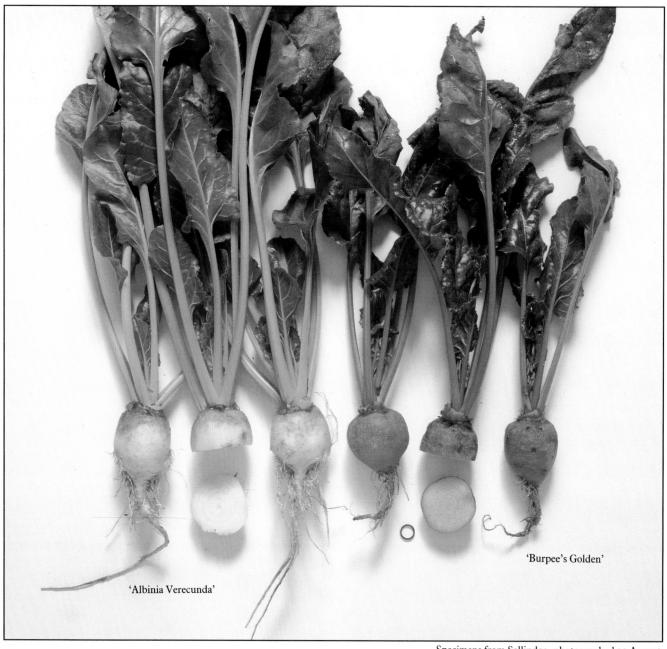

'Albinia Verecunda'

'Burpee's Golden'

Specimens from Sellindge, photographed 20 August

Cultivation of beetroot

Beetroots require light, well-drained soil which has not been freshly manured, and an open position. As for leaf beets, salt application has been found to be beneficial. Early, quick-maturing, globe beets can be planted in early spring in a warm position or in a frame which has been in position long enough to warm up the soil. It is better to plant bolt-resistant cultivars for this early crop. Seed should be sown in February or March, and the plants thinned to around 15 cm apart. The quickest varieties are ready in about two months. Later sowings, in May and June, can mature in forty-five days, though at this season the larger, longer-maturing varieties and the cylindrical ones can be planted to last the winter. These can be sown more thickly, 3 cm between the plants and 30 cm between the rows.

Most beet 'seeds' are clusters of more than one seed, so need thinning after they have germinated. So-called monogerm varieties have only one seed, so should not need thinning if planted at the right spacing. Soaking the seed (if it has not already been treated) in warm water for half an hour assists even germination. After germination the plants should not be allowed to dry out, though beetroots require less water than the leaf beets.

Pests and diseases

Beet suffers from few pests or diseases. Leaf spots may affect the leaves; they can be prevented by an application of potash before sowing. Mildews thrive in periods when the plants are growing slowly or are dry at the roots. The young plants may also damp off during very wet weather or in poorly drained soils.

'Albinia Verecunda' An old variety; roots rounded, very sweet.
'Burpee's Golden' Roots round, golden-yellow, similar in flavour to the red varieties.
'Cylindra' Roots long and cylindrical, dark red.

'Cylindra'

Leaves of Beetroot 'MacGregor's Favourite'

'Regala'

'Monopoly'

'Monogram'

'Cylindra'

'Red Ace'

'Detroit Little Ball'

'Detroit Lora'

'Mammoth Long'

Specimens from Wisley, photographed 27 September

'Detroit Little Ball' A fast-growing variety for a quick crop, and resistant to bolting. Flesh with distinct pale rings. Leaves green with red stems.

'Detroit Lora' An early-maturing and high-yielding variety, suitable to be used when small.

'MacGregor's Favourite' An old Scottish variety with a long, deep red root. The foliage is also very striking, with narrow shining-red leaves. 'Bull's Blood' is a very similar variety with broader leaves. From Nichols Garden Nursery, Albany, Oregon.

'Mammoth Long' A long-rooted variety, available from W. Robinson & Sons.

'Monogram' A monogerm variety raised by Dr C. R. Dawson and introduced by Tozers of Cobham. Roots a flattened sphere, resistant to bolting.

'Monopoly' A monogerm variety. Roots flattened or round, purplish-red, sometimes showing distinct pale rings. Resistant to bolting.

'Red Ace' An F1 hybrid. Roots round without pale rings, with tender flesh. Resistant to bolting. Very tender.

'Regala' Raised by Bejo Zaden B.V. Leaves rather small, green. Root round, purplish-red with fairly distinct zones. Resistant to bolting.

'Regala'

75

Spinach at Thomas Jefferson's garden at Montecello

Spinach

Spinachia oleracea L. (*Chenopodiaceae*)

Spinach is an annual, producing a quick crop in cool damp weather. In hot dry weather the plants often run to seed before they have made sufficient leaf growth but in a warm climate they produce an excellent crop in late winter. New Zealand spinach, described on page 69, is a good substitute for summer use in warm climates.

Spinach probably originated in southwest Asia or the western Himalayas, and was first cultivated by the Persians, spreading into China from Nepal in the seventh century and Europe in the eleventh century, being introduced first to Spain by the Arabs. The name spinach is derived from the Arabic. Spinach reached England in the sixteenth century, being mentioned first in Turner's *A New Herball* in 1551.

Other wild species of *Spinachia* are found in North Africa and Iran eastwards to the Himalayas, but it is not clear from which wild species the cultivated spinach originated.

Two main groups of varieties are cultivated at present. The prickly-seeded varieties, which generally have more lobed leaves, were in the past hardier in cold weather, and more tolerant of summer heat; they are considered more primitive. Smooth-seeded varieties, which include most modern cultivars, have broader leaves, but were formerly more liable to bolt in hot weather. Modern breeding has produced hardier, leafier plants, with resistance to bolting in summer, and reduced amounts of the calcium oxalate which causes bitterness. The iron for which spinach is famous is present in a soluble form, so any water left after cooking should be evaporated with butter and mixed back into the cooked leaves.

Cultivation

Spinach requires rich, moist soil with high nitrogen content. Seed of hardy varieties is generally sown in August or September, and will stand through the winter in well-drained soils, and with the protection of frames or cloches. It can be harvested until May. Tender varieties can be sown in early spring, from February onwards for an early summer crop, and sowings can be made through the summer in cool areas. In hot gardens summer sowings will be better in light shade. Seed should be sown thinly, and the plants thinned to 15–25 cm apart. Young plants are improved by waterings of high-nitrogen liquid fertilizer during growth, and should never be allowed to dry out. Applications of salt at the rate of 30 gm a square metre is also beneficial, especially in wet climates.

Diseases and pests

Bolting caused by drying out or hot summer weather is the most likely cause of failure. Pests and diseases are seldom serious. Aphids should be washed off with a soap solution; many varieties are resistant to mildew should that be a problem.

'Balloon' A hardy variety, photographed at Wisley. We have been unable to find this name on any list.
'King of Denmark' A variety with dark green savoyed, upright leaves; plants hardy, ready in around 46 days in North America. Available from Seeds by Size.
'Longstanding Round' A quick-maturing, round-seeded variety.
'Sigmaleaf' A robust variety, up to 30 cm high. Leaves broadly arrow-shaped with a blistered surface. Suitable for spring or autumn sowing.

Orache

Atriplex hortensis L. (*Chenopodiaceae*)
Mountain Spinach

This is a substitute for spinach, now little grown, though formerly very popular in parts of central Europe and among German immigrants to North America. It is an annual, hardier and more easily grown than spinach, but stronger in flavour especially when old. Green, red or yellow varieties are still cultivated. The lower leaves are large, and ovate-lanceolate, heart-shaped or triangular; the flowering stem can reach 2.5 m. Although grown all over Europe and Turkey, and commonly found wild having escaped from cultivation, orache is probably native only in central Asia and Siberia, where a closely related wild species grows in deserts. Other species of *Atriplex* which are common as garden weeds are perfectly edible, but seldom cultivated intentionally.

Orache is easily grown from seed sown in early spring, from March to May, or in autumn in warm climates. The plants will run to seed in mid-summer, shooting up into a narrow spire of small leaves and tiny green flowers, but can be kept low by being clipped. Only leaves should be eaten. Red orache does not lose its colour when cooked.

Spinach 'Longstanding Round'

Red Mountain Spinach (*Atriplex hortensis*)

Spinach 'Balloon'

Spinach 'King of Denmark' (behind)

Spinach 'Sigmaleaf'

Mexican Tea

Good King Henry

Good King Henry

Chenopodium bonus-henricus L. (*Chenopodiaceae*)
Mercury, Lincolnshire Asparagus

This is a very old vegetable in northern Europe, probably
introduced by the Romans into any area where the legions were
stationed. It is perennial and very easily grown, but has become
neglected in favour of spinach which stays fresh longer after
picking, and is therefore a better commercial crop. Good King
Henry wilts very quickly after picking, and is therefore suitable
only for the amateur gardener. Its leaves are used in similar ways
to spinach, but the succulent young flowering shoots are also
excellent, and can be forced under pots and then eaten with
melted butter like asparagus. They are cut when about 15 cm
long, and peeled if at all stringy.

The genus *Chenopodium* contains several vegetables and
common weeds, and both leaves and seeds are eaten. It is closely
related to *Atriplex* but the two may be easily distinguished by their
fruits, enclosed by large triangular bracts in *Atriplex*, small,
rounded and clustered in *Chenopodium. Chenopodium album*, the
Fat Hen, is a very common weed throughout Europe, and was
grown as a vegetable in eastern Europe; the seeds were found in
the stomach of Tollund man.

There are three South American species of *Chenopodium* which
were important crops in the past:

Quinoa, *Chenopodium quinoa*, is an annual, very similar to *C.
album*. It is used mainly as a grain for making bread or porridge.
The seeds are about twice as large as those of *C. album*, and the
inflorescence remains intact after it is ripe. Quinoa was a staple
crop at the time of the Spanish conquest of the Andes, and is still
grown in parts of Peru and Bolivia. It is gaining popularity in
England as a cover crop and food for pheasants. It is grown as a
fast-maturing summer annual.

Canahua, *Chenopodium pallidicaule*, is another grain, rarer and
now even less often grown. It makes a small bushy plant, with
leafy flowering branches. It is also grown in the Andes.

Huauzontle, *Chenopodium nuttalliae*, is grown as a vegetable in
southern Mexico. The immature flowering or fruiting stalks are
eaten, apparently fried in batter. Huauzontle is very similar to
quinoa, and the two may have originated from the same species,
one as a vegetable in Mexico, the other as a grain in Peru.

Mexican Tea, *Chenopodium ambrosoides* L. is similar in
appearance to Quinoa, and is now found throughout North
America, and in the warmer parts of Europe. It was used in the
past as a vermifuge.

Cultivation

A plantation of Good King Henry can be productive for several
years, so it is worth preparing the ground for it with care. The
position should be slightly shaded in mid-summer, in well-drained
soil. Old manure or compost should be dug in before planting,
and a mulch of manure is beneficial during the growing season.
Young plants are generally bought in pots, and can be planted at
any time of year. Established plants can be divided and replanted,
and this is best done in spring. Seed can be sown in spring, and
the young plants set out about 40 cm apart. About thirty plants
will produce a good supply for four people.

Glasswort

Salicornia europaea L. (*Chenopodiaceae*),
Sea Asparagus Marsh Samphire

Marsh samphire is a most excellent vegetable, common in muddy
salt-marshes by the sea throughout Europe, North America and
northern Asia, on temperate coasts in the southern hemisphere,
and in saline areas inland. As far as I know it has never been
cultivated, possibly because it is so easy to collect in quantity from
the wild. It is often sold by fishmongers in London in late summer

Glasswort or Marsh Samphire, Chichester Harbour

when it is at its best. Its alternative name of Glasswort derives from its use, when collected and burnt, in the manufacture of glass.

Marsh samphire is delicious boiled until soft, with the water in which it has come to the boil poured away to reduce the saltiness. It is then eaten with melted butter like asparagus. The fleshy outer part of the stems slips off, leaving the thin woody stalk behind.

Salicornia europaea is an annual, very variable in size and branching, and numerous microspecies have been named. The best are bushy plants up to 40 cm high, with ascending branches which keep them out of the mud. *S. ramosissima* Woods has this habit, and grows in the uppermost parts of salt marshes, so it is not inundated at every tide. Species from inland saline areas are presumably never covered by water while in growth. *S. rubra* Nels is found in inland areas in the prairie states and southern Canada. It turns red in autumn.

Cultivation

This would be an interesting exercise for those with an experimental bent, or with gardens close to a source of saline water. The plants grow best in a rich organic soil with ample nitrogen, and regular watering. Fertilizer derived from seaweed would seem appropriate. Seed of the tallest plants from near high-tide mark would make the best starting stock; seed should be collected in late autumn, and sown in spring. Plants should be spaced about 10 cm apart to ensure that they develop to their full size. One of the main points to be discovered would be the amount of salt needed for good growth, and whether the plants need inundation or not. Once the plants have reached about 15 cm tall the top 10 cm can be harvested, and the lower branches will grow up again.

A good edible *Salicornia*

Young leaves of *Boussingaultia*

Malabar Spinach

Basella rubra L. var. *alba* (*Basellaceae*)
Ceylon Spinach

These two tropical climbers are grown as substitutes for spinach.
They are fast-growing annuals, twining up any supports, and
producing an ample supply of fleshy leaves, which have a slightly
slimier texture than spinach when cooked. In good growing
conditions the leaves may be 15 cm long. Var. *rubra* or 'Rubra'
generally known as Ceylon spinach, has reddish leaves and deep
red fruits formed by the fleshy petals which can be used as a food
dye, or as rouge. Var. *alba*, commonly called Malabar spinach,
has green leaves. Both varieties are probably native to southern
India, but are now widely grown in China and southeast Asia.
Basella also has medicinal properties; the leaves are a gentle
laxative; the roots are used in China to treat diarrhoea.

Cultivation is easy, provided the plants have sufficient heat.
Sow in spring indoors, as a temperature of 18–21°C is needed for
germination – which is improved if the seeds are soaked before
sowing. After germination a temperature of 15–20°C is needed for
good growth, so in all but the warmest summers in northern
Europe the plants are best in a greenhouse. In warm North
American conditions a crop is ready in about seventy days. The
plant is perennial, but soon suffers from botrytis in cold autumn
weather, so is best grown from seed as an annual, though it can
also be propagated by cuttings.

Madeira Vine

Boussingaultia cordifolia Ten. syn. *Anredera cordifolia* (Ten.)
Steenis

This is a similar looking plant to *Basella* but has numerous
underground potato-like tubers and even more rampant climbing
stems, which can reach six metres. It is a native of South America,
from southern Brazil to northern Argentina, and is sometimes
grown in England as a curiosity and for its mignonette-scented
flowers. In southern Europe it is grown as a vegetable and has
become naturalized in Madeira, the Azores, France, Spain and
Portugal, and, as Ken Beckett records, on Easter Island. It is
easily propagated by the tubers which form on the stem as well as
underground, and is nearly hardy, surviving in frosty areas with
the protection of a mound of dry peat or straw and ashes. The
leaves are eaten like spinach.

Ulluco

Ullucus tuberosus L. (*Basellaceae*)
Other local names: papa lisa (S. Peru); melloca (Ecuador)

Ulluco is an important root crop in the High Andes, along with
potatoes, anu and oca (pp. 64–65). It is closely related to *Basella*,
with similar cordate, truncate, rather fleshy leaves, and tiny
pinkish-yellow flowers on short racemes arising from the leaf axils.
The tubers are similar to small potatoes, and may be yellow,
yellow with magenta spots or magenta-pink. They may be either
spherical or elongated.

Ulluco is grown from Colombia south to northern Argentina,
and is the hardiest of these Andean vegetables, surviving −5°C.
Ulluco tubers are also dried and made into lingli, similar to the
chuno made with potatoes. In cultivation it requires similar
treatment to oca, and does not begin to form tubers until the day
length is reduced to nine hours in autumn. (Not illustrated).

Purslane

Portulaca oleracea L. (*Portulacaceae*)

Although this is an easily grown and reasonably nutritious
vegetable, which has been cultivated and eaten since ancient
times, it has never been much improved by plant breeders, and
remains only rarely grown and eaten. It can be eaten raw, or
lightly cooked like spinach, though the taste is not memorable. Its
name in Malawi translates as 'Buttocks-of-the-wife-of-a-chief' as
Dr Herklots records in his *Vegetables of Southeast Asia*, alluding to
the plant's rounded and fleshy leaves.

Purslane is a common weed throughout the warmer parts of
Europe, Asia and eastern Africa. It is naturalized in North
America and elsewhere in the tropics. The cultivated plant, subsp.
sativa (Haw.) Celak., is more upright, with larger leaves than the
wild creeping form.

It is a more popular vegetable in France and the Mediterranean
countries than in the colder climate of England and a golden-
leaved variety is cultivated there, where it is mostly eaten in
salads.

Purslane is easily cultivated. It is generally sown in spring and
harvested through the summer, until cut down by frost. Pick the
tender young shoots at about 3–5 cm long.

Miner's Lettuce

Montia perfoliata (Donn) Howell syn. *Claytonia perfoliata* Donn
(*Portulacaceae*)
Winter Purslane

This small plant is very common along the west coast of North
America, from Baja California north to British Columbia, and
inland to the desert, growing in shady places which are damp
during the winter. It formed a valuable part of the diet of the
miners in the gold rush of the 1850s, helping to prevent scurvy in
times when fresh vegetables were scarce. It is now frequently
naturalized in western Europe, especially in sandy areas such as
the Breckland of East Anglia.

The seed should be sown in July and August, in a sheltered
position, and in the shade of a deciduous tree. The young plants
should not be allowed to dry out, and when they have grown
sufficiently, they may be harvested until they flower in late spring.
They can be eaten raw or steamed.

Talinum triangulare (Jacq.) Willd., another member of the
family *Portulacaceae*, sometimes called Surinam spinach, is a
succulent perennial, native of the West Indies and tropical South
America. It has upright stems, fleshy oblanceolate leaves, and
small pink or red flowers. The young side shoots are broken off
and eaten steamed or lightly boiled. Apart from tropical America,
Talinum is cultivated in West Africa and the east Indies.

Ceylon spinach

Miner's lettuce in flower

Purslane grown as a summer salad

Miner's lettuce in young leaves

Purslane: detail of leaves

Red-flowered peas in Baoxing, Sichuan

Detail of red-flowered peas in China

Pea

Pisum sativum L. (*Leguminosae*)
Snow Pea, Mangetout, Ho Lan Tau (Chinese)

Peas have been grown in southern Europe and the Near East for thousands of years, and eaten either as fresh green peas when immature or, when ripe, as dried peas made into a soup or potage. Mangetout, sugar peas or snow peas, in which the pod lacks the stiff parchment-like walls and so is edible, were recorded by Gerard in 1597. In parts of China the young green tops of the pea plants are often picked and stir-fried, and cooked like this they taste excellent. Several varieties are used, and plants are grown specially for the purpose, the shoots being picked regularly and the plants prevented from flowering. The young tendrils of leafless varieties such as 'Bikini' can also be eaten in this way or lightly boiled.

Peas are related to beans, groundnuts and clovers and belong to the family *Leguminosae*. *Pisum* belongs to the tribe *Vicieae* or vetches, which contains broad beans, chick peas and lentils. Only two species of *Pisum* are accepted in modern floras, *P. sativum* L. and *P. fulvum* Sibth. & Smith, which can be recognized by its orange-buff flowers. Both species are native to the eastern Mediterranean, from Turkey eastwards to Syria, Iraq and Iran, growing in rocky places, and as weeds in fields of wheat or barley, or among vines.

In Turkey, which is probably where peas were first cultivated, *Pisum sativum* can be divided into two subspecies and numerous varieties. The wild subspecies *elatius* (Bieb.) Aschers. & Graebn.is found from southern Europe and the Crimea eastwards to Georgia and Turkmenia. It has papillose seeds, always bicoloured flowers and pods 7–12 mm broad. Var. *pumilio* Meikle (syn. *P. humile* Boiss. & Noë) is a short, small-flowered variety of subspecies *elatius* found mainly in eastern Turkey, Cyprus and Iran. Subspecies *sativum*, which has smooth or wrinkled seeds and pods more than 12 mm broad, contains the cultivated varieties, var. *sativum* with white flowers, plain green stipules and large seeds, and var. *arvense* (L.) Poiret with bicoloured flowers, stipules with a red blotch and small seeds 4–8 mm across. Var. *arvense* is also reported by Peter Davis to be wild on Karaçadağ, a rocky basalt plateau on the northern edge of the Syrian desert in southern Turkey. Wild forms of peas have hard seed-coats, and can remain dormant in the soil for several years.

History

Pea seeds have been found in deposits from Neolithic settlements in Jericho, and in deposits dating from around 5700 BC in Erbaba in Anatolia (central Turkey) and about 5600 BC at Tell Azmak. Other early evidence of cultivation comes from Swiss lake dwellings, caves in Hungary and in the ruins of early Troy where one large jar alone contained more than 440 lbs of peas, and visitors to Schliemann's excavations 'supped from peas from Priam's larder'. This makes the cultivated pea as ancient a crop as wheat and barley. Pea cultivation spread eastwards to India and reached China in the T'ang dynasty (AD 618–906). Peas were probably grown in England by the Romans, if not by earlier invaders from the continent, but they seem to have died out in the Dark Ages, as they are said to have been reintroduced from Holland or France in the reign of Henry VIII. Thomas Tusser, writing in 1573, mentions peas as a field crop, and Rounceval peas as a delicacy to be grown in the garden, and by 1597 Gerard knew of four varieties, including 'Pease without skins in the cods' an early mangetout-type.

Peas were some of the first plants to be used for genetic experiments. Thomas Andrew Knight (1759–1838) started his pea breeding about 1787. His primary aim was to produce better varieties of apples, especially for the production of cider in his native Herefordshire, but the length of time taken for any results to become apparent was so great that he decided to try some experiments on garden peas at the same time, as they were annuals with large flowers and clearly observed characteristics. His results, showing the independent inheritance of single characteristics, were similar to those of Gregor Mendel around seventy years later, but he did not recognize how fundamental they were to the laws of genetics.

Mendel used peas as the subject of his studies into genetics, although he had originally intended to improve the garden qualities of the peas grown in the monastery gardens in Brno in Czechoslovakia. Other breeders also had new and better peas as their primary goal. Thomas Laxton, who followed the work of Knight, published his own results in 1872. He also worked on pelargoniums and strawberries, but his sons concentrated on raising new varieties of apples, pears and plums. The seedsmen Hurst & Son, who had their trial grounds at Kelvedon in Essex, raised new pea varieties as well as other vegetables in the 1920s. Some pea varieties raised by both these are still grown today.

Recent breeding has concentrated on the production of varieties suitable for freezing which can also be grown on a field scale and harvested mechanically. As much as possible of the crop must be ready on the day of harvest. The use of varieties with no leaflets has improved the resistance of the plants to leaf diseases caused by the plants lying over each other in the field.

At present there are several major groups of pea cultivars:
Pod peas for dried peas, such as 'Holland Brown'.
Pod peas for garden peas or petit pois, such as 'Trio', 'Little Marvel', 'Hurst Beagle', 'Waverex', etc.
Pod peas without leaflets, such as 'Bikini', 'Novella'.
Mangetout peas with flat pods, such as 'Snowflake', 'Oregon Sugar pod' or 'Agio'.
Mangetout peas with swollen pods, such as 'Sugar Snap', 'Sugar Ann' or 'Early Snap'.

'Purple Podded' An old variety, tall-growing to 150 cm, with deep purple rods, and peas wrinkled when ripe. Best sown in spring.

Cultivation

Peas do best in a rich, light, but moisture retentive soil, and will not thrive either in heavy, waterlogged soils which cause basal rotting of the plant or in soils that are very dry. They dislike very hot weather, and do best in spring, cool summers or early autumn. In mild climates the early varieties can be sown in autumn to overwinter and produce an early spring crop, and these early peas are often covered by cloches, which also protect them from pigeons and other birds.

Suitable varieties for autumn sowing are 'Hurst Beagle', 'Feltham First' and 'Winfrida', the last the hardiest of all. Later sowings can be made from February onwards, and a succession of sowings can provide a crop into autumn. The latest sowing will be in July, of a fast-maturing variety which will crop before the frost in warmer areas. Varieties such as 'Hurst Beagle' mature in about ninety days from an early spring sowing, fifty-five days in warm weather. 'Extra Early Alaska' can mature in fifty-one days. 'Snowbird' is a mangetout variety, recommended for an autumn crop, maturing in about fifty-eight days.

Seeds should be sown in a v-shaped drill in a single row spaced 5 cm apart and about 4 cm deep. Alternatively, for shorter denser rows, the seed may be sown in three rows in a wide, flat-bottomed drill, the seeds and the rows about 12 cm apart. Newly planted seed and young plants will need to be protected against mice and pigeons, and the plants will benefit from support as soon as tendrils appear. Varieties vary in eventual height from 30 cm in the dwarf types to 2 m or so in 'Tall Telephone'. Either much-branched sticks or supported netting can be used for the peas to climb into. In dry weather, both mulching and watering will improve the crop, especially from flowering time onwards. In most varieties, continued picking of the young pods prolongs the cropping time.

'Purple Podded': an old variety at Inverewe

Detail of a pale pink flower

Peas in China, grown for their leafy shoots

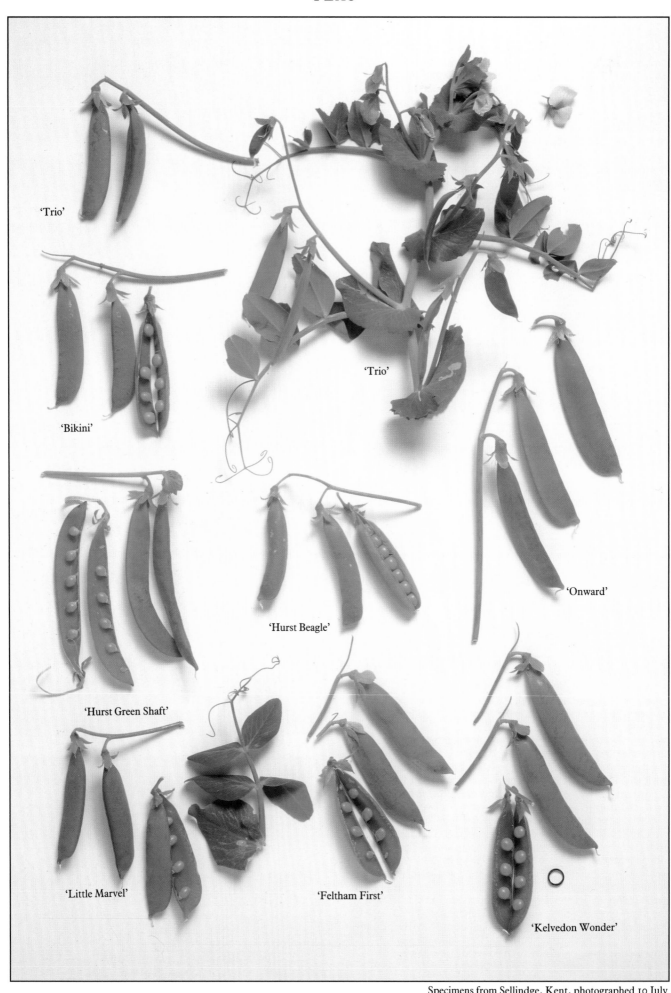

'Trio'

'Bikini'

'Trio'

'Onward'

'Hurst Beagle'

'Hurst Green Shaft'

'Little Marvel'

'Feltham First'

'Kelvedon Wonder'

Specimens from Sellindge, Kent, photographed 10 July

'**Bikini**' Plants leafless with much-branched tendrils and leaf-like stipules.

'**Feltham First**' 58 days in North America; plant 45 cm, pods 9 cm; heavy cropper. Suitable for autumn or March sowing. A particularly hardy variety.

'**Honey Pod**' (snap) Pods 6.5 cm long, round in cross-section.

'**Hurst Beagle**' 55 days (90 days in UK), seeds wrinkled; plants 50 cm; sweet and juicy pods 9 cm, 6–9 peas per pod. Susceptible to wilt.

'**Hurst Green Shaft**' Raised by Hurst Gunson Cooper Taber Ltd. Plant 171 cm. Pods 10 cm long, straight; peas dark green. Good yields; good resistance to pea wilt. 102 days in UK.

'**Kelvedon Wonder**' Raised by Hurst in 1925. 65 days; 8 cm pods. Plant cold tolerant, suitable for autumn, spring or midsummer sowing for an autumn crop.

'**Little Marvel**' 62 days; sweet and tender; 8 cm pods. A popular variety with plants 46 cm high.

'**Markana**' Like 'Bikini' this is a leafless variety with extra branched tendrils. 'Mora' is similar but earlier. Pods 9–10 cm, in pairs.

'**Onward**' 72 days; plant 75 cm. A heavy cropper; for spring sowing; recommended for freezing.

'**Sugar Bon**' Raised by Gallatin Valley Seed Co. Plant 1 m; pods 7 cm curved, fairly round. Matures in around 80 days in southern England, 60 days in North America.

'**Trio**' 74 days; plant 92 cm; seeds extra sweet. Pods are produced in bunches of 3–5. Peas keep well.

'**Waverex**' Tolerant of cool weather. Short pods, suitable for picking young, as petit pois. A German variety.

Pea 'Sugar Bon' (*left*) 'Waverex' (*right*)

Leafless pea 'Markana'

Mangetout pea 'Honeypod'

'Purple Podded' (detail) (see p. 83)

Broad beans in a market in Bolivia, photographed by Sam Phillips

'Red Epicure' in flower at Barnsley House (p. 88)

Dwarf broad bean, 'The Sutton'

Broad Bean

Vicia faba L. (*Leguminosae*)
Fève de Marais, Grosse Fève (French)

The broad bean is the hardiest of beans and the only one which can be sown in autumn, survive the winter frosts and be harvested in early summer. Most cultivars are large upright annuals with hairy pods. The slightly flattened green or white beans are coarse and strong-flavoured when mature, but delicious when young. The very young pods can also be eaten whole.

The wild ancestor of the broad bean is not now known, but the species is assumed to have originated in the eastern Mediterranean region in neolithic times. It is most closely related to the wild species *Vicia narbonensis*, now found in southern Europe, North Africa and southwest Asia. This species differs in being a slenderer plant with tendrils and seed pods which are hairless when mature. It also has a different chromosome number, $2n=14$, while *V. faba* has $2n=12$.

The earliest evidence of the cultivation of broad beans comes from pre-pottery neolithic B levels at Jericho and Hungary. They have been found in ancient Egypt dating from 1800 BC, and are mentioned in Greek and Roman literature. They are found in Iron Age deposits in lake dwellings near Glastonbury, and in northern Europe. Primitive varieties had small black seeds, and black seeds are mentioned by Homer and have been excavated at Troy.

Broad beans grown in the present day are divided into four groups of varieties:
var. *faba* or *major*, the broad bean, most commonly eaten as a vegetable;
var. *equina*, the horse bean, grown for animal feed;
var. *minor*, the tic bean;
var. *paucijuga*, close to *minor*, and grown mostly in Central Asia; unlike the other varieties it is largely self-pollinating.

Varieties cultivated as vegetables are generally divided into two groups, 'long-pod', which has long pods with up to eight seeds per pod, and 'Windsor' which has shorter pods with about four seeds per pod. There are also white-flowered and pale-seeded types which have a low tannin content, and so are less strongly flavoured when mature.

Broad bean seeds can be sown either in November, though they are vulnerable to slug and bird damage during the winter, or in January or February on warmer soils. The long-pod types such as 'Aquadulce' are usually recommended for winter planting. They will grow slowly during the winter, and will benefit from the protection of a frame or clothe. Later varieties, and particularly the Windsor and the dwarf types, can be sown in March or April. The ideal soil is rather heavy and well manured, but not poorly drained. Alternatively the plants may be sown indoors in pots and planted out during a mild spell in March.

'Bonny Lad'   Plant compact, c. 35 cm tall. Pods 12–15 cm long, with four to five green seeds.
'Brunette'   Plant 45–60 cm; pods 10–12 cm long, thin-walled with small seeds. A quick-maturing variety.
'Bunyard's Exhibition'   Grown since 1917. Plant to 120 cm. Pods 30–35 cm with seven beans.
'Imperial Green Longpod'   Plant 90–135 cm; long pods to 50 cm, with up to nine green seeds.
'Masterpiece Green Longpod'   Plant 80–90 cm; pods 20 cm, with around seven green seeds.
'Suprifin'   Plant to 90 cm; pods 20 cm, abundantly produced.
'The Sutton'   A dwarf plant 30–48 cm, with reduced internodes. Pods 12–15 cm, with around five small beans. An easy plant and a good cropper. Suitable for sowing in succession through the summer, and under cloches through the winter for a very early crop.
'Witkiem Major'   Plant 90 cm; pods thick, 20–25 cm; seeds green. Good yields from a spring sowing.

'Masterpiece Green Longpod'

'Imperial Green Longpod'

'Bunyard's Exhibition'

'Suprifin'

'Brunette'

'Bonny Lad'

'The Sutton'

'Aquadulce Claudia' (p. 88)

'Witkiem Major'

Specimens from Sellindge, Kent, photographed 10 July

'Red Epicure'

Dwarf broad bean 'Ite'

'Relon'

'Aquadulce Claudia'   An early, long-podded variety, grown since 1930; hardy and suitable for autumn sowing from late October to November. Plant c. 1 m tall. Pods 20 cm long, with around 5 seeds.

'Express'   Plant 90 cm; pods 16–20 cm with around 4 pale green seeds; frost hardy and quick-maturing, in about 70 days under warm conditions.

'Feligreen'   A new low tannin variety from Nickerson Zwaan.

'Fonseca' A very large-seeded variety raised by S. Pigot in Portugal.

'Giant 4-seeded Green Windsor'   This old variety produces extra large beans, up to 6 in a characteristic curved pod.

'Hylon'   A late-maturing variety with exceptionally long pods, with around seven white seeds.

'Ite'   Plant 75 cm; pods 15 cm, prolific, with small but well-flavoured beans. About 10 days later than 'Express'.

'Jubilee Hysor'   Sow after March in England. Late-maturing, with 6–9 large, white seeds.

'Red Epicure'   Plant 90 cm; pods green, but seeds and flowers deep red. Available from Unwins.

'Reina Mora'   A Spanish variety.

'Relon'   Plant to 90–130 cm; late-maturing with very long pods, 42–55 cm with around 8, but often 11, green beans.

'Feligreen'

'Aquadulce' outgrowing its frame

'Relon'

'Hylon'

'Jubilee Hysor'

'Reina Mora'

'Fonseca'

'Express'

'Red Epicure'

'Giant 4-seeded Green Windsor'

A wild purple-podded bean on *Salvia iodantha* south of Lake Chapala, Mexico

French Bean

Phaseolus vulgaris L. (*Leguminosae*)
Common Bean, Kidney Bean, Flagelot, Haricots Verts

The four cultivated species of *Phaseolus* bean all originated in central and South America. *Phaseolus vulgaris* is now found wild in western and central Mexico and Guatemala, growing in the mountains at 500–2000 m, and in the Andes in Peru, Bolivia and Argentina. The wild species are all climbers; the Mexican variety has small seeds usually 5–7 mm long. In October 1991 we found one form with narrow purple pods about 7 cm long, and about seven buff, dark-veined seeds 6–8 mm long when fresh, growing

over tall shrubby purple-flowered *Salvia iodantha*, by a country road at 2000 m in the hills south of Lake Chapala. The Andean variety, var. *aborigineus*, has larger seeds, 8–10 mm long, and is now found as far south as the San Luis area of Argentina.

Both varieties were probably domesticated in ancient times, before being introduced to Europe and Asia at the time of the Spanish conquest, but its original country of domestication is uncertain. There have not been any archaeological finds of beans with seed sizes intermediate between the wild and cultivated beans. Seeds of cultivated forms 12–13 mm long are recorded from deposits at Cuitarrero cave in Peru dated around 6000 BC, and from cave deposits in the Tehuacan valley in central Mexico in 4000 BC. Equally ancient seeds were found in the Jujay region of

Semi-climbing wax bean 'Mont d'Or'

Bamboo wigwams for climbing beans

Argentina. Bean cultivation spread into western North America and finds in New Mexico have been dated to around 300 BC.

French beans were brought to Europe in the early sixteenth century and were grown in England by Gerard before 1597, the date of the first edition of his herbal. The early varieties were all climbers, and dwarf French beans were not grown commonly until the early eighteenth century.

Cultivated beans are now very variable, and distinct cultivars are found in many parts of the world. The main variations are in habit, pod colour and texture, and in seed colour. The bean plants may be dwarf, commonly called bush beans, or climbing, commonly called pole beans in America. The intermediate habit, so-called determinate growth, in which the flowering stems, and therefore the beans, are held up above the leaves, is becoming commoner; examples with this last growth habit are 'Golden Butter' or 'Mont D'Or' and 'Purple Teepee'.

Variations in pod texture are also important. The wild species have very papery pods, which split open when the seeds are ripe. Cultivars which have papery pods are grown only for use as shell beans or haricots; those with leathery pods can be used as green or snap beans when very young, but are used for shell beans when mature. Cultivars with fleshy stringless pods, such as 'Blue Lake', are used mainly as green beans, and the pods remain palatable much longer than other groups. Apart from length, pods also vary in cross section, being flat, oval or round.

Pod colour varies also; green is the usual colour, but yellow pods, the so-called wax beans, are common, especially among bush beans. Purple-podded beans are also frequently grown, both climbing or bush. The variety 'Tongues of Fire' has greenish pods streaked with red, and the beans are a similar colour. Seed coat colour is the fourth main variable, and appears to be independent of other characters. Seeds may be black, white, red, buff, brown or various combinations of these colours.

Cultivation

French beans are fast-growing annuals, and as they originate from a tropical climate require warm soil in which to germinate and grow. It is not worth planting the seeds too early, as they then grow so poorly that they are prone to disease and pests, such as root rots and slug damage.

Most varieties need a soil temperature of at least 13°C, to ensure good germination, but varieties such as 'Loch Ness', 'Savor' and 'Purple Podded' are recommended for colder soils. The bush varieties are generally planted in rows, the seeds sown 3.75–5 cm deep, 5–7.5 cm apart, with 45 cm between the rows. Alternatively the seeds can be sown in groups of about six, with about 30 cm between the groups, or singly in blocks, allowing 15 cm between the plants. Wider spacing is often recommended, but this close spacing gives higher yields. It is beneficial to earth up young seedlings by drawing 5–7.5 cm of soil around the base of the stems and, in dry areas, to provide a good mulch.

In cold areas or on heavy soils, the plants can be germinated indoors in pots and planted out when they have two well-developed leaves. This should be necessary only for the first sowing of the season, and later sowings can be made directly into the soil. Most bush varieties bear in forty-five to sixty days, and pole varieties in about sixty days.

The pole varieties can either be planted in double rows 60 cm apart, the seeds 15 cm apart, and provided with a support of crossed poles, or planted on wigwams, two seeds at the foot of each of five poles at least 2.4 m tall. Alternatively they can be planted up a well-supported wire-netting fence, which should also be 2–4 m tall.

French beans are self-pollinating, and generally produce heavy yields, provided that the young beans are picked regularly and the plants are growing well. If the weather is dry, the plants should be well watered while in flower.

Shell beans, which are grown for their seeds, are harvested when the pods are nearly ripe, and the whole plant is hung up to dry under cover in a well-ventilated place.

'German Pole' bean from Virginia (text on p. 93)

Climbing French bean 'Blue Lake' (text on p. 93)

Seedling French beans planted in groups of about five

'Blue Peter'

'Robsplash'

'Kingston Gold'

'Lazy Housewife'

'Purple Podded'

'Selka Improved'

Specimens from Wisley, photographed 4 September

Climbing bean 'Blue Coco'

Climbing bean 'Kentucky Wonder Wax'

'Anelli' (syn. 'Hillary')   An old variety; pods green; seeds red-brown, with dark brown curving lines; for use fresh or dry.

'Blue Coco'   Pods purple; seeds pale brown, similar to 'Purple Podded' but flatter; from Seeds Blum, Boise, Idaho.

'Blue Lake' (syn. 'White Creaseback') Pods c. 15 cm, green, stringless and very fleshy, with a groove along the back; seeds elongated, white. A very good and easy grower which is quick-maturing. A North American variety, which probably originated with the Indians along the upper Missouri river, and was grown in the South at an early date. (Shown on p. 91.)

'Blue Peter'   A climbing purple-podded bean, received from Harry Hay.

'German Pole'   An old variety from the southeastern United States, received from Jane Price, from Tom's Creek in Blacksburg, Virginia. Slow to mature in cool weather. Seeds pale brown with darker mottling, especially at one end. Flavour best when nearly mature. (Shown on p. 91.)

'Kentucky Wonder Wax' (syn. 'Golden-podded wax')   An old variety, dating from the 1850s. Pods golden, oval in section; seeds large, red-brown. The original Kentucky Wonder had green pods similar to 'Blue Lake', but orange-brown seeds.

'Kingston Gold'   A flattened podded golden bean, grown at Wisley. We have been unable to find this name elsewhere.

'Lazy Housewife' (syn. 'Lazy Wife', 'Coco Blanc')   An old variety from Germany introduced to America in around 1810. Flowers white; pods fleshy and stringless; white seeds with grey pattern; better as a dry bean than a green bean. A late-season variety, producing pods at least 80 days from planting.

'Mont d'Or' (syn. 'Golden Butter') (snap) Pods pale golden, slightly flattened, on a tall upright or semi-climbing plant, remaining soft until nearly mature. Seeds short and plump, deep reddish-brown to black. Originated in Lyon before 1874.

'Purple Podded'   An old French variety, with purple pods and pale brown seeds. From Suttons and Thompson & Morgan.

'Robsplash'   From W. Robinson & Sons Ltd, Sunny Bank, Forton, near Preston, Lancs.

'Selka Improved'   A French variety, with very long, flat, stringless pods to 30 cm long, with distinct flavour; seeds white, elongated.

'Wren's Egg' (syn. 'London Horticultural', 'Araucano', 'Speckled Cranberry Egg', 'King Mammoth')   A vigorous grower with pink flowers. Pods pale green, splashed with red or carmine when mature, flat, oval in section. Seeds buff, splashed or streaked with dark red, with a deep orange eye ring. An ancient variety, possibly originating in Chile.

Climbing bean 'Anelli'

Climbing bean 'Wren's Egg'

93

'Jumbo'

'Daisy'

'Cyrus'

'Constanza'

'Delinel'

'Loch Ness'

'Tendercrop'

'Masterpiece'

'Pros Gitana'

'Royal Burgundy'

Bush French beans: specimens from Wisley, 10 August

'**Constanza**' (snap) Pods golden-yellow, round in section; seeds white, elongated; plant c. 35 cm tall.

'**Cyrus**' (snap) pods slender, straight and round; seeds long and narrow, purplish with heavy dark stipples and lines; plants to 45 cm, prolific.

'**Daisy**' (snap) pods c. 15 cm, round in section with a groove on the upper side, held up above the leaves.

'**Delinel**' (snap) Raised by Vilmorin-Andrieux SA. Plant around 35 cm high, with pods round in section, 15–20 cm long, bright green, curved, in loose clusters. Quick-maturing and resistant to mosaic and anthracnose., Available from Marshalls and Vesey's seeds, Houlton, ME.

'**Jumbo**' (snap) Pods 30 cm long, dark green, flattened; seeds large, reddish-brown with dark curving streaks. Plants with a long season of cropping if the pods are picked regularly when immature.

'**Loch Ness**' (snap) Pods round, fleshy, stringless, to 15 cm long; plant upright to 50 cm. This looks like a bush form of 'Blue Lake'.

'**Masterpiece**' (syn. 'Jaune de Perreux') (snap) Introduced by Vilmorin in around 1907, and Suttons in 1910. Suitable for forcing in hothouses when it is ready in about 52 days. Pods flat. Seeds pale reddish-brown, darker round the eye. There is a recent stringless development of this variety.

'**Michelet Teepee**' A new, semi-dwarf variety from Bakker.

'**Pros Gitana**' (snap) Pods round to oval, stringless, c. 10 cm long, produced in large numbers and used for eating whole.

'**Purple Teepee**' (snap) Pods purple, c. 15 cm long, slightly curved, on slightly elongated stems held above the foliage and clear of the ground.

'**Royal Burgundy**' (snap) Pods purple, curved, round, about 15 cm long, stringless; seeds pale reddish-brown. Plant rather tall, to 45 cm, and tolerant of cool weather. Dwarf purple-podded beans are said to have originated in Germany.

'**Royalty**' (snap) Purple podded; pods purple, curved, round in section, about 12 cm long, stringless, of good flavour. Seeds pale yellowish-brown. Raised in 1957 at the University of New Hampshire from a local heirloom purple-podded variety, crossed with 'Florida' 501. A good garden variety, especially for cold, wet soils.

'**Tendercrop**' (snap) Pods c. 12 cm straight, fleshy and stringless, round in section, seeds long and narrow, purplish with heavy dark stipples and lines. Raised in 1958 at the USDA, Beltsville; parentage 'Tropcrop' × 'Tenderpod'. Suitable for northern conditions and resistant to virus.

'**Venture**' (snap) Plant stiff, with upright stems. Pods slightly curved, round in section, around 16 cm long, stringless; seeds white. A new fast-maturing form of 'Blue Lake', ready for harvest in as little as 48 days.

Dwarf French beans, 'Masterpiece'

'Daisy' (in flower)

'Daisy' (in pod)

'Purple Teepee'

'Royalty'

'Venture'

'Michelet Teepee'

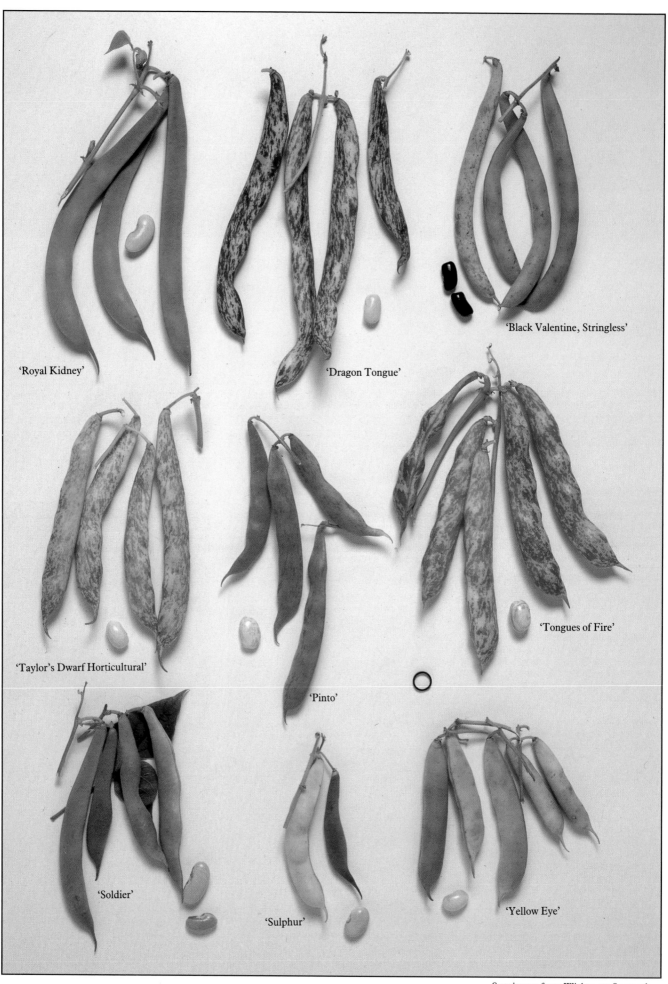

'Royal Kidney'

'Dragon Tongue'

'Black Valentine, Stringless'

'Taylor's Dwarf Horticultural'

'Pinto'

'Tongues of Fire'

'Soldier'

'Sulphur'

'Yellow Eye'

Specimens from Wisley, 20 September

A good row of bush beans

Dwarf bean 'Hama'

'Jacob's Cattle'

'**Black Valentine, Stringless**' (syn. 'King of the Garden', 'May Queen') (snap or soup) Pods green, c. 15 cm long, slightly flattened; seeds elongated, black. The original stringy variety was introduced by Peter Henderson & Co. in 1897, though the name was in use earlier for a similar bean.

'**Dragon Tongue**' (syn. 'Dragon Langue') (wax) Pods flat, pale yellow striped purple; seeds rather elongated, reddish-brown, lightly streaked and stippled with dark brown. A Dutch variety.

'**Hama**' A new dwarf French bean from Nickerson Zwaan.

'**Jacob's Cattle**' (syn. 'Trout', 'Dalmatian' or 'Coach-dog Bean', 'Forellen') (soup) An old variety from New England; the beautiful seeds are white, heavily mottled with crimson. A field bean, commonly used dry.

'**Pinto**' (snap or soup bean) Plant semi-trailing; pods short, c. 12 cm; seeds pale reddish-brown with dark brown stippling. A variety from Colorado and the southwestern States. Mexican Pinto, with cream-coloured seeds stippled black, is traditionally used for chilli con carne.

'**Royal Kidney**' (soup) Flowers pink; pods flat, green, tough and fibrous; seeds large, maroon when ripe. A variety of Red Kidney. The earliest large-seeded red kidney was raised in Marion, New York, by John Q. Wells in 1904.

'**Soldier**' (syn. 'Johnson Bean') (soup) Seeds elongated, white with a few irregular red-brown markings near the eye. Plant about 45 cm tall, pods long and slender. An old variety from Maine and New Hampshire. Good for baking.

'**Sulphur**' (syn. 'California Cream', 'China Yellow') (soup or snap bean when young) Plant producing good yields in cool temperatures; flowers pink; seeds yellowish to pale reddish-brown, rather small, tender even when mature. An old variety of field bean, now seldom grown.

'**Taylor's Dwarf Horticultural**' (syn. 'Speckled Bays', 'Shelley') (snap or soup bean) An old variety from the early nineteenth century, with stems to 45 cm; pods pale, streaked, c. 15 cm long, flattened-ovate in section; seeds reddish-brown with a few, darker markings. 'Dwarf Cranberry' and 'Dwarf Wren's Egg' are similar, closely related varieties. (Not illustrated.)

'**Tongues of Fire**' (soup) Pod flat, c. 15 cm long, with a pale pod streaked with red; seeds rather round, pale reddish-brown with streaks and stipples of darker brown. Beans of good flavour and texture. Said to have originated in Tierra del Fuego.

'**Yellow Eye**' (syn. 'Molasses Face') (soup) Seeds white, with a reddish-brown zone around the eye. Pods pale green, stringy and coarse. A field bean, usually grown on a large scale.

Wild runner beans in flower in the forest on Collima Mountain, Mexico

Runner bean

Phaseolus coccineus L. syn. *Phaseolus multiflorus* Lam. (*Leguminosae*)
Scarlet Runner, Haricots d'Espagne

The runner bean is native of Mexico, from mountains west of Durango southwards; it is especially common in the central volcanic mountain belt west of Mexico city, and in the high mountains of southern Mexico. It is also recorded in Guatemala. It is a perennial with starchy tuberous roots, and grows in cool, partially shaded places, usually on the north-facing sides of barrancas or deep valleys in mixed pine-oak forest, scrambling into coarse vegetation composed largely of shrubby and large-leaved *Senecio* and *Salvia* species. It seems to be commonest from 1800 to 2500 m, growing in the same places as wild dahlias, begonias and orange lobelias, and in these areas the scarlet flowers of the bean may be conspicuous along roadsides. They are probably pollinated mainly by hummingbirds which are common in this zone, as well as by bumble bees. The flowers have been reported to be purple, but all those seen flowering in the northern half of Mexico in October 1991 were the usual scarlet, and there is another report that the red flowers dry purplish.

The wild beans themselves have the flavour and texture of cultivated runner beans, but are only about 8 cm long, with about eight rather round seeds, 7–10 mm long, which were pale brown with heavy blackish-brown stippling and a black eye in the only ripe sample we could find in early November.

Runner beans were cultivated by the pre-Spanish civilizations in Mexico and were found in cave deposits in the Tehuacan valley in Puebla province. This is a famous site for early agriculture in the Americas, from 7000 BC onwards, and includes some of the earliest records of maize cultivation. The cultivated runner bean, however, dates only from 2200 years ago. It was probably introduced to Europe in the sixteenth century, but one of the first records in garden literature is in Johnson's 1633 edition of Gerard's *Herball*, where it is mentioned as an ornamental introduced by John Tradescant. In his garden catalogue of 1656, John Tradescant the Younger lists two varieties grown in his garden at Lambeth, one with black, the other with variegated seeds. Philip Miller is said to have been the first English gardener to cook the green pods, perhaps from plants growing in the Chelsea Physic Garden, in the early eighteenth century.

Modern breeding has not been extensive, but has concentrated on producing longer pods, which are slower to develop fibres and 'stringiness'. The variety 'Butler' is said to have extra-long (35 cm) stringless pods and red flowers, and 'Desirée' is a white-flowered stringless variety, with slightly shorter pods.

Only green pods are known, but flower colour and seed colour are both variable. Most varieties are vigorous climbers, like the wild species, but one or two are genetic dwarfs.

Wild runner beans compared with 'Scarlet Runner'

'Hammond's Dwarf' in flower (text p. 101)

Flowers of 'Sunset' (text p. 101)

Traditional arrangement of poles for runner beans

Cultivation

Runner beans are easy to grow, but often slow to produce pods in hot dry weather. Unlike French beans, which are regularly self-pollinating, runner bean flowers require pollination before they will form pods. The flowers are commonly visited by bumble bees, but may still fail to set. The old remedy of spraying the flowers with water is said to be useless, but the plants themselves require deep rich soil and ample water in the growing period. A heavy watering at the root will help flowering and pod formation, and mulching the roots will retain the moisture. In their native mountains the roots are kept cool and damp by surrounding shrubs, and they receive torrential rain in July, August and September, after a rather hot and dry spring. Frosts are almost unknown, at least until December. High temperatures are definitely a limiting factor in pod formation, as Herklots records that the plants will grow and flower well in Hong Kong, but only set an occasional pod.

Seed may be planted into its final position in late May or June, or earlier if the soil has warmed up. In cold areas seeds may be planted individually in pots, and the plants put out when all danger of frost is past, as the plants are killed by −3°C or less. They are usually placed 15 cm apart, with 60 cm between the rows. The position should be sheltered from drying winds and the plants will benefit from shade at mid-day.

Old gardening books recommend digging a trench 60 cm deep and wide, filled with half-rotted farmyard manure to within 15 cm of the top, and planting the seeds 5 cm deep in the shallow surface layer of soil, but the plants will make ample growth in any rich, moist soil, and too rich soil may produce many leaves but few pods. Some system of staking is required, either wigwams of poles or canes at least 3 m high, or the traditional method of two rows of crossed poles lashed to horizontals where they cross. Any other type of support must be equally strong to bear the heavy vines, and they make an attractive covering for a fence or pergola.

The pods should be picked when they have nearly reached their full length, usually about 20–30 cm, and before they become stringy or the seeds hard. It is very important to continue to pick all the pods as they become ready, or the plants will stop flowering. In most gardens the plants will then continue to bear until cut down by the first air frost. Pods are usually sliced before cooking. The seeds themselves may be eaten but require a considerable amount of boiling.

Diseases are few, but the germinating seeds may be attacked by slugs or mice, and root rots may kill some of the plants in wet and poorly drained soil. Failure to set pods, discussed above, is the commonest problem.

'Scarlet Runner' trained on a wigwam

Runner bean 'Painted Lady'

'Achievement'

'Desirée'

'Scarlet Runner'

'Scarlet Runner'

'Streamline'

Specimens from Sellindge 15 August

'Liberty'

'Scarlet Runner' in flower at Sellindge

'Desirée'

'Pickwick', a dwarf runner

'Achievement' Flowers red; pods 40–45 cm long; seeds purple, with few dark markings.

'Desirée' Flowers white; pods 25–30 cm, stringless; seeds large, white. Said to be relatively drought resistant.

'Hammond's Dwarf' A non-climbing variety, with stems up to 45 cm tall, and benefiting from some support. Flowers red, held above the leaves; pods c. 20 cm long; seeds pinkish-brown, with scattered streaks and spots. Known since the late nineteenth century. See p. 99.

'Liberty' Flowers red; pods 45–50 cm long, but stringy when mature.

'Painted Lady' Flowers with a red standard and white wings and keel; pods 20–30 cm long; seeds pinkish-brown, with dark streaks and stipples, mainly around the eye. A very old variety, known since the early nineteenth century. Shown on p. 99.

'Pickwick' A new non-climbing variety, with stems c. 45 cm tall; pods 20–23 cm long, stringless; seeds purplish with dark streaks and stipples, especially around the eye.

'Scarlet Runner' (syn. 'Scarlet Emperor') Flowers red; pods 25–30 cm; seeds purplish with dark streaks and stipples, especially around the eye. An old variety from the nineteenth century.

'Streamline' A variety with very long pods which do not become stringy. Seeds pinkish-brown, heavily mottled with black.

'Sunset' Flowers pink; pods 30–35 cm; an early-maturing variety of good flavour.

The **'Black-seeded Runner'** (not shown) is a very old variety, described 1654. The pods are flamed brownish-red, the seeds large, coal-black. 'Mrs Cannell's Black Runner' is possibly the same.

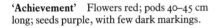

'Sunset' flowering at Wisley

A bean field on the central plateau in Mexico

Lima Bean

Phaseolus lunatus L.
Sieva Bean (small seeded), Madagascar Bean or Butter Bean,
Potato Limas (large, plump seeded)

The Lima bean is found in two varieties, large-seeded and small-seeded, and both climbing and bush varieties are grown. It was first seen by Europeans in Lima in Peru, but is generally a tropical and lowland species, found below 1200 m, and requires a hot growing season of around eighty days for the climbing varieties and sixty-five days for the quickest-maturing bush varieties. It is seldom successful outdoors in England, and in North America is found mainly in the southern States.

The Lima bean is naturally a perennial, and appears to be native from Guatemala southwards to Peru, the large-seeded forms in the south, the small in the north. Both large- and small-seeded forms were grown by pre-European cultures in America. The large-seeded are recorded from Huaca Prieta in Peru, in deposits dated to 2500 BC, and the small-seeded in Mexico, in the Ocampo caves (AD 100) and the Tehuacan valley (AD 700). There are other pre-European records from the Rio Zape area of Durango province, and other varieties were grown by the Maya in Yucatan, in the West Indies and by the Hopi tribe in Arizona and New Mexico.

The Spaniards soon distributed the Lima beans throughout their colonies in the East Indies, and they are now commonly grown there and in Africa and Madagascar.

Most modern varieties have been bred for the hotter states of North America. Varieties with coloured seeds, which may be green or pale brown, sometimes striped or splashed with red, require soaking and boiling to remove poisonous cyanogenetic glucosides, but these are absent from the white-seeded varieties.

Dwarf bean in Mexico

Climbing, large-seeded lima in Malawi

Bean from market in Ili, Sinkiang

Lima bean, 'King of the Garden'

The pods themselves are generally not eaten, but the seeds may be eaten either fresh or dried. For fresh beans the pods should be picked when they are mature and the seeds have swelled, but before the pods turn yellow.

Lima beans require more heat than French beans to germinate and grow well, but the cultivation requirements of the two groups are otherwise similar. 'Fordhook 242' is the most reliable of the bush varieties with large, white seeds.

'Cliff Dweller'   A strong-growing, but slender climbing variety, with small pods and small seeds, speckled with purple.
'King of the Garden'   A strong-growing climbing variety, with large pods to 20 cm long and large, white to pale-green seeds.

A fourth species of American bean, sometimes cultivated, is the Tepary Bean, *Phaseolus acutifolius* Gray. This is a quick-maturing annual, grown mainly in the drier areas of the southwestern United States and western Mexico, adjacent to the Gulf of California, but it is also grown in the far south of Mexico in Chiapas and in Guatemala. Again the earliest archaeological records of the species in cultivation are from the Tehuacan valley in Puebla, Mexico, dating from around 3000 BC. Recently its cultivation has been associated especially with the Papago Indians, and they are sometimes called the 'bean people'.

The wild form is recorded from western Texas to southern Arizona and Mexico at 1000–1800 m, flowering from August to October. The cultivated form, var. *latifolius* Freeman, is of uncertain origin, but may well also be native of Arizona, where it is sometimes found wild. The flowers are white or pale purple; the pods up to 7 cm long. The seeds are white, yellow, brown, green, bluish-black or variously speckled, and high in protein. The species is also notable for its low water requirements.

'Golden' and 'Sonoran Brown' are two cultivars suitable for hot, dry conditions.

Lima bean, 'Cliff Dweller'

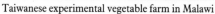

Taiwanese experimental vegetable farm in Malawi

Flowering plants of ground nut

Ground nut

Arachis hypogaea L. (*Leguminosae*, tribe *Stylosanthae*)
Peanut, Monkey Nut

The ground nut is a tropical crop, widely grown in America from North Carolina southwards, in the warmest areas of Turkey and possibly Sicily. India, China and West Africa are leading producers. In Malawi peanuts are often planted as ground cover in maize fields, both fixing atmospheric nitrogen and shading the soil. They are not suitable for growing in temperate regions as they require temperatures around 15°C and a growing season of at least 105 days. The plants are generally trailing, with leaves on short stalks with four leaflets, though bush varieties have now been developed. The seeds, which are produced in pods which bury themselves under the ground, contain large amounts of both oil and protein, and it is for their oil that most ground nuts are cultivated.

The genus *Arachis* contains forty to seventy species, all native to South America, and especially diverse in the Matto Grosso area of Brazil. Both annual (from dry areas) and perennial (from wet areas) species are known. *Arachis monticola*, an annual species from northwestern Argentina, is closest to the cultivated species and presumed to be its ancestor. Two subspecies of *A. hypogaea* are recognized, subsp. *hypogaea* which fruits on the lateral branches only, and subsp. *fastigiata* which fruits on both the main axis and on the lateral branches. The earliest archaeological records of cultivated ground nuts are from Peru, dating from 3000 to 2000 BC, but the crop is thought to be more ancient than these dates suggest, and to have originated in southern Bolivia and northern Argentina.

By the time the Spaniards reached America, ground nuts were grown as far north as Mexico and the Caribbean; they were soon spread by the Spaniards and the Portuguese both to Africa and to the Philippines and eastern Asia. The first introduction to temperate North America seems to have been from Africa in the seventeenth century, not directly from the south.

A similar species, the Bambara groundnut, *Voandzeia subterranea* (L.) Thouars, is a native of West Africa, named after a town near Timbuktu. It is tolerant both of drought and of poor soil, and is recorded by Herklots as grown in Nigeria south to Malawi, in Brazil, Madagascar, India and the Far East. The stems creep and root at the nodes and the leaves, which are on long upright stalks, have three narrowly lanceolate leaflets. The small flowers are pale yellow. The subterranean seed pods contain one or rarely two seeds which may be black, red-brown or pale buff.

Cowpea and Asparagus Bean

Vigna unguiculata (L.) Walp. syn. *Vigna sinensis* (L.) Savi ex Hassk. subsp. *unguiculata* (*Leguminosae*)
Yard-long Bean, Blackeye Bean, Crowder

Cowpeas are grown mainly in India and West Africa, but are also important in some areas of America and as green vegetables in the East Indies and China. They are commonly grown in the warmer parts of North America, where they are known as southern blackeye peas, blackeye beans, and crowders.

Vigna unguiculata is thought to have been cultivated first in Ethiopia from 4000 to 3000 BC. The wild form, subsp. *dekindtiana*, is found in the semi-arid savannah area of Africa, from northern Kenya and southern Ethiopia westwards to northern Nigeria, but it is in Ethiopia that the cultivated cowpeas are most diverse. The cultivated African cowpea (subsp. *unguiculata*) arrived in India via Arabia in 1500–1000 BC, at the same time as sorghum, and in Asia was developed into the three modern cultivated subspecies. By 300 BC the cowpea had reached Europe, and was being grown by the Romans by the end of the Classical period. Introduction to America probably occurred by two separate routes in the seventeenth century, to North America from the Mediterranean, and to South America from West Africa, with the slave trade.

The subspecies are as follows:
Subsp. *unguiculata*, the cowpea, crowder or blackeye bean is now widely cultivated as a vegetable in America and in West Africa. It is also grown throughout China, and seeds of the variety shown here were bought in the market in Kuldja, near the border with Kazakstan. Many modern varieties are dwarf, not climbing. The pods are 20–30 cm long.

Cowpea from China at Harry Hay's

Cowpea in Malawi

Yard-long bean in flower

Yard-long beans bought in the market

Subsp. *cylindrica* (L.) Skeels, was developed in India primarily as a fodder crop. The plants are upright and non-climbing, the pods 7.5–13 cm long.

Subsp. *sesquipedalis* (L.) Fruw., the asparagus bean or yard-long bean is cultivated mainly in southwest Asia, for its very long immature pods, which may reach 90 cm in length. It requires a long warm summer to grow and produce satisfactory pods, and only fruits in an unheated greenhouse in England in unusually hot seasons. We failed to produce a good crop in a house mixed with cucumbers, peppers and aubergines, but Joy Larkcom succeeded with it in a polytunnel in the warm summer of 1989. The beautiful flowers open in the morning, when they are pale violet and yellow, and have become pale bluish and closed by midday. In the greenhouse we found it was very susceptible to red spider, and the humid conditions needed to keep the red spider at bay encouraged botrytis on the stems in cool weather.

Cultivation

All varieties require much the same conditions as sweetcorn, though there are fewer which have been raised to ripen their pods in a cool summer climate. The quickest maturing American varieties are 'Dixielee', grown for green pods, which can be ready in 65 days, and 'Extra Early Blackeye' which is ready at 50 days. 'Queen Anne', another blackeye bean, is ready between 56 and 68 days. The yard-long bean is rated around 75 days in a warm American summer, and there is a purple-podded yard-long available in America from Seeds Blum, which is said to stay purple when cooked.

Field of chick-peas in Mexico in October

Chick-peas in pod in Malawi

Asparagus pea

Chick-pea

Cicer arietinum L. (*Leguminosae*)
Indian Gram, Garbanzo bean

The chick-pea is an annual, with an upright base to the stem and arching, spreading branches. The leaves have five to seven pairs of small leaflets and the whole plant is covered with sticky glandular hairs. The flowers are small and solitary; the pods with one or two large round seeds. It is commonly cultivated in rather hot, dry climates from southern Europe and North Africa to China, and especially in India, where it is grown through the winter to be harvested in the warm dry spring before the onset of the monsoon. It is also an important crop in Mexico, being grown at rather high altitudes through the wet summer for harvest in late autumn. Western varieties tend to have large smooth seeds, shaped like an owl's head; the eastern varieties from southern India and Ethiopia have smaller wrinkled seeds more like a ram's head, hence the name '*arietinum*', as well as smaller leaves and flowers. A second species, *Cicer microphyllum*, is cultivated in the Himalayan region.

Chick-peas are usually grown on a field scale for their seeds which are high in protein (c. 20 per cent), carbohydrate (50–60 per cent) and oils (c. 5 per cent). The small-seeded varieties are usually sold as split peas, and made into dahl or flour for poppadoms. The larger-seeded varieties are often roasted and eaten whole, or combined with oil to make hummus.

Herklots records that the Indians collect acid from the glandular hairs on the leaves for use as vinegar or to make a cooling drink, by spreading a cloth on the plants overnight and wringing out the dew in the morning.

The genus *Cicer* contains about forty species, found mainly in central and western Asia. Like the pea, it belongs to the tribe *Vicieae* of the family *Leguminosae*, but it also has a lot of similarities with the genus *Ononis*, the Restharrow, usually included in the tribe *Ononideae*. Nine species are recorded from Turkey. *Cicer arietinum* is not known as a wild plant, but one wild species, *C. echinospermum* P. H. Davis, found in oak scrub and grassy and rocky places in southeastern Turkey, is close to it, differing mainly in its spiny seeds.

Chick-pea, 'Kabuli Black'

Asparagus pea

The oldest archaeological record of the chick-pea is from neolithic B levels in Jericho; there are also early records from Turkey, dated to 5450 BC, and it was grown at a very early date all round the Mediterranean and in Ethiopia. It has been recorded at Atranji Khera in Uttar Pradesh in remains dating from c. 2000 BC, along with barley and rye, and there were also later and probably independent introductions to southern India.

Chick-peas are easily cultivated in warm areas on sandy soils. In the Mediterranean they are usually sown in February, when they should have enough water to form good bushy plants. They are quite drought resistant. In colder climates they need the same treatment as kidney beans, in as warm a position in the garden as possible. After the pods have formed they may be allowed to get dry before harvesting, as the seeds remain enclosed in the dry pods.

In the variety 'Garbanzo' (not shown) the seeds are large, and pale brown; the plant erect and bushy.
'Kabuli Black': seeds large, black skinned; plant spreading.

Asparagus pea

Tetragonolobus purpureus Moench. (*Leguminosae*)

This is a small creeping pea with red flowers and winged pods which are delicious if eaten young, at about 2.5 cm long; they are up to 7 cm long when ripe. A well-grown plant may be 60 cm or more across, and about 15 cm high. *Tetragonolobus* belongs to the tribe *Loteae* of the *Leguminosae*, and is closely related to the genus *Lotus*, which contains common northern European wild plants such as bird's foot trefoil, but differs from *Lotus* in having transverse septae between the seeds, and winged pods.

Asparagus pea is an annual plant, native to the Mediterranean region, where it grows in fields and scrub, growing through the winter and flowering in spring. The closely related *T. requienii*, also from the Mediterranean area, differs in having unwinged pods and usually yellow flowers. A third species, *T. maritimus*, is a perennial, also with solitary yellow flowers. It grows in damp grassy places, often in slightly saline soil throughout Europe, east to the Caucasus. It is found in a few places, mainly on chalky soils, in southern England, but is thought to have been introduced by man.

Cultivation

Asparagus pea needs a warm, open sunny position, in light, rich soil. Seed can be sown in April and May, and in cold areas may be started indoors. The young plants should be spaced out 20–30 cm apart, leaving about 40 cm between rows, and well watered while they are growing. Because the pods are so small, several plants are needed per person. Picking should begin as soon as the pods reach 2.5–4 cm long, and if picked regularly the crop will be prolonged. Ideally the pods will be produced from June to August.

Hyacinth bean in the kitchen garden at Longwood, Pennsylvania

Sword bean in Mexico

Hyacinth Bean

Dolichos lablab L., syn. *Lablab niger* Medik. (*Leguminosae*)

This very beautiful climbing bean is grown as an ornamental, as well as having edible pods and seeds. It also has a thick, edible root. It is thought to have originated in India, but is now found throughout the tropics, and is naturalized in many areas including the southeastern United States. The leaves are often purple, the flowers purple, red or white; some varieties are annual, others biennial. The pods have a line of rounded tubercles on their edges, and are flat and curved with a persistent style. The seeds may be white, yellowish or black, and variously spotted, with a long white hilum.

In temperate climates the seeds should be sown in late spring, and may flower by late summer if they have sufficient warmth. In the tropics seed is sown in the hot, wet summer and the plants flower in the cooler autumn and again in spring. The plants require well-drained soil.

Jack Bean

Canavalia ensiformis (L.) DC. (*Leguminosae*)

Canavalias are woody perennial climbers found in both the American and Asian tropics, and sometimes cultivated as annuals. The immature pods, which are 25–30 cm long, and 2–2.5 cm broad, are eaten in the same way as French beans or snap beans, and the seeds, while still green, can be eaten when well cooked. The white seed coat of the mature beans is said to be poisonous.

The jack bean is native to the West Indies, Mexico, Peru and Brazil. We found it growing on the edge of the evergreen oak forest on the lower slopes of Volcan Tequila in central Mexico, flowering and fruiting in October, the woody shoots climbing up into the trees. The young pods are slightly furry, and ridged along one edge. It has a long history of use in North America, and has been found in archaeological deposits in the southwestern United States dating from about 1300. It is now grown in Asia as well as in America, as green manure and as shade for pineapples and other crops, as well as for food.

The sword-bean, *Canavalia gladiata* (Jacq.) DC., is closely

related but has wider pods to 40 cm long, 5 cm broad. It is known only as a cultivated plant, and is grown mainly in India, Malaya and southeast Asia. Both flowers and seeds may be red or white, and the white-seeded forms which are commonly cultivated in Japan are better as food. The seeds may be poisonous when not well cooked, and Dr Herklots recommends that in any case only a few be eaten first, then more on subsequent days if no ill effects, such as headaches and diarrhoea, are experienced.

Potato Bean

Apios americana Medik. (*Leguminosae*)
American Ground nut, Indian Potato

The Potato Bean is native throughout eastern North America, from New Brunswick west to Colorado and south to Texas and Florida. It has numerous small edible tubers on the roots, leaves with five leaflets and racemes of small purplish flowers. The tubers are sweetish, and usually eaten boiled. The closely related *Apios fortunei* Maxim., with tuberous roots and greenish-yellow flowers, is found in Japan and China. The potato bean was an important food plant of the North American Indians, and enabled the Pilgrim Fathers to survive their first winter in America

The Four-angled Bean

Psophocarpus tetragonolobus (Stickm.)
DC Goa Bean or Winged bean
(Not illustrated.)

This is possibly a native of Madagascar, but is most commonly grown in Java, Malaya and Thailand, Burma, India and Ceylon. It has tuberous roots which can be eaten raw or cooked, as can the young shoots. The main edible part is the winged seed pods which are eaten when 10–15 cm long, about half grown. The seeds are edible, both when green and when ripe. Even the beautiful pale blue flowers may be put into salads.

Seeds are generally sown in good soil at the beginning of the summer rains. They reach flowering size in three to four months; after fruiting, the plants survive the dry season as root tubers.

Jicama

Pachyrrhizus erosus (L.) Urban
Xiquima, Yam Bean

Pachyrrhizus erosus is a native of Mexico and central America, but is now commonly cultivated throughout the tropics. The closely related *P. tuberosus* is native to the headwaters of the Amazon, and is cultivated in the Andes in Ecuador, and is also grown in the West Indies and China. (Illustrated on p. 133.)

Pigeon Pea

Cajanus cajan (L.) Millsp. syn. *C. indicus* Spreng. (*Leguminosae*)
Red Gran, No-eye Pea, or Dahl

This is a tall perennial pea, which forms a short-lived shrub with stiff stems to 3 m tall in suitable climates. It is especially suitable for cultivation in poor soils and with limited supplies of fertilizer. It is most commonly grown in India, with lesser but still important crops in the Caribbean, Uganda, Malawi and southeast Asia. The peas may be eaten green, but most are used in the form of 'split peas' eaten as dahl.

 Cajanus cajan is the only member of the genus, but is closely related to the mainly Indian genus *Atylosa*, and it was probably in India that the crop originated. No single species is a likely ancestor. The earliest evidence for its cultivation is uncertain. Burkill recorded seeds from Egyptian tombs dating from about 2000 BC, but this early date is not supported by other evidence. However, at some early date the pea was taken from India to Africa, and later from West Africa to the Caribbean where it is still called Pois Angola. It also spread east to Malaysia and to China in about AD 500, but India remains the most important area for its cultivation. At present there is considerable breeding effort designed to increase yields and improve disease resistance. It also has potential as a fodder crop for cattle.

 Cultivation is by seed which is planted in groups of two or three, 1–1.5 m apart in spring, or at the beginning of the wet season. Different varieties mature at different times; the shorter early-maturing types are called tur, the late-maturing types arhar. The plant is commonly grown as an annual, the mature stems being cut down and used for firewood after the pods have been harvested. All varieties have three stalked leaflets, and racemes of small flowers in the leaf axils. There are two main varieties in Jamaica; the petals are pure yellow in var. *flavus* the No-eye pea, which has yellow peas, or veined with red in var. *bicolor*, the Congo pea, which has spotted and coarser peas.

Kudzu Vine

Pueraria lobata (Willd.) Ohwi (*Leguminosae*)
Fan Kot (Cantonese)

This is a rampant climber, with stems to at least 10 m. It is native to China and Japan, but long cultivated in the Philippines and Polynesia, and now naturalized and threatening to become a pest in the southeastern United States. It has large spindle-shaped tubers which may weigh up to 30 kg, illustrated on p. 133. The flowers are reddish-purple, in dense racemes; the small pods are covered with brown hairs. Herklots describes how, in Hong Kong, the plants are often cultivated in the same beds as taro and ginger. All three crops are planted at the same time in spring and harvested in winter. The tubers are starchy, and more often used as a source of starch for thickening soup than eaten by themselves.

Apios americana with leaves of Osmunda

Pigeon pea in Malawi

Flowers of Kudzu vine

Drying lentil plants in China; the mountains of Lijiang behind

Soy bean

Glycine max (L.) Merr. (*Leguminosae*)

The tropical beans shown on these pages are never really satisfactory in Europe, but grow well in climates with hot, humid summers such as the southeastern States of America, in parts of Africa and in eastern Asia.

The soy bean is probably the most important economically, and is grown mainly for the extraction of protein and oil. A few varieties, such as 'Butterbean', 'Frostbeater' and 'Envy' are suitable for eating as green beans, cooked when the seeds are full sized but still green. In North America they take a minimum of seventy-five days to reach harvesting stage, so they should be sown about three months before the first frost of autumn. These quick maturing modern varieties are also adapted to flowering and fruiting in the shortening days of July and August. The original varieties only flowered during the lengthening days of early summer, so were unable to produce crops in cooler and shorter northern summers.

Soy beans are an ancient Chinese crop, probably first cultivated in the eastern part of northern China in the eleventh century BC, and had spread throughout China and southeast Asia by the third century BC. The wild ancestor of the soy bean is probably *Glycine soja* Sieb. & Zucc. syn. *G. ussuriensis* Regel & Maak, a twining annual found in northeastern China and adjacent Russia, Korea, Taiwan and Japan. The main differences which have been selected for in the cultivated soy bean over the millenia are larger seeds, non-climbing habit, increased oil content but reduced protein, and non-shattering seed pods. Soy beans were first known in Europe through the writings of Engelbert Kaempfer, who was

physician to the governor of the Dutch East India Company on Deshima Island off the coast of Japan in 1690–92. The Japanese carefully guarded their culture from foreign influence and allowed the foreigners ashore only on the yearly embassy to Tokyo, and it was only by bribing their guards and picking plants along the route that Kaempfer was able to get his botanical specimens.

Lentil

Lens culinaris Medik. (*Leguminosae*)

The lentil is one of the most ancient crops, grown in the eastern Mediterranean since at least 6700 BC, from which date seeds have been found at Çayonü in Turkey. The lentil plant is like a slender annual vetch, with small pale mauve or white flowers 6–8 mm long in groups of one to three, and short pods with one or two seeds; the seeds in cultivated varieties are 3.5–6.5 mm across.

The genus *Lens* belongs to the tribe *Vicieae* of the *Leguminosae*, and is intermediate between the large genera *Lathyrus* and *Vicia*. There are four wild species in addition to the cultivated lentil, all native to Turkey, with some also found in southern Europe and other parts of the Near East. *Lens orientalis* (Boiss.) Hand.-Mazz., which is closest to the wild lentil, is found from Greece eastwards to the southern Caucasus and northern Iraq, growing in steppe, pine forest and oak scrub, as well as in weedy arable fields. It has smaller seeds 2.5–3 mm across, and somewhat shorter pods than the cultivated species. The earliest seeds found on archaeological sites are the size of *L. orientalis*, but by the fifth millenium BC the crop has seeds 4.2 mm across, within the range of the modern cultivated species. Lentils appear to have been an important crop

Beans sown in a jar

Ready for eating, showing weight

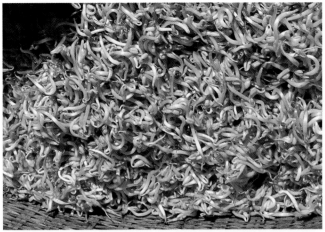

Bean sprouts in a Chengdu market

Plants of lentil in south-west China

at this period, associated with the growing of wheat and barley.
There has been little increase in seed size since classical times,
although lentils are widely grown in India, Pakistan and Ethiopia,
as well as the Mediterranean region, Argentina, Chile and
Washington State. They survive in poor sandy soils, and in areas
with little rainfall in summer.

Bean Sprouts

The following species can be used for bean sprouts, though mung
beans are probably most commonly used.

Mung Bean, Green Gram *Vigna radiata*(L.) Wilczek syn.
Phaseolus aureus Roxb., *Adzukia radiata* (L.) Ohwi.

Adzuki Bean *Vigna angularis* (Willd.) Ohwi & Ohashi.

Soya bean (see above); Horse Bean *Vicia faba* var. *equina* (see
page 86–7); Pea (see p. 82–3).

The method for their sprouting recommended by Joy Larkcom
gives excellent results.

A few preliminary points are important: the seeds must be alive
to germinate, and must not have been treated with any fungicide
(fungicide-treated seeds are sometimes dyed pink as a warning);
mould is the great danger, so any damaged or mouldy seeds must
be removed; the seeds should be washed very well, preferably in
chlorinated water, before starting; a warm, dark place, such as an
airing cupboard, is suitable to grow them in.

The method recommended by Joy Larkcom is as follows:

Place a layer of mung beans about 1 cm deep in the bottom of a
wide-mouthed container, such as a jamjar, or a clean plastic pot
with small holes in the base. Put a layer or two of muslin on top of
them, and rinse them in cold water. On the muslin place a weight
(I put the old iron weights in a polythene bag to keep them dry). A
weight of 500 gm seemed to work well on a 500 gm jamjar; a 1 kg
weight fits an 11–12 cm pot. The beans are then rinsed in cold
water night and morning, disturbing them as little as possible. If
they are in a glass jar make sure they are well drained. At 20°C,
they will be ready after three to six days, and may then be stored
in the fridge if they reach the right stage at an inconvenient
moment.

Soy beans can be sprouted in the same way, but do not need a
weight, and need a higher temperature of 21–25°C.

Adzuki beans need an even higher temperature, around 30°C,
and even more frequent rinsing. They are used when only
1–2.5 cm long.

Both horse beans, which are a small-seeded form of the broad
bean, and peas can be eaten when sprouted. They do not need
darkness, and will grow at a lower temperature, around 12–15°C.
Horse beans are usually eaten when just sprouted; peas can be left
until the leafy shoot is showing its first leaves.

Soy beans with plastic mulch

Ripe soy beans

French sorrel

Wild sorrel

Large-leaved sorrel

Different species of sorrel

Evening Primrose plants in autumn

Evening Primrose flowers

Udo

Aralia cordata Thunb. (*Araliaceae*)

Udo is a large perennial with arching stems to 1.5 m, much divided leaves and numerous small umbels of greenish-white flowers in late summer, followed by very tiny, probably poisonous, black fruits in autumn. It is related to common ivy, and is found throughout Japan, Sakhalin, Korea and in northern China, growing in open woods and ravines in the mountains. It is commonly cultivated in Japan, where the young shoots are blanched.

Cultivation

Young plants can be raised from seed, and will grow fast in moist, leafy soil in a partly shaded position. The young shoots emerge in late spring, and should be blanched in a tall seakale pot or drainpipe, as they are harvested when about 60 cm long. They are usually eaten raw, thinly sliced into soup. Although I have grown the plant as a curiosity after collecting seeds in Japan, I have been unwilling to sacrifice the flowers, so cannot report on its flavour, but it is said to be mild and resemble asparagus.

Sorrel

Rumex acetosa L. (*Polygonaceae*)

This is a popular vegetable in France and among keen cooks in England, but is otherwise seldom grown now, though it was popular here until the eighteenth century. The leaves have an acid, slightly sharp taste, and can be used sparingly in salads, in soup, or puréed like spinach to make a sauce for fish such as salmon or shad.

Large-leaved sorrel is an improved form of *Rumex acetosa*, a perennial native of hay fields and grassy places throughout Britain and Europe. It grows best in moist conditions and cool soils. Most of the leaves come from the base of the plant which puts up a simple flowering stem with a few leaves.

French sorrel is *Rumex scutatus* L., a native of mountains in central and southern Europe, Turkey and northern Iran, growing in rocky subalpine meadows and on screes. It has creeping underground shoots, and smaller, squarer leaves than ordinary sorrel, and is said to have a finer, more lemony flavour. The flowering shoots are leafy and much branched, and yield a supply of edible leaves. It thrives in drier and better-drained soil than *Rumex acetosa*, and it is probably for this reason that it is more popular in France. There is an attractive grey-leaved variety grown in gardens as an ornamental. Propagation is easy from rooted pieces.

A third species, *Rumex patientia* L., the herb patience, was cultivated in the past, and seed is still available. The plant is a perennial and grows to 2 m, with long leaves to 30 cm, which can be cooked like spinach when young. It is a native of eastern Europe, Turkey, northern Asia and North Africa, growing on wasteland and open steppe.

Buckwheat in flower

Floating plants of Water chestnut

Buckwheat

Fagopyrum esculentum Moench. (*Polygonaceae*)

Buckwheat is grown for its seeds which are triangular in section and form a nutty grain. It is widely eaten in eastern Europe and Asia, and among those of east European descent in North America. The grains soften after much boiling and have a good, nutty flavour. It is also made into flour, which has a high protein content.

Buckwheat is an annual, probably derived in cultivation from the perennial species *Fagopyrum dibotrys* (D. Don) Hara, syn. *F. cymosum* (Trev.) Meissn., which is native of the Himalayas and also grown for food.

A third species, *F. tartaricum* (L.) Gaertn., is also cultivated; it thrives and produces crops in very poor soils and in a relatively short growing season, so is popular in mountain areas such as Tibet and the drier parts of the western Himalayas. Buckwheat has been cultivated for at least 1500 years in China, and its cultivation spread to Europe in the fifteenth century. It probably originated as a crop in northern India, and spread outwards from there.

Buckwheat has proved a difficult crop to improve by normal breeding techniques, but recent work will no doubt produce higher yielding varieties with larger grains. Seeds are generally planted in spring and the plants harvested in autumn.

Evening Primrose

Oenothera biennis L., *O. erythrosepala* Borbas (*Onagraceae*)

Mme Vilmorin-Andrieux's classic, *The Vegetable Garden*, published in English by William Robinson in 1885, describes evening primrose roots as excellent vegetables, equal with and rather similar to salsify. Several closely related species of *Oenothera* are equally suitable, as they produce a rosette of leaves and a deep fleshy tap root at the end of their first year, and flower in the second year. All species were originally native to North America, but have long been naturalized in Europe, where new species such as *Oenothera biennis* have evolved.

Cultivation is easy in any soil, but the plants produce a better and less forked root in deep, fine soil without stones. Rich soil is not necessary, as the plants are very happy growing in deserts or in sand dunes by the sea. Seed can be sown in early spring, and the plants thinned to about 25 cm apart, when they will make flat rosettes of narrow leaves. They can be dug from October onwards and treated like salsify. As far as I know, no breeding work has been done on *Oenothera* in connection with its use as a vegetable. The seeds, however, contain valuable edible oil, and breeders are attempting to raise plants whose seed can be harvested mechanically.

Water Chestnut

Trapa natans L. (*Trapaceae*)
Ling Kok

Although it is such a very different-looking plant, *Trapa* is closely related to *Oenothera*. It grows in still water, the leaves forming floating rosettes with the small white flowers and spiny edible seeds hidden among them.

Water chestnut is also the name for another vegetable, the corm of *Eleocharis dulcis*. It is illustrated and described on pages 236–7.

There is little agreement among botanists on the number of *Trapa* species that exist, and they differ mainly in the shape of their fruits. They are native throughout southern Europe eastwards to China, and were formerly found in England; semi-fossilized fruits of *Trapa* have been found in interglacial peat deposits in East Anglia. It has gone wild in parts of the eastern United States and become a pest, as it can very quickly form mats on the surface of the water.

Trapa is now grown as a vegetable mainly in China, though also in southern Europe for the overseas Chinese market. The usual cultivated variety has two large recurved horns on the large black fruit, not four slender horns as are found on the smaller fruits of wild European plants. The seeds must be boiled for at least an hour before eating, as they are poisonous when raw.

Cultivation

It is necessary to obtain seeds which have been kept moist, because they lose their viability once they dry out. They must be planted in shallow water at a temperature of around 18°C, and they probably need at least that to grow properly. The seeds form in succession beneath the surface, amongst the leaves.

Udo (*Aralia cordata*) in flower

'Lancer'

'Gladiator'

'Tender and True'

'White Gem'

'The Student'

Specimens from Wisley, 27 September

Wild parsnip in chalk grassland   Leaves and flowers of skirret   Roots of skirret

Parsnip

Pastinaca sativa L. subsp. *sativa* (*Umbelliferae*)

Like the carrot, the parsnip is a biennial, producing its long edible tapering root the first year and flowering the following year. There are few varieties of parsnip, and it has never been bred for different colour or shape as has the carrot. Modern varieties aim to be resistant to canker, and produce a fat, wedge-shaped root.

Cultivated parsnips have been developed from the wild parsnip which is found throughout central and southern Europe, and as an escape from cultivation in Scandinavia, North and South America, Australia and New Zealand. In the British Isles the wild subsp. *sylvestris* (Miller) Rouy & Camus is found mainly southeast of a line from the Humber to the Severn; here the yellow umbels of flowers are often conspicuous on grassy roadsides, especially on chalky soils in the late summer. In Ireland, Scotland and Wales wild parsnips are usually escaped plants of subsp. *sativa*. The genus *Pastinaca* contains about fourteen other species, mainly in southern Europe and western Asia, but they do not seem to have played any part in the development of the edible parsnip.

Parsnips were probably grown as a vegetable by the Greeks and Romans, though there is some confusion whether the references in the literature refer to parsnips or carrots. The word *daucos*, mentioned by the Greek authors Hippocrates and Dioscurides, refers to a medicinal umbellifer from Crete, and the word *pastinaca*, used by Pliny in the first century AD, refers to either parsnip or carrot, possibly both. Parsnips were definitely grown as a vegetable in Germany in the mid-sixteenth century and were especially valued for their sweetness, hardiness and ability to overwinter in the ground. They were commonly eaten with salt fish in Lent, but their popularity declined as that of the potato increased. The high sugar content of parsnips was exploited by using them to make wine, jam, or a sweet flour used for cakes.

Cultivation

Parsnips need a very deep, well-dug and fine soil which has not been recently manured. Fresh manure tends to cause forking of the roots. Short-rooted varieties are better for heavy or shallow soils, long-rooted for deeper, lighter soils. Seed has short viability, so it is safer to buy fresh seed yearly, or at least to be aware of a possible cause if it does not germinate well. Seed should be sown in April or May, unless the soil has warmed up earlier, and placed in a shallow drill. Three seeds planted in groups 8–15 cm apart, depending on the size of the variety used, can be thinned to one

plant per position. Harvesting is usually in winter, from October onwards. The variety 'Improved Hollow Crown' is said to mature faster than most others.

Extra long parsnips for showing can be grown in drainpipes as carrots are. They will need regular watering. 'Lisbonnais' and 'Tender and True' are long varieties suitable for exhibition.

Celery fly and carrot fly, both covered under their respective vegetables, can also affect parsnips. Canker produces cracks and black areas near the tops of the roots which eventually rot. It is worst on acid soils. No cure is known, but late sowings in May and June may be less affected. The varieties 'Gladiator' and 'Avonresister' are highly resistant, as is the new variety 'Andover' raised in the United States. It has very long narrow roots, in contrast to the short roots of 'Avonresister'.

'Gladiator'   An F1 hybrid, early-maturing; roots wedge-shaped; smooth white skin; canker-resistant with sweet flavour.
'Lancer'   Available from Dobies.
'Tender and True'   Raised by Sutton's Seeds Ltd. Roots can be very long with little hard core. A traditional variety.
'The Student'   Available from Unwins.
'White Gem'   Broad roots, said to have a particularly good flavour. High yielding, with some resistance to canker.

Skirret

Sium sisarum L. (*Umbelliferae*)

Skirret is an ancient vegetable, now seldom seen. It is a perennial, producing a cluster of fleshy roots about 1 cm in diameter. They are said to taste sweet and floury. Skirret is a native of damp places in central Europe, from Hungary and Bulgaria eastwards to Siberia and central Asia, and south to North Iraq and Iran. The wild plant is known as var. *lancifolium* (Bieb.) Thell., and does not have tuberous roots. The origin of the tuberous-rooted variety is unknown, but it has been grown at least since the sixteenth century, and possibly even by the Romans.

Another *Sium* species, *S. latifolium* L., the water parsnip, is native to the British Isles, growing in fens and dykes in shallow water. It has tall furrowed stems to 1.5 m and conspicuous sepals. Skirret differs in not producing submerged leaves, in having a finely ridged stem and very small sepals. It is usually shorter and slenderer.

Skirret should be grown in rich, moist soil. It may be raised from seed, but is best grown by planting offsets from a good tuberous form in the spring.

Sea carrot *Daucus carota* subsp. *gummifera*

Summer carrots at Sandling Park

Carrot

Daucus carota L. subsp. *sativus* (Hoffm.) Arch. (*Umbelliferae*)

The carrot is a biennial; in the first year the plant produces the fleshy, usually orange tap root which is eaten; if left in the ground, the plant will flower the following spring. Wild carrots usually have white roots, but cultivated carrots have been developed in shades of orange, red, yellow, white or even crimson in the Japanese variety 'Kintoki', which contains the red pigment Lycopene, found also in tomatoes (*Lycopersicum*). The roots contain significant quantities of sugar, and of carotene, an orange pigment which is converted by the mucous membrane of the intestines into vitamin A.

The carrot is a member of the family *Umbelliferae*, which also contains the parsnip, celery and parsley, as well as hemlock, *Conium maculatum*, which was used to kill Socrates, and other equally poisonous parsley-like plants. Wild carrot is found throughout Europe from the British Isles eastwards, and in Asia as far east as northwestern China. In North America it has escaped from cultivation and become a pernicious weed in many areas. Other species of wild carrot are found mainly in the Mediterranean, and these and distinct subspecies of *D. carota* are often found on coastal cliffs or dunes. This is also the habitat of a wild subspecies of *D. carota* found in Britain, subsp. *gummifera* Hooker fil., which is commonest along the south coast. It is a short, stout plant, with shiny leaves and an umbel which is almost flat when in fruit.

It is likely that carrots were first cultivated in the eastern Mediterranean region, and were certainly grown by the Romans. Orange carrots are thought to have been developed from red, anthocyanin-containing carrots. Wild carrots with red or purple roots are still found in Afghanistan, and it may be there that the coloured cultivated carrot originated, yellow ones occurring as anthocyanin-free mutants from the purple. Yellow carrots are first recorded in Turkey in the tenth century, and both yellow and purple were grown throughout Europe until the seventeenth century, when the orange carrot was developed in Holland. By the late eighteenth century four varieties were distinguished – 'Long Orange', 'Late Half Long', 'Early Half Long' and 'Early Scarlet Horn' – and all modern Western carrots are derived from these four.

Some old varieties are still cultivated: 'Early Scarlet Horn' is still a good variety for forcing. 'Muscade' is an annual variety, originating from North Africa, which produces its root very fast and was bred to grow quickly in the cool winter months of the Mediterranean climate. 'Belgium White' has a long white or pale yellow root. Modern breeding has concentrated on reducing the proportion of the root which forms the tougher core, on sweetness, on uniformity of shape and heaviness of crop.

A recent development has been the breeding of varieties resistant to carrot root fly, the most serious pest of carrots. This has been based on the partially resistant variety 'Sytan', (available from Marshalls), and promising results have also been obtained using the Libyan species *Daucus capillifolius*, crossed with 'Sytan' and other varieties.

A carotene-rich variety, 'Juwarot Double Vitamin A', is still available. Deficiency of vitamin A is the cause of xerophthalmia, which can cause blindness in children, and was formerly frequent in India, Africa and southeast Asia. In traditional Chinese medicine the dung of fruit-eating bats is applied to the eyes. This is rich in carotene derived from the undigested skins of fruit.

Wild carrots on Salisbury Plain

Cultivated carrots in flower

Netting used as protection against carrot root fly; the barrier is 75 cm high

Carrots damaged by root fly

'Early French Frame', photographed 1 May

Carrots planted next to onions

Carrots 'Giganta' grown in sand in a drain pipe

Carrot cultivars are now divided into six main groups:
Amsterdam   Quick growing and maturing for early crops; roots generally small and slender, tapering.
Nantes   Also used for early crops; roots long and more cylindrical than Amsterdam.
Round or Stump-rooted   For early crops, and good for heavier or very shallow soils where long carrots do not develop well. Typical varieties are 'Paris Market' or 'Kundulus'.
Chantenay   For use in summer; thick, rather short, tapering roots.
Berlicum   For late summer use and for storing; long, thick cylindrical roots.
Autumn King or Imperator   Mainly used for storing; long roots, tapering from a broad shoulder.

Cultivation

Carrots do best in sandy soil, especially that which is chalky or well limed. Soils should be well manured the autumn before sowing, because fresh manure encourages the plant to produce forked roots. The soil should be prepared so that it is very loose and friable, and deeply cultivated. Seed should be sown 2 cm deep, aiming to produce about twenty plants per 30 cm square for medium-sized carrots, more for very small carrots and about ten plants in the same area for large carrots. In the garden, seed is generally sown more thickly than this, as the young carrots which are thinned out can be eaten. After they have been thinned, the soil should be drawn up along the row, so that carrot flies do not find an easy route to the remaining crop.

Carrots can be left in the ground over winter, especially if the soil is very sandy. If the soil is heavier or slug-infested, it is better to store them in boxes of barely moist sand in as cold a place as possible. Young carrots are excellent when frozen whole. Suitable varieties for growing as young carrots are the early round or stump-rooted ones, and the Japanese variety 'Suko'.

Long show carrots (and parsnips), with roots up to 1.5 m long can be grown by sowing ten or so seeds in the middle of a tall drainpipe filled with finely sifted sandy soil. They should be well watered to ensure that the soil in the lowest part of the pipe stays moist to encourage the root to grow straight and deep. Harvesting can be a problem; either the pipe must be laid on its side and carefully emptied, or it must have been split into two lengthwise and tied together before planting.

Pests and diseases

Carrot root fly is the commonest and worst pest; the maggots, which are about 8 mm long, eat into the outer layers of the carrot and leave unsightly cracks and lines which can be the starting point for rot. Young plants may be killed. The leaves of mature plants infected with carrot fly tend to become reddish. The fly is very hard to control. Early sowings should be made in mid-March to avoid the early crop of flies, and later sowings, in mid-June, again have a good chance of avoiding an attack. The variety 'Sytan' is partially resistant. Parsley, parsnips and celery are also affected.

Other methods of control are the placing of barriers 60–80 cm high around the rows, because the fly travels along near the ground and is easily diverted. Planting sage or onions among the carrots, or sowing scorzonera and carrot seed together, are also suggested; perhaps their smells confuse the flies. Alternatively a soil insecticide can be worked into the upper layer of the soil before sowing late crops.

'Early French Frame'   A quick-maturing variety for sowing in early spring in frames or greenhouses and pulling when very young. Also suitable in succession outdoors, from May onwards, and for heavy or shallow soils where normal long carrots will not produce a good root. 'Kundulus' is a similar variety.

'Giganta'   A selection of 'Autumn King', suitable for growing for show.

'Nandrin'

'Cluseed New Model'

'Redca'

'Berlicum Berjo'

'Supreme'

'Comet'

'Nevada'

'Campestra'

'Autumn King Vita Longa'

'Cardinal'

Winter carrots: specimens from NIAB, Cambridge, photographed 20 November

Carrot 'Cellobunch'　　　　　　　　　　　　　'Early Horn'

Carrot 'Caropak'

'Autumn King Vita Longa'　Long roots tapering from a rather wide top. For sowing in May and harvesting in December onwards as a maincrop.

'Berlicum Berjo'　Root 21 cm long 3.5 cm diameter; cylindrical. For sowing in May and harvesting in December or earlier.

'Campestra'　Raised by Campbells Soups Ltd. Foliage; large root 20 cm, 4.3 cm diameter, deep orange slightly tapering; core small, orange. Autumn King type, but slightly shorter. For sowing in May or early June and harvesting from September to December and later.

'Cardinal'　A Berlicum hybrid, with long cylindrical roots. For sowing in early to mid-May and harvesting in December and later.

'Cluseed New Model'　A Chantenay Red Cored variety. Maincrop. A short root, tapering from wide top, ready in October and November when sown in early May.

'Comet'　A Chantenay Red Cored variety, raised by Nickerson Zwaan.

'Early Horn' (syn. 'Early Scarlet Horn')　An early-maturing variety, suitable for sowing under glass in January for harvesting in May or June, or sooner when very young. Partially resistant to carrot root fly.

'J.N. Cellobunch'　An F1 hybrid with long, narrow roots c.20 cm. Inclined to bolt in Britain. Imperator-type.

'J.O. Caropak'　An Imperator-type with good resistance to bolting.

'Nandrin'　An early maincrop variety, suitable for sowing outdoors in April–May, for harvest in autumn.

'Nevada'　A late variety, suitable for sowing in January for harvest in November. Of good sweet flavour.

'Redca'　A coreless, Nantes-type carrot with good juice content. Suitable for pulling young at 15 cm long, after about 70 days in North America.

'Supreme'　A Chantenay Red Cored variety, with good quality roots, tapering sharply from a wide shoulder.

Specimens from NIAB, Cambridge, 20 July

Carrot 'Centennial'

'Blanche' An old Belgian, white-rooted variety.

'Centennial' An Imperator variety, inclined to bolt in Britain.

'Condor' First early when sown in October for harvest in May under polythene, or in January or February for harvest in June. An F1 hybrid.

'Jaune Obtuse' An old yellow-rooted variety, partially resistant to carrot root fly.

'Nairobi' Second early when sown in January, under polythene, for harvest in June. An F1 hybrid.

'Nandor' Second early when sown in January, under polythene, for harvest in June. An F1 hybrid Nantes type. Good for pulling young. With a very soft core. Partially resistant to carrot root fly.

'Napoli' First early carrot when sown in October under polythene, for harvest in May.

'Nelson' First early sown in October under polythene, for harvest in May.

'Parano' Raised by Nunhems Zaden BV, Haarlem, Holland. F1 hybrid: c. 50 cm long – core orange.

'Presto' Second early when sown in January for harvest in June.

'Primo' Second early sown in January under polythene, for harvest in May. An F1 hybrid. Partially resistant to carrot root fly.

CARROTS

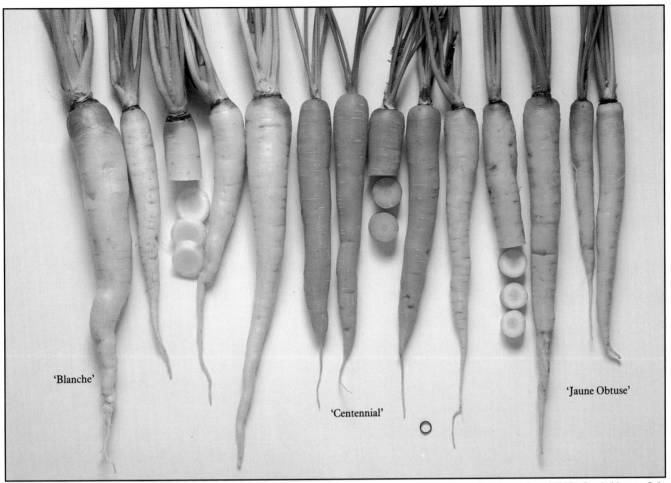

'Blanche'

'Centennial'

'Jaune Obtuse'

Specimens from NIAB, Cambridge, 20 July

White carrot 'Blanche'

Yellow carrot 'Jaune Obtuse'

123

Wild celery at Sandwich, Kent

Specimen from Wisley, photographed 1 November

Celery

Apium graveolens L. (*Umbelliferae*)

Apium graveolens is an important vegetable, and is now eaten in three distinct forms: celery, the commonest, consists of the swollen and succulent petioles or leaf stems, and is generally called var. *dulce*; celeriac is the swollen rootstock, and is called var. *rapaceum*. Leafy celery, formerly known as smallage or soup celery, was used as a herb for flavouring and is called var. *secalinum*. This last is similar to the celery grown in China, where the leaves and stems are all cooked together, in a green and unblanched state. This celery, which is very strong-tasting, together with steamed dough, was given me as my first lunch when working in the herbarium in Beijing.

Wild celery is native to Europe and Asia, growing in marshes and often in the mud on the edges of tidal rivers, usually near the sea or in slightly saline conditions. The plant is a biennial, with much-branched stems and short-stalked or sessile umbels of white flowers. Its smell is extremely pungent. Celery was probably first used as a flavouring and as a medicinal herb, before the milder forms with the thick stalks (petioles) and celeriac were selected. Stalk celery was probably first grown in Italy in the sixteenth century, and was considered a new vegetable by John Evelyn, writing in the 1690s. It is now grown in red, yellow, green and self-blanching forms, as well as the traditional form which needed earthing up to produce good white stalks.

Celeriac is even more recent, not becoming known in England until the 1720s when, as Jane Grigson records in her *Vegetable Book*, it was introduced from Alexandria by Stephen Switzer, and offered in his seed catalogue. Modern varieties tend to be larger and less knobbly than older ones, but all are white, and ideally crisp and solid throughout the bulb. Unlike carrots, the swollen part of the celeriac is not the root, but the lowest part of the stem, and it is therefore technically a corm. It is covered with the leaf-scars of the old leaves, and all the roots emerge from the base.

Cultivation of Celery

Celery needs a rich moist soil to grow well, and is especially successful in low-lying alkaline peaty areas such as the Fens in eastern England, and in Florida. It was also grown successfully on the thin layer of peat and marl-rich soil left after the bogs in central Ireland had had their peat stripped. To grow well it needs at least 2.5 cm of rain per week (equivalent to eighteen litres per square metre). If too dry the stalks are stringy and tough, not crisp and succulent.

Seedlings are best raised indoors, the seed planted at about 10–15°C. For the earliest crops February is recommended, but late March and early April are better for most purposes. It is important that the seedlings are not subjected to a temperature of less than 10°C for more than twelve hours, or they are likely to bolt before they are mature, and damage at planting out can also cause bolting. Soil should be rich, high in nitrogen and with a pH above 6.6. Liquid feeding is beneficial from about four weeks after planting, or a nitrogenous fertilizer (sodium nitrate is particularly recommended) applied as a top dressing.

Self-blanching celery is best grown in blocks instead of rows, as a certain amount of blanching improves the stalks. Plants may be spaced about 30 cm apart each way, but closer spacings produce a heavier crop of smaller hearts.

Varieties of celery which need blanching are usually grown in a trench 40 cm wide and 30 cm deep, and planted in a single row, the plants 20 cm apart. Alternatively, a wider trench can be dug, with the plants 20 cm apart in two rows, the plants placed alternately. Watering is again important, and earthing up should begin when the plants are about 30 cm tall and be continued every three weeks or so, adding about 8 cm of soil each time. Before earthing up begins the plants should have their outer leaves removed, and be reduced to a single head. Blanching may also be done on the level, by tying heavy brown paper, several layers of newspaper or black polythene around the stems, again blanching by degrees. Of the different types of celery, yellow is the least hardy, and pink the hardiest.

Celery being blanched with brown paper

Cultivation of Celeriac

It is difficult to grow celeriac to the large size bought in the greengrocer's. The secret of growing a large corm is to give the plant a long growing season and ample water so that it never becomes dry in the summer. A rich soil with plenty of organic matter is also needed.

Seed is generally sown indoors in early spring, as early as February, and hardened off before planting out in May, 30–40 cm apart each way if planted in blocks. Celeriac will tolerate light shade. The outer leaves should be removed in midsummer, and the plants may then be mulched with compost or old manure to assist good growth and retain moisture. Make sure there is only a single growing point per plant, and any lateral shoots should be removed as they appear. The plants are hardier than celery and will last well through the winter if stored in a cool place in sand, or protected with straw.

Chinese celery This is grown for its leaves and young stalks and the whole plant is eaten except for the roots. Seed may be sown in the open in late spring and summer, and the plants grown as fast as possible, given ample water and fertilizer. Leaves and stalks can be cut from the plants as needed, or the whole plant may be harvested, and coarsely chopped before cooking.

Pests and diseases

Celery fly, a leaf miner, can be a serious pest, attacking the leaves of young plants and slowing down their growth. The damaged leaves, with large yellow or brown areas, are easily seen. Any damaged leaves should be picked off and burnt as soon as they appear. If the attack is serious, the plants can be sprayed with a systemic insecticide. Other vegetables such as parsnips and the herb lovage can also be affected. Carrot root fly can also attack celery, causing general weakness of the plants. Methods of control are described under carrots.

A fungal disease, caused by a *Septoria* species, can also result in spotting of celery leaves. It is usually controlled by treating the seeds before sowing, and any affected plants should be burnt. Spraying with benomyl or a systemic fungicide can give some control.

Chinese white-stalked celery

Chinese leaf celery

'Ivory Tower'

'Giant Pink'

'American Green'

Specimens from NIAB, Cambridge, photographed 1 November

Celeriac

Celery 'Golden Self-blanching' at Villandry

Celery

'American Green' (Tall Utah 52–70) syn. Greensnap.   A green-stemmed variety which does not need blanching. 'Tall Utah' is a selection of the 'American Green' type.

'Giant Pink'   A pink- or red-stemmed variety with dark green leaves. The stems are paler if blanched, and deeper coloured in cold weather.

'Golden Self-blanching'   This variety has very pale, golden-yellow leaves and golden stems. It is best eaten young, in late summer, and is not frost hardy.

'Ivory Tower'   A quick-maturing, self-blanching, pale-leaved variety with narrow petioles. Needs to be well grown as the petioles become pithy and stringy if left dry.

Celeriac

'Iram'   Medium-sized, globe-shaped roots with few side shoots.

'Marble Ball'   White, round roots: there seems little between these two varieties. Illustrated on p. 124.

'Tellus'   Leaf stems brownish-red. Medium-sized, globe-shaped roots. Quick-growing.

'Tellus'

'Iram'

Specimens from Wisley, photographed 27 September

Marshall's 'Moss Curled'

'Paramount Imperial Curled'

'Green Velvet'

'Plain-leaved'

'Clivi'

'Hamburg'

Specimens from Sellindge, Kent. Photographed 15 October

Parsley going to seed in summer

Parsley

Petroselinum crispum (Miller) A. W. Hill (*Umbelliferae*)

Three forms of parsley are eaten: crisped-leaf parsley, flat-leaved parsley and Hamburg parsley (var. *tuberosum*), in which the swollen root is used as well as the flat leaves. All three are biennials, easily grown in any good soil, and very hardy. The leaves are rich in vitamin C, and are used as flavouring or as an ingredient in salads. The roots of Hamburg parsley are eaten cooked, and are a traditional ingredient of Polish or Russian bortsch. Jane Grigson also found them in a recipe for hare soup from Bulgaria and a Croatian soup of pig's trotters, and gives an amazing recipe for Hamburg beef and eel soup which uses them.

Parsley is not known as a wild plant, though it is thought to have originated in southern Europe. It is now commonly found having escaped from cultivation, so its natural range as a wild plant is obscured. A second species, *Petroselinum segetum* (L.) Koch, is a native of western Europe east to central Italy, and is found in hedges and grassy roadsides. It smells like parsley, but has white flowers and simple pinnate leaves. Parsley was known as a herb by the Greeks, and two varieties are mentioned by Theophrastus, writing in about 320 BC. It was cultivated in southern Europe from then onwards, and reached England, apparently from Sardinia, in 1548. Hamburg parsely is a more recent introduction, the seeds being brought from Holland by Philip Miller about 1727.

Beware of eating wild parsley found in roadside ditches or damp woods. It is likely to be the very poisonous hemlock water dropwort, *Oenanthe crocata* L., which has young leaves similar to a bright green flat-leaved parsley.

Cultivation

Sow seed of parsley in spring for use in summer, or in July and August for plants which will survive the winter and do well the following spring. They will tend to go to flower in midsummer. The seed can be slow and erratic in its germination, and it is helpful to soak it overnight before sowing. The seed also loses its viability after a year or so, and needs to be fresh for satisfactory growth. The plants can be raised in boxes before being planted out, or can be sown in a row in the open garden and thinned out to about 15 cm apart.

Flat-leaved parsley is even easier to grow than the curly-leaf varieties, and has a slightly stronger flavour. In Turkey it is commonly used in place of basil to flavour a tomato salad and is considered to be an aphrodisiac.

Of all the crisped varieties, 'Krausa' is said to have an exceptional flavour.

Hamburg parsley needs a growing season of at least three months and a deep well-tilled soil like that recommended for carrots. It is available both with short, wedge-shaped roots as shown here, and with a long tapering root about 15 cm long, like a white carrot. The plants can either be planted close and harvested young and small, or spaced 15 cm apart and allowed to grow until the winter. Boiled and eaten as a vegetable, this parsley has a slightly sweet flavour, nutty and between a delicate parsnip and a carrot.

Carrot fly can infect parsley, causing poor growth, and slugs may attack the roots, especially those of Hamburg parsley, eating away the soft outer layer and making the skin brown rather than white.

'Clivi' A dwarf variety with basal leaves which stay green, and do not go yellow when they get old.
'Green Velvet' A close relative of 'Moss Curled', said to have piquant flavour.
'Hamburg' A very ancient variety, with edible roots tapering from a wide top, like small parsnips. Late Hamburg parsley, illustrated by Vilmorin, had roots like very long carrots. 'Berliner' is similar. The leaves are also edible, similar to those of plain-leaved parsley.
'Moss Curled' A very vigorous variety, probably the best for overwintering.
'Paramount Imperial Curled' A dark green variety, with tightly curled leaves, from Sutton's Seeds.
'Plain-leaved' or 'Flat-leaved', Sheep's or common parsley This is the variety used in south-eastern Europe and in Asia. It has a stronger flavour than the curled varieties, and is commonly used in Italian cooking. Beware of confusing this with Hemlock Water Dropwort, as mentioned above.

Flat-leaved and curled parsley in the field

Parsley 'Green Velvet'

Thomas Jefferson's vegetable garden at Montecello, Virginia

Florentine or Florence Fennel

Foeniculum vulgare Miller var. *azoricum* (Miller) Thell.
(*Umbelliferae*)

Fennel is grown for its seeds, its leaves and for its swollen edible
bulb, known as Florence fennel. It is usually a biennial, forming a
bulb or thick root the first year, and flowering the following
summer. The leaves are fine and soft, the flowers yellow.

Fennel is divided into two subspecies, but they are not always
really distinct. Subspecies *vulgare* is the sweet-tasting fennel; both
seeds and leaves are used for flavouring, especially for fish dishes
which are enhanced by the mild flavour of aniseed. The thick
roots of young plants were also cooked and eaten. Var. *azoricum*,
thought by Philip Miller to originate in the Azores, is the one
which forms swollen bulbs, the edible part being the leaf bases.

Subspecies *piperitum* (Ucria) Coutinho, sometimes called
carosella, has stiffer, narrower leaf lobes and sharp-tasting seeds,
which are used to flavour herb liqueurs. It is a perennial, native to
the Mediterranean, and grows in rocky places. The purple or
bronze-leaved variety, grown as an ornamental in gardens,
probably belongs to this subspecies. It is a very deep-rooted
perennial, hardy in all but the coldest winters. Green-leaved
fennel is commonly naturalized in southern England, usually in
sandy or chalky soils near the sea, and is found on sea cliffs where
it may possibly be native. The leaves of both these varieties may
be used for flavouring.

Florentine fennel was introduced to England from Italy, where
it is much eaten both cooked and raw as an accompaniment to
cheese. It was used by the Romans and the swollen bulb variety
was probably developed in Italy. The first records of its being

grown in England are from the early eighteenth century, and in
1824 Thomas Jefferson received seeds for his garden at
Montecello from the American consul at Leghorn (Livorno), with
an enthusiastic account of the delights of Italian fennel, 'like the
largest celery'.

Cultivation

Fennel needs well-drained, light soil, but ample water and a cool
growing season to form good bulbs. It is likely to go to seed in the
long days of midsummer, before it has formed its bulb. Bulbs
grown in gardens in England seem to be more elongated and never
as round as those imported from Europe, though they are usually
tenderer and more delicious.

Seed can be sown in spring, from April onwards for a crop in
late summer, and in July and early August for a winter crop. The
varieties 'Zefa Fino' and 'Perfection', a French variety, are best
for early sowings. Both these and the commoner variety 'Sweet
Florence' are suitable for late sowings as they are then less likely to
go to seed prematurely. The plants should be kept well watered
and grown as fast as possible. Plants from seed sown directly in
the garden can be thinned to 30 cm apart, or young plants can be
raised in pots and planted out, with as little root disturbance as
possible. Fennel does not seem to be attacked by any serious pests
or diseases.

Dill, *Anethum graveolens* L., is similar in general appearance,
with thin narrow leaf-segments and yellow flowers. It is an annual,
native to China, India and western Asia, and commonly grown as
a herb for flavouring. Both seeds and leaves are used in the same
way as fennel.

FENNEL

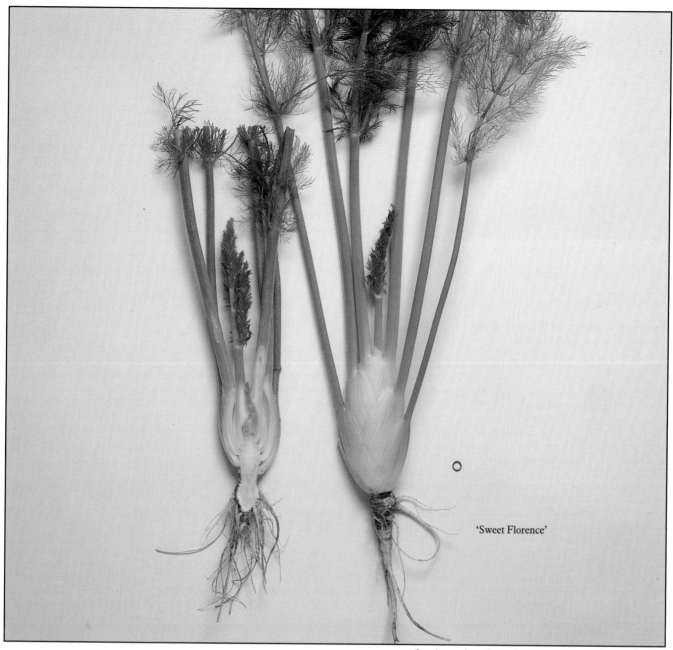

'Sweet Florence'

Specimens from Sellindge, Kent, photographed 20 August

Flowers of fennel

Fennel 'Perfection'

Good-sized bulbs of fennel

Young plants of sweet potato, with dried stalks of oil-seed rape

Cassava

Manihot esculenta Crantz (*Euphorbiaceae*)
Tapioca, Manioc, Yuca (Mexico), Aypu, Boniato (Caribbean)

Cassava is a very important crop in the tropics. The plant is not known wild, and originated in South America, probably by the hybridization of several wild species. The earliest archaeological records are from coastal Peru in around 1000 BC. It is now widely cultivated in areas where there is a warm wet growing season, followed by a dry period, and because of its easy culture is commonly planted by primitive farmers who practise shifting agriculture. Cuttings are stuck into the ground at the beginning of the growing season, and the elongated tuberous roots are harvested as soon as they are large enough, usually between eight months and a year. The roots may be up to 1.3 m long, and the primitive bitter cultivars contain poisonous cyanogenic glucosides as well as starch and protein. These tubers need thorough preparation to remove the poison – grating, washing and squeezing, followed by drying and cooking. The more advanced sweet cultivars contain little poison, and that mostly in the skin, and so are edible after simple cooking. They may be roasted, boiled or thinly sliced and fried like potato crisps.

Sweet Potato

Ipomoea batatas (L.) Poir. (*Convolvulaceae*)

Sweet potatoes are tropical tubers like elongated swedes, often with attractive red skin and yellow, sweetish, potato-like flesh. Sweet potatoes were widely grown in South America by pre-Inca civilizations, and were introduced to Spain before the true potato; indeed many early references to potato, such as those by Shakespeare, actually refer to the sweet potato. It also has a long history of cultivation in eastern Asia, being grown in Polynesia before 1250, and spreading from there to New Zealand in the fourteenth century; Captain Cook and Sir Joseph Banks found the Maoris of North Island growing it when they landed in 1769. It is supposed to have reached China in 1594.

Ipomoea batatas is related to morning glory and less closely to the bindweeds. It is thought to have been developed in cultivation from *Ipomoea trifida* (HBK) G. Don, which is native from Mexico south to Venezuela. The flowers are pinkish-purple or white. The stems are sprawling or climbing, and when on the ground will root and form tubers. The leaves are pointed and sometimes three- or five-lobed at the base. The young tips of the shoots are edible, as well as the tubers.

Propagation is either by pieces of sprouted tuber or by stem cuttings later in the year. Ample potash is essential for a good crop, and this together with its ease of cultivation has made it ideal for planting in areas where the forest is cut and burnt, and a quick-growing crop is needed. Some varieties mature in as little as two months in the tropics, though ninety days is a more usual time in North America, even for quick-maturing varieties. In order to store sweet potatoes through the winter they must be 'cured' by staying for about a week at 25°C; then they can be stored at around 14°C.

Sweet potatoes require subtropical heat for proper growth, and no varieties have yet been raised which will mature in England, though they are grown in southern Europe and there are several varieties suitable for the southeastern United States, and for the warmer parts of New Zealand. One variety shown here, 'Tokatoka Gold', has a large rounded smooth tuber, and is especially popular in New Zealand, where thin slices are used for making potato crisps.

Water Spinach

Ipomoea aquatica Forsk. (*Convolvulaceae*)
Kancon, Green Engtsai

Water spinach is an aquatic *Ipomoea* with edible young shoots and leaves, which can be eaten like spinach. It is probably a native of southern India, but is now found all over the tropics, its swollen floating stems running over the surface of the water. In many warm areas, for instance in Florida, it has become a serious weed.

It is easily raised from seed, but the seedlings need heat, above 25°C, to grow well. Young seedling plants are often grown on dry land, but then they have upright stems and narrow leaves and do not develop the swollen stem or the normal heart-shaped leaves of the aquatic form. Both forms may be propagated by cuttings. The flowers are purplish in wild forms, but white or pink in cultivated varieties. The poor little specimen shown on page 45 (bottom right), was sown outdoors in midsummer in England, but grew very poorly.

Japanese white-rooted sweet potato

'Tokatoka Gold' sweet potato

Sweet potato, white fleshed, red skin

SWEET POTATOES

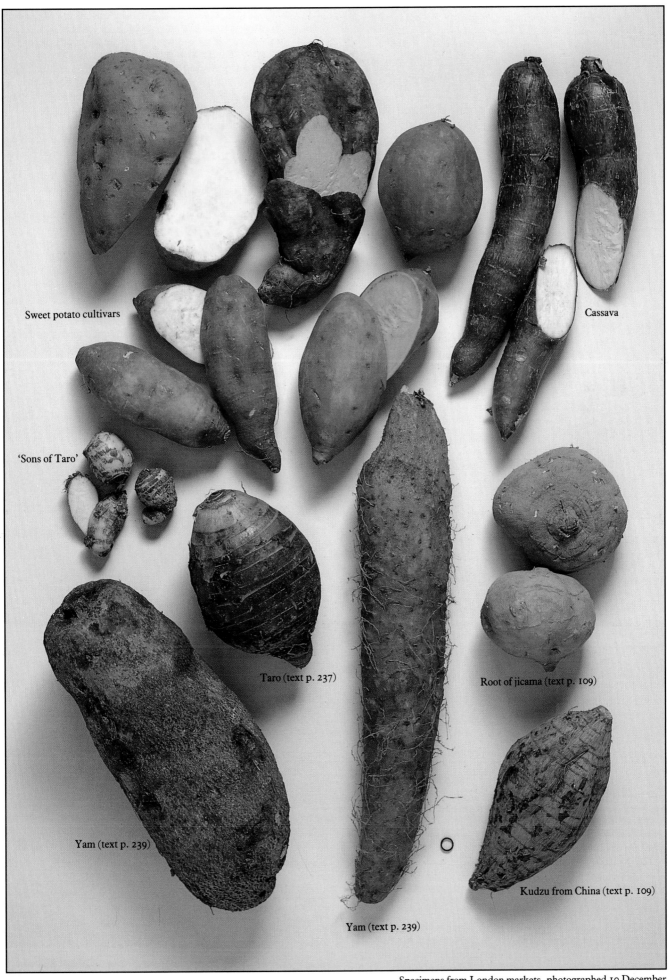

Sweet potato cultivars

'Sons of Taro'

Cassava

Taro (text p. 237)

Root of jicama (text p. 109)

Yam (text p. 239)

Yam (text p. 239)

Kudzu from China (text p. 109)

Specimens from London markets, photographed 10 December

133

Rock-ledge habitat of wild potato in Mexico

The Potato

Solanum tuberosum L. (*Solanaceae*)
Other names: Papas (Inca), Pomme de Terre, Kartoffel

The potato is without doubt the most important of all vegetables, and is at present the fourth most important food crop in the world, after wheat, maize and rice. It grows well in all temperate climates and in many parts of the tropics, especially in the mountains or when grown in the cool season. As well as vitamins and a small amount of protein, its edible tubers contain large quantities of starch, and this is the primary reason for its use as food. However, 500 g of cooked new potatoes produces the daily recommended amount of vitamin C, and significant amounts of vitamin B_1 and riboflavin. Because of the presence of the alkaloid solanin, both the tomato-like fruit and the leaves are poisonous, as are any parts of the tubers which have turned green after exposure to light.

Origin

The potato is a member of the *Solanaceae*, the same family as the tomato (*Lycopersicum esculentum*), the sweet and hot peppers (*Capsicum* species) and many other vegetables, as well as tobacco (*Nicotiana tabacum*), deadly nightshade (*Atropa belladonna*) and other very poisonous plants.

The genus *Solanum* itself contains, apart from the potato, the aubergine or eggplant (*Solanum melongena*), the huckleberry (*Solanum nigrum* var. *guineense*), the woody nightshade or bittersweet (*Solanum dulcamara*) and other poisonous species, many of which also contain the alkaloid solanin.

Tuber-bearing species of *Solanum* are found wild in the mountains of both North and South America from western Nebraska, Colorado and Utah, to Mexico, where they are frequent in the highest mountains at 2500 m and above, and lower down in

particularly cool shady places. Other species are found in central America, southwards to Chile and Argentinian Patagonia.

The taxonomy of the species which are related to the potato is very complex, and hundreds of species have been named by botanists who visited the Andes and Mexico to collect material for potato breeding in Europe and North America. J. G. Hawkes, in a lecture to the Royal Horicultural Society in 1966, recognized 170 species, and his most recent monograph recognizes 235 species, of which seven are cultivated and the rest wild.

The wild species are very diverse, both in morphology and habitat, much more so than the modern cultivated potato. For instance, *Solanum acaule* is a stemless species with a rosette of leaves at the ground, which is found in the Andes in Peru, Bolivia and northern Argentina at 3500–4600 m, and can withstand −8°C of frost. Another species, from pine and fir forest in the high mountains of Mexico, *Solanum demissum* Lindl., with tubers up to 6 cm long, is resistant both to frost and blight. We found it growing commonly on the forest floor in central Mexico, in the exact areas where the millions of monarch butterflies (*Danaus plexippus*) spend the winter. It is interesting that it was grown by John Lindley in the Horticultural Society's Garden in London in 1848 and is one of the few distinct species which have made any significant contribution to modern potato cultivars.

Another Mexican species *Solanum cardiophyllum* subsp. *ehrenbergii* is reported to be much sought after and to cost more in local markets than cultivated potatoes. A small potato with variably reddish, round knobbly tubers, which may be this species, was found in the market in Guadeljara in central Mexico in 1991, being sold under the name 'papitas' (little potatoes).

There is no single ancestor of the European potato which can be found in the wild state, but Professor Hawkes has suggested that the earliest wild potato to be cultivated was *Solanum leptophyes*, now found in rocky places in the mountains of northern Bolivia at 3200–3950 m. After this species was brought into cultivation it gave rise to the still diploid species *S. stenotomum*, which can still be found cultivated in Peru. Hybrids between *S. stenotomum* and another wild species *S. sparsipilum* (a diploid) became, by chromosome doubling, the fertile tetraploid *Solanum tuberosum* subsp. *andigena*, the ancestor of the common potato.

Other potato species in cultivation in the Andes have involved wild species. *Solanum acaule*, the wild tetraploid which grows at very high altitudes, has crossed with *S. stenotomum* to form *S. juzepczukii*, a sterile triploid which is highly frost resistant and grows at a higher altitude than any other food plant, at up to 4500 m in the Andes in central Peru. Crosses with another species, *S. megistacrolobum*, have led to other frost-hardy potatoes called Yari and Ajawiri in the areas of the high Andes where they are grown. *Solanum phureja*, on the other hand, has become adapted to more tropical climates and grows and produces tubers continually, without becoming dormant.

On the high altiplano of Peru and Bolivia around Lake Titicaca and Lake Poopo, cultivated potatoes are still extremely variable and this variability is encouraged by the local farmers who may grow fifteen or more cultivars in a single field.

Solanum demissum with *Alchemilla* in Mexico

Potatoes for sale in the market at La Paz, Bolivia, photographed by Sam Phillips

History

It is assumed that potatoes were among the crops domesticated by man when the High Andes were first colonized 7–10,000 years ago, and remains of potatoes have been found in deposits in Chilca canyon south of Lima, dating from around 4000 BC. Early definite evidence for the cultivation of potatoes is given by strikingly unusual pottery produced by the coastal Moche culture, found at burial sites in northern and central Peru, and dating from AD 1000; several of these pots were made in the form of potatoes, which were not grown in this hot and arid area but were probably imported from the high Andes. One particular large urn from the central Peruvian highlands has crude representations of anu (*Tropaeolum tuberosum*), oca (*Oxalis tuberosa*) and ulluco, (*Ullucus tuberosus*), three other important Peruvian root vegetables, as well as the potato.

The potato was widely cultivated in Inca times, c. AD 1400, and naturally freeze-dried potato, called chuno, which is still sold today, was even then an important commodity. The potatoes are sliced, or kept whole, and put out in the dry cold mountain air. The success of the potato and the other root crops was due to their ability to grow in the icy, windswept highlands which were too cold for maize, the staple crop in warmer areas.

The first reports of potatoes by Europeans date from 1537, when Cieza de Leon, as a young man, joined an expedition from

Chuno in La Paz, Bolivia, photographed by Sam Phillips

Cartagena to Cali in what is now Columbia. His travels were published in 1553, and he described the food of the native people of the Titicaca region as consisting of both potatoes and the dried form chuno. Another description by Juan de Castellonos in his *Elegias*, though written in the 1560s, was not published until 1886. He gave a good description of the potato, likening its root to a truffle, about the size of an egg, round or elongated, and white, purple or yellow in colour, 'floury roots of good flavour, a delicacy to the Indians and a dainty dish even for the Spaniards'.

The first record of potatoes in Europe is usually said to be that found in the accounts of the La Sangre hospital in Seville for 1573, when they were bought as part of the normal supply of vegetables in the autumn (but it is possible that the potatoes referred to here are sweet potatoes). This suggests that they were grown in Spain, but they were not common there much before this date as Clusius makes no mention of them in his account of his Spanish expedition in 1564. From Spain the potatoes went to Italy, and it was from here that, in 1588, Clusius received his first two tubers and a fruit, from Philip de Sivry, the prefect of Mons, who received it from a friend of the Papal Legate in Belgium. Because it was so easy to grow, its cultivation spread quickly round Europe, and in 1601 Clusius recorded that it was commonly cultivated in gardens in Germany and in parts of Italy.

Clusius also recorded that he received a drawing of potatoes from James Garret, who lived in England, some time between 1589 and 1593. This was earlier than Gerard's first published account of the potato in England, in one of his garden Catalogues in 1596. He also published an illustration in his *Herball* in 1597 showing a hairless plant with numerous small, round, irregularly knobbly tubers with few eyes, which is similar to the form shown in Clusius' woodcut, used by Gerard in later editions.

A very different form is shown in Jean Bauhin's illustration in *Historia Plantarum Universalis* published in 1651. This shows an elongated tuber with numerous deep-set eyes and very hairy stems, similar to varieties still grown in the Andes. Gerard reported that he received his tubers from Virginia, but this is now considered to be a mistake, as is the legend that the potato was introduced to England by Sir Francis Drake. Clusius visited Drake in England in 1581, but did not see the potato then; Drake brought Raleigh's colonists back from Virginia in 1586, and might have acquired potatoes on this voyage, though Gerard's own statement suggests that he received his first potatoes after 1588.

According to early descriptions the first potatoes grown in Europe were very tall, with stems 1.5–2 m long, and produced their tubers late in the autumn. This is consistent with their presumed origin in the Andes of Columbia, where they flower and produce tubers only after the autumn equinox when days become short. These illustrations and a specimen preserved by Bauhin himself in the herbarium at Basel have been identified by Hawkes as his subsp. *andigena*. Potatoes were already very variable when grown from seed, which shows they were of complex hybrid origin. There is however a suggestion that the English potatoes, which were mainly white or brown skinned, were from a separate introduction to those which reached Spain.

When the Russian botanists Juzepczuk and Bukasov visited South America in the 1920s looking for primitive potatoes, they were excited to find some varieties very similar to European potatoes growing in southern Chile, especially on the Island of Chiloe; these were also adapted to the long summer days and cool temperatures of high latitudes outside the tropics. These Chilean potatoes were recorded by early sailors such as Sir Francis Drake in 1578 who, on his voyage round the world, obtained potatoes from Indians on the island of Mocha off the coast of Chile, but there is no evidence that any were brought back to Europe.

Juzepczuk and Bukasov concluded that these Chilean varieties were the true ancestors of the European potato, but there is unfortunately no evidence that these southern potatoes were ever introduced to Europe, and any similarities are now considered to be caused by selection for the same characters. It is likely that the Chilean potatoes also originated in the High Andes of Peru, and were brought south either by the migration of people, or through trade at least a thousand years before the sixteenth century.

The European potatoes were selected and bred from those forms which happened to arrive in Europe at an early date, not from forms which were selected for being either generally superior or likely to do well in northern Europe. It was because these early varieties were not well suited to cultivation in northern Europe that the potato was slow to become an important crop. The tropical forms tended to flower and make tubers only after the autumn equinox, so they grew best in southern Europe and in western Ireland, in areas where they would not have their top growth killed by frost in early autumn. Growers from Clusius onwards grew plants from seed as well as tubers, and so selected, whether intentionally or not, varieties which produced tubers earlier in the summer.

Martyn, in the eighth edition of Miller's *Gardener's Dictionary* in 1768, describes how growers around Manchester repeatedly raised new varieties from seed, and competed with one another to get saleable tubers early in the season.

In other parts of the world potatoes were also cultivated early, and many have retained their tropical characteristics longer than in Europe. In India there are records of cultivation in 1615, probably brought there by the Portuguese, and they were observed in Formosa in 1650. Old varieties have also been found in modern times in the Canaries, whence they probably arrived direct from Peru, and in the highlands of Lesotho.

It was only during the eighteenth century that the potato became an important item of diet in the British Isles. An early attempt to promote potato growing was the treatise, written in 1664 by John Forster of Hanslop, Buckinghamshire, *Englands happiness increased, or a sure and easy remedy against all succeeding dear years; by a plantation of the roots called potatoes*, but potatoes did not become popular as the staple diet of the poor in either country until around 1800. In Scotland, the poorest crofters who had been cleared from their land in the glens, and settled around the coast, often lived in yearly danger of famine, and soon came to rely on the potato as an easy source of food.

In 1845 it was reported in *The Times* that in England the two main meals of a working man's day consisted of potatoes, not of the traditional bread and cheese, and there was alarm in some circles at such dependence on one food plant.

The early history of the potato, and many more fascinating details can be found in *The History and Social Significance of the Potato* by R. N. Salaman, who was director of the Potato Virus Research Station in Cambridge; it has recently (1985) been reissued with a critical introduction by Professor J. G. Hawkes of Birmingham University.

Abandoned lazy beds near Killary harbour in Connemara

The Irish potato famine

There is a legend, which may be true, that the first potatoes in Ireland were brought to his estates in Youghal in Co. Cork by Sir Walter Raleigh in around 1590. By the early eighteenth century the potato had become such an important crop that a partial failure in 1727 caused an uprising in Cork during the following February when supplies became scarce. The population of Ireland grew slowly, from the 500,000 or so left after Cromwell's campaigns of 1649 to 1651, until the late eighteenth century when there was a startling increase. From about 1779 to 1841 it rose by 142 per cent, and reached 8,200,000 (and even that was thought by some to be an underestimate); Ireland, according to Disraeli, had become the most densely populated country in Europe.

The population increase in Ireland occurred mainly in the rural areas and rose fastest among the poorest sections of society. This was made possible by a diet of ample potatoes and milk, which even the poorest could afford. The mild climate and abundant summer rain produced large crops. The potato thrives in peaty acid soils, and was grown by the Irish system of 'lazy beds', in which the seed potatoes were laid on four-foot-wide ridges which had been manured with dung or seaweed, and first covered, then earthed up from the trenches; they were in effect planted on raised beds with ditches in between, which both protected the plants from excess rain and allowed ground frosts to drain away harmlessly between the rows.

This method of cultivation is remarkably similar to that shown in early illustrations of potato growing in the Andes, and in both areas a narrow spade was used, like the loy still employed for cutting peat today. The remains of lazy beds can be seen on the hillsides of Connemara, and some years ago we found a similar wide-bed system of cultivation still used in a remote part of Co. Mayo.

In the early nineteenth century, the poorest families rented perhaps half an acre of land for a season to grow potatoes, and this usually enabled them to pay the very high rents and to have ample food left for themselves. The diet of boiled potatoes, with milk from a cow grazed on the mountain, proved adequate for a simple but healthy life. There was also, in most areas, an abundant supply of free fuel to be cut from the bog, both for cooking, for heating and for brewing whiskey and poteen or potato spirit. A partial failure of the year's crop, however, could mean destitution for the family, as there was great demand for land, and no security for the tenant. Periodic partial failure of the potato was a regular feature and famines in some districts often required the government's attention. A particularly disastrous failure occurred in 1739, caused by severe frost in early November and a long cold winter. It was estimated that 300,000 people, or a third of the population, perished. It is worth recalling that the potatoes grown at this time produced their tubers very late in the autumn, and therefore the mild climate in the far west of Ireland was most suitable for their growth.

Real disaster came over a century later. In 1845 the prospects for a large harvest were excellent until the end of July, and the first sign of an unusual disease was reported from the Isle of Wight at the beginning of August. A few days later the disease was noticed in east Kent, and by the end of the same week it had spread to the outskirts of London. It was also widespread in France and Holland, and Dr Lindley reported in the *Gardener's Chronicle* that the fields in Belgium were completely desolated, and there was widespread damage as far east as Poland.

There was no doubt in Dr Lindley's mind what scale of disaster this disease would cause should it reach Ireland, and the appearance of the 'murrain' was reported around Dublin on 13 September. In October most of the potatoes had still not been harvested (in 1845 the early varieties mostly escaped the blight), and there were conflicting reports on how extensive the outbreaks of disease had become. Even after the first areas had been harvested the crop appeared to be a fair one, but not for long, as 'potatoes bought a few days ago, seemingly remarkably good', soon rotted. The blight had spread to all parts of Ireland. Numerous methods for preserving diseased tubers were proposed, including treating them with chlorine gas which was to be made in the Irish cottages by mixing vitriol (hydrochloric acid), manganese dioxide and salt, but all were useless.

The cause of the blight was unknown. Dr Lindley, who was an expert on orchid growing, editor of *Gardener's Chronicle*, assistant secretary of the Horticultural Society, and one of the most eminent scientists of the time, was of the opinion that the excessively wet weather that autumn had caused the plants and tubers to absorb so much water that they rotted with 'wet purification'. The government in London sent Dr Lindley and Dr Playfair on an official mission to Ireland, and they reported that in the areas they had visited around Dublin 'we can come to no other conclusion that one half of the actual potato crop of Ireland is either destroyed and . . . we fear this to be a low estimate'. The partial destruction of the crop in 1845 was bad enough, but was followed by almost total loss in 1846, as areas which had previously escaped the blight were infected; that year disease struck earlier and in the cold wet weather at the beginning of August blackened every potato field in Ireland.

The true cause of the disease was soon discovered by the Revd M. J. Berkeley, a country parson in Northamptonshire. He was already a well-known mycologist, and an expert on molluscs and seaweeds which he had studied while a curate in Margate. Berkeley, and a correspondent in France, a Dr Montagne, who had been a surgeon in Napoleon's army, both found the hyphae and spores of the blight on the underside of infected potato leaves, and exchanged drawings. Berkeley's paper describing the fungus, *Observations, Botanical and Physiological, on the Potato Murrain*, was published in the *Journal of the Horticultural Society* in January 1846, but was not accepted by the horticultural establishment, and a fierce controversy followed between those who, like Berkeley, believed that the fungus was the cause of the decay, and those, like Dr Lindley, who believed that the fungus followed the death of the leaf tissues from a form of 'dropsy'.

It appears that the disease had been recorded first in North America in 1843, when much of the crop on the east coast from Nova Scotia to New England was destroyed, though there was an isolated outbreak in Germany near Hanover in 1830. The details of the life history of the blight fungus, *Phytophthora infestans*, were not worked out until the early twentieth century. It is now known that the spread of the disease by spores can be remarkably rapid under suitably warm and humid conditions, and humid easterly winds no doubt enabled the original outbreak to spread from northern France via Kent, to England and Ireland.

The famine that followed the outbreaks of blight in 1845 and 1846 was the worst that Ireland had ever experienced. By June 1847 over 3,000,000 people were receiving emergency rations from government-sponsored soup kitchens, mainly in the form of cooked maize meal, imported from America. Even so, it is estimated that between 1846 and 1851 over 1,500,000 died, and nearly 1,000,000 emigrated, the majority to England, but many of those who could still afford the fare, to America. The population of Connaught declined by 28.6%, and other areas of Ireland suffered similar though lesser reductions of population.

Though it is less well known, there was a similar decline in the population of the Highlands of Scotland during the same period, caused both by the destruction of the potato crop, and by the continuing activities of landlords clearing crofters from the glens to increase the population of sheep.

Development of modern cultivars

The early growers of the potato mention varieties with both purple and white flowers, and early illustrations show a variety of tuber shapes. Seed was widely used for propagation, as a way to reduce the deleterious effect of a virus, called the curl, which affected most varieties within a few years of their introduction. Gardeners working from the original potato stocks managed to produce

Effect of blight on potato leaves

Potato beds on the Connemara coast

Potato fields in Idaho

varieties which matured in July rather than October and November, and noted both these earlies, and a large black variety which was an exceptionally good keeper.

Named cultivars are not much mentioned before about 1770. Some of the most popular ones were 'The Irish Apple', a floury variety which matured late and was a good keeper; 'The White Kidney', another Irish variety and one of the earliest, ready in the west by early July; 'Ox Noble', a heavy cropper, much used for cattle feed; 'The Lumper', a very heavy cropper, much grown in Ireland before the famine, but extremely susceptible to blight; 'The Ashleaf', probably raised in around 1804, another early, much grown throughout the nineteenth century.

All these varieties originated from stocks long grown in Europe, and proved terribly susceptible to blight. One of the first breeders to try to introduce new characters from South America was the Revd Chauncey E. Goodrich of New York who, in 1851, received a small collection of tubers from the US consul in Panama who had bought them in a local market. 'Rough Purple Chile' was one of the varieties he obtained and from it was raised 'Early Rose', the seed parent of modern varieties such as 'Golden Wonder'.

Another breeder working at this time was William Paterson of Dundee. He began by gathering together, from as far away as the Cape, stocks that were not affected with virus, and so set seed freely. By large-scale seed sowing and selection he raised several distinct varieties, including, in 1863, 'Victoria', an important variety and one of the parents of 'Up-to-Date' which is still grown. Two famous varieties were raised in the late nineteenth century by James Clarke of Christchurch, Hampshire; these are 'Magnum Bonum' and 'Epicure', both of which were introduced by Messrs Suttons, and are the parents of modern varieties.

Cultivation

Potatoes are the most easily grown of all vegetables, provided they receive enough water during the growing season and are protected from frost. Nowadays the varieties are divided into three groups according to the time which they take to develop: first early, which is ready after about 100 days, and second early, ready after 110–120 days; both these are eaten small as new potatoes. Main crop are ready after about 130 days, but are generally left in the ground until autumn and used after storage. 'Seed' tubers are generally sold in early spring, and should be laid out in a light frost-free place to sprout. They may remain like this for several weeks, until the soil and weather are suitable for planting. It is important to buy healthy seed potatoes, from a reliable source, and to try to find ones which do not already have etiolated sprouts.

The ideal soil for potatoes is sandy, with a high humus content or ample moisture during the growing season, but they are tolerant of chalky soils as well. Potatoes also need ample nitrogen, so it is beneficial to manure the ground the previous autumn with either farmyard manure or garden compost, both of which also help retain moisture. It is also beneficial to apply a compound balanced fertilizer to the soil at planting time at about 170 g per

'Magnum Bonum'

Flowers of *Solanum demissum* from Mexico

square metre. Old books recommend the use of lime, soot, wood ash and especially leafmould.

The tubers are normally planted between late March and early May, about a month before the last frost. If they emerge before all danger of frost is gone they should be protected in some way, either by covering with a cloche or by earthing up. Polypropylene fleece is a modern material suitable for frost protection in spring. On ordinary soils the tubers are usually planted into a drill about 10 cm deep, and each about 40 cm apart. The emerging shoots can be earthed up one to three times during the growing season, both to encourage the formation of more tubers from the lower leaf axils, and to prevent any tubers from becoming green on exposure to light. An alternative method is to use black polythene instead of earthing up, and this is especially valuable when planting potatoes on very weedy land. The potatoes are planted as described above, but the whole row is covered with a sheet of black polythene after planting. When the emerging shoots begin to push up the polythene, they are eased up through a slit. All weed growth is thereby suppressed. The polythene is rolled back as the potatoes are harvested.

Potatoes also require ample supplies of water while in full growth. Extra watering when the tubers are about 1 cm across will improve the size of early potatoes. For main-crop potatoes, watering is required at about ten-day intervals throughout the growing season, unless there has been substantial rain.

Common diseases and pests

Although modern varieties are not so susceptible as those which were grown at the time of the Great Famine, potato blight (*Phytophora infestans*) is still a common disease, and one which restricts the growth of main-crop potatoes. Early potatoes are seldom seriously affected. 'Estima', 'Spunta' and 'Maris Peer' are among the most resistant varieties. Spraying with Bordeaux mixture as soon as the presence of blight is suspected will often prevent a serious outbreak. If the plants are badly affected, the stalks should be cut off just above ground level, so that the rain does not wash the spores into the soil, where they can affect the tubers. Outbreaks of blight usually occur in warm humid weather, and the first sign of the disease is dark brown patches on some of the leaves; a fine white fringe of fungus is just visible around the infected area.

Scab is another common disease, in which areas of the surface of the potato become brown and cracked. It is prevented by watering and by incorporating plenty of humus into the soil before planting. Viruses commonly affect potatoes, but are not serious if you do not intend to save your own 'seed' tubers for replanting. Viruses are spread by aphids, and for this reason most seed potatoes are grown in cool windy areas where aphids are uncommon.

The commonest pest of the potato is the slug, especially the small dark species with a yellow belly, which spends much of its life underground. It can be controlled with aluminium sulphate sprinkled on to the soil around the plants.

The Colorado beetle, with narrow purple and cream stripes along its body, used to be familiar to people in England because of the government's poster campaign to prevent it becoming established in the British Isles. It got its name from the State where it was first recognized in 1824, as a harmless parasite on various species of wild *Solanum*. It was not until European farmers reached Colorado following the Gold Rush in 1858, and brought the potato with them, that the beetle found a new host much to its liking. It then spread quickly eastwards, crossing the Mississippi in 1865 and reaching the Atlantic seaboard in 1873, where it caused devastation in many states. The first European record was at Tilbury in 1901, but it did not gain a permanent foothold in Europe until the 1914–1918 war, when it became established near an American army camp outside Bordeaux, becoming a serious pest by 1922. There were other lesser outbreaks in southwest England in 1942, but it has still not become established. It can be controlled on a small scale by picking off the adult beetles and the larvae, or by spraying with an insecticide such as would control Japanese beetle.

Planting potatoes at Sellindge

'Magnum Bonum' (Early Rose × Paterson's Victoria); raised by James Clarke of Christchurch, Hants, who left no record of its origin; it was introduced by Suttons in 1876. This had some partial resistance to blight and is important as the parent of varieties such as 'King Edward'. It is often assumed to have been a seedling of a self-set fruit of 'Early Rose'.

Solanum demissum Lindl. A dwarf wild potato found in central Mexico at around 3000 m. It grows on the floor of the *Abies religiosa* forest with *Alchemilla procumbens*, and various shrubby *Cestrum*, *Senecio* and *Eupatorium* species which provide nectar for the Monarch butterflies through the winter. Though this area is very cold in winter, the temperature rarely drops much below freezing for more than a few days each year. *Solanum demissum* has been used in modern breeding programmes and is found in the ancestry of many modern varieties of potato.

Potatoes planted under black polythene mulch

'Epicure'

'Duke of York'

'Up-to-Date'

'Dr MacIntosh'

'Sherine'

'Nadine'

'Mona Lisa'

Specimens from Peter Maine, photographed 15 October

'**Dr MacIntosh**' (Herald × *Solanum phureja* hybrid) and contains genes of *S. demissum*. Raised by T. P. McIntosh in Scotland in 1944. Grows best in a wet season. Flesh waxy. Maincrop.

'**Duke of York**' (Early Primrose × King Kidney)   Raised by W. Sim at Fyvie, Aberdeenshire, in 1891. First early; plant spreading, with plain green stems; leaves with some secondary leaflets; Introduced by Messrs Daniels in 1891). Very prolific and a good forcer. Recommended for all soils, especially heavy.

'**Epicure**' (Magnum Bonum × Early Regent) Raised by James Clarke of Christchurch, Hants, and introduced by Suttons in 1897. First early, flowers white, few, stems purplish. Leaves with narrow primary leaflets and prominent secondary leaflets. Tubers round, with deep-set eyes. In its time an exceptionally hardy and prolific first early, of excellent flavour. Useful for digging early, a heavy cropper.

'**Golden Wonder**' A russet sport of 'Maincrop'   Introduced by James Clarke of Christchurch, Hants, but raised by J. Brown from a berry of 'Early Rose' in 1904. A tall, erect plant with rugose leaves, and white flowers. Formerly very highly regarded as a table variety.

'**Mona Lisa**' (Bierma A1–287 × Colma) Raised in Netherlands in 1982. Early main crop.

'**Nadine**' (from a *Solanum vernaije* polycross) A new variety raised in Scotland. A second early, with round tubers and waxy flesh.

'**Russet Burbank**' (syn. 'Netted Gem' (said to be a seedling of 'Early Rose'))   Medium-sized, used especially for baking. Main crop, maturing late. Tubers long, flesh white. Popular in North America.

'**Sefton Wonder**'   An old variety, dating from before 1926.

'**Sherine**' (from a *Solanum vernayji* polycross) A new variety; a second early.

'**Up-to-Date**' (Old Blue Don seedling × Paterson's Victoria)   Introduced by Archibald Findlay in 1891. Main crop, flowers pale purple with a white tip. This was known as a very fine table variety, waxy when cooked.

'Sefton Wonder'

'Golden Wonder'

'Russet Burbank'

Specimens from Peter Maine, photographed 15 October

Potato fields in Maine

Detail of flower

'Stroma'

'Diana'

'Vanessa'

'Salad Red'

'Cavalier Red'

'Kerr's Pink'

'Antar'

'Fanfare'

Specimens from Peter Maine, photographed 15 October

POTATOES

'Mein's Early'   'Penta'

'Pentland Beauty'   'Pink Duke of York'   'Ulster Ensign'

Specimens from Peter Maine, photographed 15 October

'Antar' An old variety, from Peter Maine.

'Cavalier Red' An old variety, from Peter Maine.

'Diana' (Desirée mutant × ZPC61–98) Raised by De ZPC in the Netherlands in 1962.

'Fanfare' Raised by De ZPC in the Netherlands.

'Home Guard' (Doon Pearl × Cumnock) Raised by McGill and Smith Ltd in 1943. First early; flowers few, white. Leaves with many secondary leaflets. An open leaf with kinked margins to the leaflets. Tubers oval, white, somewhat floury when cooked. Not good in dry conditions.

'Kerr's Pink' (Fortyfold × Smith's Early) Raised by Mr J. Henry of Ottawa, late of Brae, Cornhill, Banffshire, in 1907. Originally known as 'Henry's Seedling' and locally known as 'Brae Seedling'. It came into the possession of Mr Kerr, seedsman of Banff, who introduced it in 1917 under its present name. Main crop; flowers white, freely produced; leaves greyish, with rather large secondary leaflets and a coloured midrib. Tubers rounded with pink skin and creamy flesh. Floury when cooked, a popular variety in Scotland.

'Mein's Early' Raised by Laing & Mather An old variety, from before 1920. 'Mein's Early Round' may not be the same as 'Meins Early'.

'Penta' (Bellona × Estima) Raised by J. P. Dijkhuis in the Netherlands in 1983.

'Pentland Beauty' Raised by the Scottish Plant Breeding Station in 1955.

'Pink Duke of York' An old variety from Peter Maine.

'Red Gold' An old variety from Peter Maine.

'Salad Red' An old variety from Peter Maine.

'Stroma' (V32 × Desirée) Second early. A modern variety.

'Ulster Ensign' Raised by John Clarke of Broughgammon in Northern Ireland.

'Vanessa' (Bierma B 584 × Desirée) Raised by De ZPC in the Netherlands in 1973. First early; flowers few, light purple with a white tip; leaves with rounded leaflets, and numerous secondary leaflets. Light yellow flesh, waxy when cooked.

'Home Guard' (just dug)

Potato 'Red Gold'

143

'German Black'

'Edgecote Purple'

'Salad Blue'

'Mauve Queen'

'Blue Kerr's Pink'

'Morven'

Specimens from Peter Maine, photographed 15 October

Specimens from Peter Maine, photographed 15 October

'All Blue' An American variety. Blue skin, blue flesh, good flavour baked or boiled. Available from Seeds Blum.

'Angus Beauty' An old variety from Peter Maine.

'Blue Kerr's Pink' A blue-skinned form of 'Kerr's Pink'.

'Caribe' Raised by a Mr Finlay. An old heritage variety, grown in New England in the nineteenth century for export to the Caribbean. Flesh creamy-white, floury; skins purple. Early maturing and producing large tubers for keeping. It is a good cropper, and especially recommended as an exhibition potato on account of its nice shape and appearance.

'Catriona' (syn. 'Torquil') (parentage unknown) Raised by A. Findlay at Auchtermuchty, Scotland, in 1920. Introduced 1920.

'Di Vernon' The low spreading habit distinguishes it from 'Kate Glover', the tubers of which are mottled with more red than purple. From 'Catriona' it is distinguished by its more open leaf and recumbent habit. The vigour of 'Di Vernon' is less than that of 'Catriona' and its stem is more pigmented. The colour and shape of the tubers of the two varieties are identical. Parentage not disclosed. Raised by Mr A. Finlay of Auchtermuchty, introduced 1922.

'Edgecote Purple' Raised by Mr Wilde of Edgecote. Purple-tongued flower, dusty and feathery appearance of foliage. Long, rather thin tubers. Yellow flesh, with excellent flavour for which this variety is famous.

'German Black' An old variety from Peter Maine.

'Mauve Queen' Raised by Mr R. Scarlett, before 1916, and introduced by Dobies.

'Morven' (Maris Piper × Desirée) × VRTIS (an *S. vernanyi* polycross).

'Pink Fir Apple' (syn. 'Tannenzapfen' (literally fir cone) Introduced in 1979. Main crop; plant slender and upright, flowers few, white, leaves secondary leaflets. A salad variety with yellow waxy flesh and strong flavour.

'Purple-eyed Seedling' An attractive variety, commonly used for showing.

'Salad Blue' A variety from Peter Maine.

'Pink Fir Apple'

'All Blue'

'Caribe'

'Wilja'

'Estima'

'King Edward'

'Desirée'

'Romano'

'Pentland Dell'

'Maris Piper'

'Pentland Squire'

'Pentland Crown'

'Maris Peer'

Specimens from Peter Maine, photographed 15 October

POTATOES

'Kirsty'

'Lola' (see p. 149)

'Kondor'

'Marfona'

'Ratte'

Specimens from Peter Maine, photographed 15 October

Flowers of 'Maris Peer'

'German Lady's Finger'

'Desirée' (Urgenta × Depesche)   Raised by ZPC in Holland in 1962. Main crop; plant spreading with purple-black stems and petioles, leaves with few secondary leaflets; flowers purple fading to white. Flesh pale yellow, holding together well in cooking.

'Estima' (Oldenburger 51640 × G 3014)   Raised by J. P. and P. R. Dijkhuis in Holland in 1973. Second early, flowers few, white; leaves smooth and glossy, with average-sized secondary leaflets. Plant with good resistance to blight, producing heavy crops of light yellow tubers.

'German Lady's Finger'   Tubers elongated to 12 cm long with golden skin and yellow flesh. Good yields for a finger potato.

'King Edward (syn. 'King Edward VII', 'Fellside Hero') (Magnum Bonum × Beauty of Hebron)   Raised in c. 1902 by a gardener of Northumberland whose name appears to have been lost, called by him 'Fellside Hero' and introduced by J. Butler in 1910.

'Kirsty' (Pentland Crown × seedling 3683a)   Raised by Dr J. H. W. Holden at the Scottish Crop Research Institute, Midlothian, in 1982. Early/main crop. Tubers white, large, rounded, shallow eyed. Soft creamy flesh; good for baking (Marshalls).

'Kondor'   A new variety, available from Marshalls.

'Marfona' (Primura × (Craigs Bounty × Profijt))   Contains genes of both *S. demissum* and *S. phureja*.   Raised by J. P. G. Konst & Zn at Zwaanshoek in 1975. Second early. Tubers large, white, good for baking. A robust variety good on poor soils.

'Maris Peer'   Raised by the Plant Breeding Institute at Trumpington, Cambridge. Maincrop. A prolific flowerer, and popular potato for field growing.

'Maris Piper'   Raised by the Plant Breeding Institute at Trumpington, Cambridge, in 1962. Second early; flowers very prolific, purple with a white tip; leaves with few small secondary leaflets. Flesh white, waxy when cooked. Not resistant to drought.

'Pentland Crown' (complex hybrid of several cultivars)   Raised by the Scottish Plant Breeding Station in 1958. Main crop; flowers few, white; leaves grey-green with several prominent secondary leaflets. Plant drought-resistant. Flesh white, floury when cooked.

'Pentland Dell' (Roslin Chania × Roslin Sasumua)   Raised by the Scottish Plant

Breeding Station in 1960. Main crop; flowers many, white; leaves with few leaflets and a rounded terminal leaflet; secondary leaflets few and small. Flesh white, floury when cooked.

'Pentland Squire' (Pentland Crown × Pentland Dell)   Raised by the Scottish Plant Breeding Station in 1970. Main crop; flowers few, white; leaves like Pentland Dell, but darker green and heavier. Flesh white, rather floury when cooked.

'Ratte' (syn. Asparagus potato Quenelle de Lyon, Princes, Corne de Mouton)   Raiser and parentage unknown, but introduced in 1872. Main crop; a salad variety, mainly grown in France, with numerous small and elongated yellowish tubers, waxy when cooked.

'Romano' (Draga × Desirée)   Raised by R. J. Mansholt in the Netherlands in 1979. Main crop; flowers rarely produced, purple with a white tip; leaves with large broad overlapping leaflets, and several secondary leaflets. Tubers red-skinned with cream flesh. Plant with some resistance to blight.

'Wilja' (Climax × (Craig's Bounty × Prorijt))   Raised by J. P. Konst in the Netherlands in 1967. Second early; flowers white, rarely produced; leaves with overlapping leaflets and large secondary leaflets. Light yellow flesh, rather waxy when cooked.

POTATOES

'Dunluce'

'Alhambra'

'Rubinia'

'Accent'

'Arran Pilot'

'Lola'

'King Edward'

'Manna'

Specimens from Sellindge, photographed 1 July

148

'Ausonia'

'Costella'

'Sante'

'Ailsa'

'Kingston'

Specimens from Peter Maine, photographed 15 October

'Alhambra', just dug

Potatoes at Sellindge

Flower of 'Rubinia'

'Accent' (Alcmaria × ALM 66–42) Introduced by Marshalls in 1992. First early. Flesh pale cream, waxy.

'Ailsa' (G4324 × Maris Piper) Main crop.

'Alhambra' (Desirée × Maris Piper) Main crop.

'Arran Pilot' (Mauve Queen × Pepo) Raised by Donald Mackelvie in 1930. First early; flowers few, purple with a white tip; leaves with few, small secondary leaflets. A reliable and easy variety with waxy tubers of good flavour. Resistant to drought. Can be dug after 100 days.

'Ausonia' (Wilja × M63–665) Second early.

'Costella' (TSK 063–665 × Wilja) Second early.

'Dunluce' (Saskia × (Black 2093b11 × Clarke F97)) Raised by James Clarke at Ballymoney, N. Ireland, in 1976. First early; flowers purple with a white tip, but rarely produced; leaves with large, overlapping main leaflets and few small rounded secondary leaflets. Plant leafy and low growing, with a good crop of large, very smooth white tubers. Flesh light yellow, floury when cooked.

'King Edward' (syn. 'King Edward VII', 'Fellside Hero' (Magnum Bonum × Beauty of Hebron) Raised in c. 1902 by a gardener of Northumberland whose name appears to have been lost, called by him 'Fellside Hero' and introduced by J. Butler in 1910.

'Kingston' (Pentland Crown × Maris Piper) contains genes of *S. demissum*. Raised by the Plant Breeding Institute at Trumpington near Cambridge in 1981. Main crop: flowers white, few and seldom formed. Flesh light yellow, waxy when cooked.

'Lola' (syn. 'Lolita' (Spunta × Claustar) contains genes of *S. demissum* Raised in 1981. First early. Flesh pale yellow, somewhat floury.

'Manna' (ZPC 50–35 × ZPC 55–37) Raised by ZPC in the Netherlands in 1978. First early; flowers pale purple, few; leaves rough textured with large leaflets and secondary leaflets. Flesh light-yellow, waxy when cooked.

'Rubinia' (mutant of Arka) Raised by J. P. G. Konst and Zn in 1983. First early. Secondary leaflets. Flesh creamy yellow, smooth, rosy-pink skin.

'Sante' (Y66–13–636 × ALM 66–42) Main crop.

Tomato

Lycopersicum esculentum L. (*Solanaceae*).
Other names: Tomatl, Nahuatl (Mexico); Tomate (Spain)

Origin

The tomato is closely related to the potato and the other species of *Solanum*, but differs in its anthers which dehisce by pores rather than by splitting. All species have yellow flowers, and red or, rarely, yellow fruits.

There are now considered to be about ten species of the genus *Lycopersicum*, all native to western South America, and all short-lived perennials which can be grown as annuals. The wild form of the tomato, *L. esculentum* subsp. *cerasiforme*, is close to the small-fruited cherry tomato, and is now found wild in Mexico and Central America, as well as in South America. The large-fruited tomatoes were almost certainly developed from this subspecies. A second species, *L. pimpinellifolium*, is sometimes cultivated; it is found wild near the Pacific coasts of Ecuador and Peru.

Tomatoes were widely cultivated in both Mexico and South America at the time of the Spanish invasions, but it is uncertain in which country they were first domesticated.

The early introductions to Europe were probably from Mexico, in the Vera Cruz and Puebla area, and were mainly of large-fruited varieties. The tomato was probably brought to Europe soon after the completion of the conquest of Mexico by Cortes in 1523, but the earliest record is by the Italian botanist Matthiolus in 1544. He described the yellow-fruited variety, hence the Italian name pomodoro. A fine plate in *Hortus Eystettensis*, published in 1613, shows a form with very large yellow fruits, irregularly lobed, and it is known that early introductions included white forms as well as two varieties of the usual red.

When first introduced the tomato was regarded by Europeans with considerable suspicion, as most of the fruits of solanums then known were poisonous. It also acquired a reputation as an aphrodisiac and the names Love Apple and Pomme d'Amour.

Varieties

Most tomato varieties belong to three groups, and in addition there are several odd varieties of lesser importance. The large-fruited beef tomatoes, such as 'Delicious', have fruits around 10 cm across, which are often rather lobed. There are about one and a half fruits to the kilo. The medium-sized, round fruited varieties such as 'Moneymaker' have fruit about 5 cm across, weighing in at around ten per kilo. Small-fruited cherry tomatoes have fruits about 1.5 cm across, produced in great profusion. The larger varieties of cherry tomato such as 'Gardener's Delight' weigh in at about forty-five to fifty per kilo, and are generally sweeter and have more flavour than the large-fruited or medium-sized varieties. The smallest such as 'Sweet 100' weigh about eighty per kilo. Other varieties, of lesser importance, have fruits

Weedy tomatoes in Mexico

'Yellow Currant' compared with 'Brandywine' (see p. 157)

elongated, plum-shaped and rather square (for canning), striped, or hollow like sweet peppers, and in various other colours from white to pale pink, green and yellow.

Recent advances in breeding have been for disease resistance, for increase in yield and for ease of harvesting by machine and handling on a large scale such as is needed in the tomato-growing areas of California.

Another development has been the breeding of varieties with determinate growth; the plant stops growing after a certain number of nodes have been produced. This is useful for a field crop where all the fruit are harvested at once, and has been utilized to produce dwarf varieties for small gardens or patios.

These developments have tended to ignore the interests of the amateur grower who values flavour and a long season of ripening above other characteristics.

One very beneficial new development is the shortening of the stigma to within the anther tube, so that self-pollination and therefore fruit set are reliable. In the primitive varieties the style was exerted from the anther tube, and required insect pollination. Specially produced F1 hybrids are also valuable for the amateur, for their ease of cultivation and early ripening.

Cultivation

Tomatoes are half-hardy annuals, or short-lived perennials in warm climates. They do best in a hot climate, with water in spring while the plant is growing, and drier sunny conditions while the fruits are ripening.

In climates which have spring frosts, the seed should be sown indoors in heat and the plants grown on individually in pots before planting out in late May or June, or when all danger of frost is past. This will usually be six to eight weeks after sowing, and the first flower buds should be just opening. Plants may be grown in a greenhouse, but usually the flavour of the fruit is much better when the plants are grown outside, provided that they ripen properly. The advantages of greenhouse cultivation are earlier and heavier crops, a longer period of fruit production in autumn, and a wider choice of suitable varieties.

Soils suitable for tomatoes are fertile, well drained and moisture retentive. In soil that is not too rich, the plants will grow well and there will be a good balance of leaf and fruit. Plants require feeds of potash when young, and a balanced feed with more nitrogen later on. It has been found that more potash is needed in dull, wet seasons. Tomatoes grow very well in bags of peat or peat-like composts, though in these cases correct feeding is very important. In my own experience, however, I have the impression that the flavour of plants grown in ordinary soil is better. This is probably because the plants grown in ordinary soil received less water and nitrogen.

Bush varieties need no training, but are better if they have a clean mulch around the plant so that the fruits do not lie directly on the earth. The tall indeterminate varieties, which will go up to 2 m or more, need tying on to a stake, and the side shoots need

'Gardener's Delight' in growbags against a wall

pinching out as they are formed. When grown outdoors, the tip is usually also pinched out after about four trusses have been formed, on the assumption that only those are likely to ripen satisfactorily. The leaves below the lowest truss are usually removed at the same time, or when the lowest truss begins to ripen, so that air circulation is improved around the base of the plants.

Fruits which are picked green at the onset of cold weather can be ripened in a warm place in the house.

Troubles, pests and diseases

Greenback In this ailment the fruits remain green and unripe on the base around the stalk, and the unripe area appears hard. It is worst when the fruits are exposed to strong sunlight, and is also associated with a shortage of potash; some varieties are more susceptible than others.

Blossom end rot This is caused by stress in the plants when the fruit is young and the plant is growing vigorously with many leaves. The apex of the fruit dies and goes a dark brown, and the rot can spread into the rest of the fruit. It usually affects plants growing in pots or growbags when these have been allowed to dry out, but it can also be caused by too much water, and the death of a proportion of the roots.

Bacterial wilt This is a serious disease in tomatoes grown in wet tropical climates but is not serious in cooler areas.

Verticillium wilt This used to be called sleepy disease; the plant dies slowly from the base upwards and finally droops completely. It is caused by a fungus attacking the roots and base of the stem. It is associated with cold and wet soil. A large plant can sometimes be saved by earthing it up with good soil, so that new roots can form above the affected area.

Mosaic virus Various viruses can affect tomatoes, causing mottling and curling of the leaves. Newer varieties are less susceptible than many older ones. The viruses are spread by aphids and by handling, and can originate in other plants of the *Solanum* family grown nearby, and in cucumbers. One may even originate in tobacco; for instance, a cigarette smoker training the plants can transmit the virus through his fingers.

Fruit split Fruits often split around their widest part; this usually happens when they are ripe or nearly ripe and are suddenly subjected to heavy watering. It is common in the autumn on plants grown outside after a heavy period of rain following a hot, dry spell.

Greenfly, whitefly, red spider These three insects affect tomatoes, and can be serious in a greenhouse. Regular and frequent spraying with soap can control all three, and the last two are attacked by their respective predators which can be introduced into the greenhouse.

Wild tomato in Mexico

Detail of flowers of modern cultivar

'Striped Cavern'

'Beefsteak'

'Blizzard'

'Dombito'

'Shirley'

'Super Roma'

'Sioux'

'Counter'

'Moneymaker'

'Eurocross'

Specimens from Sellindge, Kent, photographed 16 August

Tomatoes in a polytunnel

'Ida'

'Alicante'

'Zapotec Ribbed'

'Alicante' A tall-growing variety, for indoor or outdoor use. Fruit medium-sized, prolific; flavour better when grown under cover in cool climates.

'Beefsteak' (syn. 'Crimson') A tall-growing plant, with large fruit, ripening from 80–90 days in North America.

'Blizzard' An F1 hybrid, best grown under cover in Britain. Tends to suffer from B.E.R.

'Counter' An F1 hybrid, best grown under cover in Britain. Tends to suffer from B.E.R.

'Dombito' An F1 hybrid, making plants of intermediate height, best grown under cover in Britain; fruit large, thick-walled, but with less flavour than 'Supermarmande'.

'Eurocross' An F1 hybrid; plants tall, best grown under cover and with heat in Britain; fruit medium-sized, resistant to greenback, high-yielding but of poor flavour. Tends to suffer from Blossom End Rot.

'Ida' An F1 hybrid, with large fruit, for greenhouse cultivation in Britain. Plants compact and high-yielding, with disease resistance to TMV and common fungal root rots. Available from Suttons. 'Ida Gold' is an orange-yellow variety, with low-acid juice.

'Moneymaker' Raised by Mr F. Stonor. Fruit medium, 4–6 cm; tall-growing, for indoor or outdoor use; flavour very good, especially when grown under cover. Not susceptible to Blossom End Rot.

'Shirley' An F1 hybrid, disease resistant for growing under glass. Plants compact, early maturing.

'Sioux' Tall-growing, for indoor or outdoor use; fruit medium; not acid, deep red, ripening from 70) days. Tends to get Blossom End Rot.

'Striped Cavern' Tall-growing, for indoor or outdoor use. Fruit striped, especially noticeable when green, and an ideal size and shape for stuffing. Does not get Blossom End Rot.

'Super Roma' A pear-shaped tomato, used for making paste, but with little flavour.

'Zapotec Ribbed' A variety grown by the Zapotecs in southern Mexico. Fruit about 9 cm across, scarlet with deep ribs.

'Yellow Perfection'

'Tornado'

'Moneycross'

'Sweet Chelsea'

'Ronaclave'

'Gardener's Delight'

'Sweet 100'

'Suttons Ornamental' Mixed

'Tigerella'

'Plumito'

'Red Robin'

'Yellow Canary'

'Alfresco'

Specimens from Wisley, photographed 3 September

'Ailsa Craig' Raised by Mr A. Balch, Springfield Farm, Forres, Scotland. Fruit medium, 5 cm across; tall-growing, for indoor or outdoor use; flavour not special.

'Alfresco' An F1 hybrid, bush variety.

'Gardener's Delight' (syn. 'Sugar Lump') Fruit small, 2.5–4 cm across. Plant very tall-growing, for indoor or outdoor use. Fruits produced over a long period, from 50 days onwards; flavour excellent.

'Gemini' An F1 hybrid, from Dobies.

'Moneycross' Tall-growing, for indoor or outdoor use.

'Plumito' From W. Robinson & Sons.

'Red Robin' A very dwarf plant, suitable for growing in pots or window boxes, with small fruit about 2.5 cm across.

'Ronaclave' Tall-growing, for indoor or outdoor use.

'Suttons Ornamental' This is a mixed group of varieties with small fruit of various colours and shapes. Fruit of good flavour.

'Sweet Chelsea' An F1 hybrid, indeterminate variety. An American outdoor variety which will need staking, and in good hot conditions will begin to fruit in 45 days.

'Sweet 100' Tall-growing, for indoor or outdoor use; fruit very small, but prolific; good flavour, especially outdoors; sweet but less striking than 'Gardener's Delight'.

'Tigerella' Fruits red with yellow stripes, medium-sized; tall-growing, for indoor or outdoor use.

'Tornado' An F1 hybrid, large-fruited outdoor bush tomato, introduced by Marshalls in 1988. Good flavour. Fruit should begin to ripen about 75 days after planting out.

'Yellow Canary' A small-fruited yellow variety.

'Yellow Perfection' Tall-growing; fruits yellow, medium-sized, with very good strong flavour, both indoors and out. Leaves somewhat potato-like.

'Ailsa Craig' 'Gemini'

'Sweet 100' 'Yellow Perfection'

Dwarf tomato 'Red Robin'

'Tornado'

155

Tomato 'Britain's Breakfast'

'Ruffled Yellow', photographed by Leslie Land in Maine

'Yellow Currant'

'Green Grape'

'Brandywine' An old Amish heirloom variety dating from 1885, named after the river; tall-growing, mid-season (c. 74 days), but susceptible to disease, with large fruits around 350–450 g; dark reddish-pink, with a wonderful flavour described as 'tomato heaven'.

'Britain's Breakfast' An elongated tomato, not grown in Britain!

'Evergreen' Indeterminate, mid-season. Leslie Land writes: 'New to me this year. Not a new variety but not antique. One of the best-tasting tomatoes I've ever grown, both very sweet and very tomatoey – tastes like a red tomato. Outside gets yellow-flushed when fruit is ripe, interior remains bright emerald. Colour dulls in cooking even more than red tomatoes do, alas. Shape seems to be somewhat high-shouldered and irregular, but that may have been this very dry year. Fruits 170–225 g, 7.5–11.5 cm diameter.'

'Golden Boy' A new gold-fruited tomato, with fruit of good size and flavour.

'Green Grape' A new variety of cherry tomato, fruits quite large, about 2.5 cm across, and not especially lovely; plant a quite small bush. Taste *delicious*! (when fully ripe, chartreuse outside and bright green within).

'Lemon Boy' An F1 hybrid. A tall indeterminate plant with large, good quality fruit, orange-yellow in colour.

'Marmande' A traditional, large-fruited variety from France, good flavour. Best grown outdoors, and suitable for a cool site.

'Nepal' Indeterminate, mid-late season, fairly heavy bearer of very uniform round red fruits. Excellent flavour, fair resistance to the usual tomato plagues. Supposedly from Nepal and thus somewhat less affected by cool summers than your average tomato (I can't say I've noticed this, particularly, though it does on the basis of this summer seem to have pretty good drought-resistance.) Fruits very consistent 225 g weight. 8.5–11 cm across. This variety is listed by Suffolk Herbs in England, and by Johnny's Selected Seeds in North America.

'Ruffled Yellow' Fruits of an unusual shape, rather hollow and suitable for stuffing.

'Subarctic Plenty' Fruit small to medium-sized: bush habit and very hardy, for growing outdoors and in areas with a short growing season. Flavour not particularly good.

'Supermarmande' (syn. 'Marmalade Super') Fruit large, rather flattened; tall-growing, for unheated indoor or outdoor use, good flavour both indoors and out. Said to be earlier and more disease-resistant than 'Marmande'.

'White Beauty' Tall-growing; fruits white, pale creamy-yellow when ripe, rather large, 170–225 g 7.5–11.5 cm across, very sweet and less prone to mealiness than other yellow varieties. Resistant to Blossom End Rot. American variety, ready in about 84 days.

'Yellow Currant' A very small-fruited yellow variety. The seeds generally produce a mixture of yellow and red fruits, about 1.5 cm across.

The traditional variety 'Marmande'

'Evergreen', photographed by Leslie Land

'White Beauty', photographed by Leslie Land

'Nepal', photographed by Leslie Land

'Brandywine', photographed by Leslie Land

'Lemon Boy' and 'Golden Boy'

Tomatillo in Mexico

Garden Huckleberry or Sunberry

Solanum nigrum var. *guineense* syn. *Solanum melanocerasum*
(*Solanaceae*)

This is an improved form of the common weed black nightshade,
in which the fruits are somewhat sweeter and slightly larger than
the wild forms. It is cultivated mainly in North America, and the
fruits are made into pies. The plants of modern varieties are
quick-growing annuals, large and bushy, around 1.5 m high and
wide. Seed should be sown in late spring or early summer as it
germinates only in warm conditions. Plants can be thinned to
30 cm apart and given ample fertilizer and water until a large plant
has developed.

Cape gooseberry

Cape Gooseberry

Physalis pruinosa L., syn. *P. peruviana* var *edulis* (*Solanaceae*).

The Cape gooseberry is a tall, branching perennial, usually grown
as an annual in cold winter climates. The plant will survive about
−5°C, provided it is dry at the roots. The flowers are pale creamy
yellow with a dark centre, the fruits orange-yellow when ripe,
enclosed in a dry papery bladder-like calyx. The fruits remain in
good condition for months. They can be eaten raw, made into jam
or, after the bladders have been split and peeled back, dipped into
chocolate.

In spite of its English name, the Cape gooseberry is native of
South America, though it has long been grown in southern Africa,
and has become naturalized there, as well as in Australia and in
southeastern Europe. About a hundred wild species of *Physalis* are
found in central and South America, but the two shown here are
the only ones commonly grown for food. Species like small
versions of *P. peruviana* are common in the mountains of Mexico.
Two others, *P. pubescens* L. and *P. angulata* L., natives of the
southeastern United States and Mexico, are cultivated in the
Ukraine. An Asiatic species, *Physalis alkekengii* L., is found wild
from eastern Europe and Turkey east to Japan, and is commonly
grown as a hardy perennial, called bladder cherry or Chinese
lanterns. Its bladders go bright red in autumn and remain on the
stems where they are very decorative. Other perennial species are
native of North America, but do not have the bright red bladders.

Cultivation is easy, and the plants require the same conditions
as outdoor tomatoes. They are tolerant of drought, but produce
more and better fruit when well watered in hot, dry weather.

Cape gooseberry flowers and young fruit

Garden huckleberry

Tomatillo

Physalis ixocarpa Brot. ex Hornem., syn. *P. philadelphica* Lam.
(*Solanaceae*). Other names: Jamberberry, Strawberry Tomato,
Jamberry.
Other local names: Tomate (Mexico), Tomate verde (the word for
tomato in Mexico is jitomate).

This is similar to the Cape gooseberry, but the fruits are larger,
completely filling and often splitting the calyx when ripe. The
plant is smaller and lower, especially when the branches are
weighed down with the green or purple-flushed fruit. It is a very
popular vegetable in Mexican cookery, where it is used in place of
tomatoes to make an excellent sharp sauce for grilled meat. A
variety with sweeter, yellowish fruit can be eaten raw.

The tomatillo is a native of Mexico, and has long been
cultivated there, but is seldom seen elsewhere in spite of its
excellent flavour. It is also found as a weed in southern California.
It should be easy to grow in warm, rather dry conditions, similar
to those needed for tomatoes. Seed of both the sweet and the sharp
varieties is available in America, the latter under the name
'Tomatilla de Milpa'; in North American conditions they begin to
fruit in about seventy days. Plants need wide spacing, about 50 cm
apart, or supporting on sticks.

Garden huckleberry

Sweet tomatillo or Jamberry in California

Aubergine 'Easter Egg'. Specimen from Wisley, photographed 10 August

Eggplant or Aubergine

Solanum melongena L. (*Solanaceae*)
Brinjal, Melongene

The aubergine is a perennial, which may be subshrubby or herbaceous, but is usually grown as an annual. Modern varieties make bushy plants up to 1 m tall, with few, very large fruits, but more primitive varieties are taller and almost shrubby. The leaves are softly hairy, and the flowers are purple. Early varieties also tended to be very spiny, especially on the fruit-stalk, but these spines have been all but eliminated in modern cultivars.

The wild form, *Solanum melongena* var. *insanum*, is native to India, where it grows on dry hills. It is very prickly, and has fruits which are yellow when ripe and very bitter to taste. Herklots records that closely related species are found as weeds in southeast Asia, and their small fruits are eaten by the villagers: these species include *Solanum ferox* L. which has hairy fruit and *S. torvum* Swartz, with branching clusters of round fruits. The fruit shapes of primitive aubergines cultivated in villages in Thailand are very variable, from flattened spherical to egg-shaped, and not more than 5 cm across. In colour they vary from deep magenta-purple to pure white, pale and dark green shading to white, green and golden-yellow.

History

The earliest records of cultivation of the aubergine are from China in the fifth century BC, and it was certainly also grown in India at an early date. It was probably first known in Europe in the thirteenth century, but not widely cultivated until the sixteenth. It was introduced to Europe by the Arabs who grew it in Spain, and it is known to have been grown by them in the fourth century AD.

The first varieties to be grown in England were used more as ornamentals than as vegetables, and had white, egg-shaped fruits, hence the English name; aubergine is the French name, derived from the Catalan *alberginia*, which is itself a corruption of the Arabic al-badingan.

Many of the modern large-fruited varieties are dark purple/black-skinned F1 hybrid strains, raised from two inbred lines to produce hybrid vigour. The large number of seeds in each fruit makes hand-pollination economic.

Cultivation

Aubergines require much the same conditions as indoor tomatoes. Seed should be sown in heat, at around 20°C, in spring, and the seedlings planted out in a greenhouse in May, or in the open ground once the soil has warmed up. Temperatures should stay above 15°C for satisfactory growth, with higher temperatures in daytime. Soil should be well drained, and well manured, with high potash to encourage good root growth. Aubergines do well in growbags in peat composts, but tend to become unnecessarily leafy, and require frequent watering in hot weather. Pinching the top out when the plant is about 40 cm tall will encourage bushy growth, but the modern varieties are not expected to have more than five large fruits per plant, and any more which have set should be removed. Feed with high potash tomato fertilizer when the fruits are swelling.

Both whitefly and red spider mite are likely to affect aubergines grown under glass, and red spider is often bad in frames or dry places outside. Both these pests breed at great speed in dry, warm conditions, and can be controlled by frequent wetting of the leaves and by spraying with a soap solution, as well as by establishing a good population of a suitable predator. Greenfly are also common on the undersides of the leaves, and any which are seen can be sprayed with soap solution before they have done any damage.

The warm humid conditions ideal for aubergines are also perfect for botrytis, which can attack the dead petals, or places on the stem where there is a wound, especially in autumn if the weather becomes wetter and cooler. Good ventilation after spraying and the removal of any dead leaves will prevent any outbreak of botrytis becoming serious.

'Caspar'   This variety has pure white fruit about 15 cm long, and white flesh.
'Easter Egg'   This is a modern variety of the original oriental egg-plant from India, whose egg-like fruits were the origin of the name. Fruits ripen in 52–65 days in hot climates, on a plant about 60 cm tall. The fruits should be picked when about 7.5 cm long.
'Striped'   These striped varieties were bought in a market in southern France. They seem to originate in Italy, and are grown under names such as 'Listada de Gandia' and 'Rose Blanca'. Seed of both these is available from Seeds Blum. 'Violette de Firenze' is similar, with large fruit, sometimes pale violet, sometimes striped.

White-fruited (possibly 'Caspar') and striped aubergines in France   Detail of aubergine flower

'Little Fingers'

'Elondo'

'Black Prince'

'Black Enorma'

'Rima'

'Slice Rite'

Specimens from Wisley, photographed 10 August

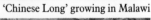

'Slice Rite' in flower

'Chinese Long' growing in Malawi

'Rima'

'Easter Egg'

'Chinese Long'

'Black Enorma' An F1 hybrid. Plant compact up to 70 cm; fruit large, black and almost spherical, ready in 75 days in North America.

'Black Prince' An F1 hybrid. Plant similar to 'Black Enorma', but fruit slightly more elongated, ready in around 62 days in North America.

'Chinese Long' Numerous oriental varieties have very long, narrow fruit. This is a slow variety to develop, 125 days in North America, with fruit about 25 cm long. 'Long Bridge' is quicker to mature, in 85 days, and has even longer fruit.

'Easter Egg' This is a modern variety of the original oriental egg-plant from India, whose egg-like fruits were the origin of the name. Fruits ripen in 52–65 days in hot climates, on a plant about 60 cm tall. Best grown in a warm greenhouse in Britain.

'Elondo' An F1 variety available from Thompson and Morgan.

'Little Fingers' A variety developed by the Harris Moran Company in California, but suitable for growing in an unheated greenhouse in Britain. Fruit ready in around 68 days in North America. Narrow fruit c. 16 cm long.

'Rima' A Dutch variety, raised by Sluis and Groot research, which performed best in a trial in an unheated polytunnel at Wisley. Plant around 80 cm, much branched; fruits about 20 cm long, 6 cm in diameter, dark purple.

'Slice Rite' An F1 variety, maturing in around 74 days in North America. We found this variety rather slow to develop in a greenhouse in southern England, and rather tough skinned, but it does extend the season by ripening after the other large, black-skinned varieties had finished.

Villandry in late summer

Peppers

Capsicum annuum L. (*Solanaceae*)

Both hot and mild peppers are derived from the species *Capsicum annuum*, which is native to Mexico and central America. Two varieties are recognized: var. *annuum* which includes all the cultivated types and var. *minimum*, sometimes called var. *aviculare*, which includes the wild and weedy types. The latter is known as the bird-pepper or chillipiquin and is now found wild in the southern United States from Florida to southern Arizona, and thence south to South America, growing in canyons and disturbed ground.

Capsicum baccatum L., which is distinguished by the yellow or brownish spots on the flower and prominent calyx teeth, is grown in temperate and subtropical South America.

Seeds of peppers have been found in archaeological deposits in Tehuacan, in Mexico, dating from around 7000 BC, but these may well have been of fruits collected from the wild. The earliest records of the cultivation of peppers date from about 2000 years later, and peppers are illustrated on pre-Columbian ceramics. It is likely that the hot types, not the large sweet peppers, were the first to be cultivated. However, by the time peppers were introduced to Europe most of the main types grown nowadays were already established.

The first records of peppers grown in Europe date from around AD 1500. They were very soon widely grown. The hot varieties were dried, powdered and then used as a substitute for true pepper, the tropical climber *Piper nigrum*, then a very expensive import from the East Indies. Peppers also soon became widely grown in eastern Asia, and they play a very important part in the cuisine of India, Malaysia and the southern parts of China.

Hot peppers, Chilis, Cayenne peppers These are usually rather small and red when ripe. The degree of hotness depends on the presence of capsaicin, which varies according to variety and is affected by the climate. Hot weather conditions produce hotter peppers. They become hotter and sweeter as they ripen, and the seeds are hotter than the flesh. The larger, hot varieties may be

elongated, as in 'Anaheim', bell-shaped as in 'Poblano' or yellow when ripe, as in 'Hungarian Wax'. (There is also a sweet Hungarian Wax, often called 'Banana'.) 'Pasilla' is a type with elongated blackish-brown fruit.

Sweet Pepper, Pimento, Bell Pepper This type of pepper is most popular in temperate countries and is widely grown in greenhouses in northern Europe, and in the open in southern Europe, the Middle East and in North America. The large, hollow fruits are generally red when ripe, but may be yellow, and there are varieties which are blackish-purple when mature.

Peppers are fast-growing annuals, and grow best in the drier parts of the tropics and in warm summer weather. In temperate climates seed should be sown under glass in March or early April; the young plants can be put into growbags when they are about 8 cm tall, and kept as warm as possible until hot weather has arrived, when they can be transferred to a sheltered place outside. Alternatively, young plants can be kept in pots until about 12 cm tall, and then hardened off and planted into frames in late June. Feeding is beneficial for building up a good-sized plant, but may be reduced when fruiting begins.

Poor growth outdoors is usually a result of cold. In greenhouses and in wet seasons in the tropics, grey moulds such as botrytis can kill the stems. Better air circulation should prevent this.

Tabasco

Capsicum frutescens L.
Chili, Goat or Spur Pepper

This species originated in tropical South America, and is also commonly grown in southeast Asia and India. The earliest evidence of its cultivation is in archaeological deposits in coastal Peru.

It is rather similar to *Capsicum annuum*, but the greenish-white flowers are held on upright stalks with only the flower itself nodding. The fruits are upward-pointing. In warm climates this plant will form a low bushy shrub. The cultivar 'Tabasco', named after a town in southern Mexico, is commonest in cultivation, and

Pimento 'Cabri'

Capsicum annuum, 'Tomato'

'Yatsufusa', a Japanese variety

'Super Chilli'

C. frutescens, Tabasco

'Albino' (p. 168)

is mostly used in the production of the famous sauce; the species is also offered under the name Thai Hot Chili. Cultivation is as for *C. annuum*.

    Capsicum chinense Jacq. is often distinguished from *C. frutescens* by the peduncles which are spreading or declined at flowering, and by having two or more flowers at each node, but the two species are very close. Jacquin, who first described it in 1776, wrongly thought that it originated in China though it is probably native to the western Amazon basin . Cultivars included under *C. chinense* are 'Rocotillo', 'Habanero' (p. 168) and 'Uvilla Grande'.

Rocoto, *Capsicum pubescens* Ruiz & Pavon, is cultivated in the High Andes and in mountainous parts of Mexico. Its wild ancestor is unknown, but it was much cultivated by the Incas, and is still grown in a few areas in Peru and in the Patzcuaro area of Mexico. The flowers are large and purple, the seeds dark brown in contrast to other species which have straw-coloured seeds. The fruits are usually rather round and are usually yellow or orange, but may be red; they are the size of a small plum, with thick walls, and extremely hot to taste.

    This species is described by Jean Andrews in her fascinating book *Peppers*. She says that it requires a long growing season with a daylength of between eleven and thirteen hours, and so is unsuitable for growing in high latitudes. In Mexico it is generally cultivated at between 1200–2000 m, and so tolerates cool, humid climates.

'Cabri' An American variety, with unusually shaped fruit.
'Super Chili' A modern hybrid variety with fruits about 7 cm long, freely produced on a compact plant to about 60 cm tall. Taste hot.
'Tomato' An ancient variety, and one of the first to come to Europe, being illustrated in *Hortus Eystettensis* in 1613. The bell peppers may have been developed from this. Fruit thick-fleshed, sweet when ripe.
'Yatsufusa' A Japanese variety of hot chili pepper, with fruit about 9 cm long.

Shrubby *Capsicum frutescens* in Mexico

Capsicum annuum, 'Cayenne' (p. 171) at Ryton

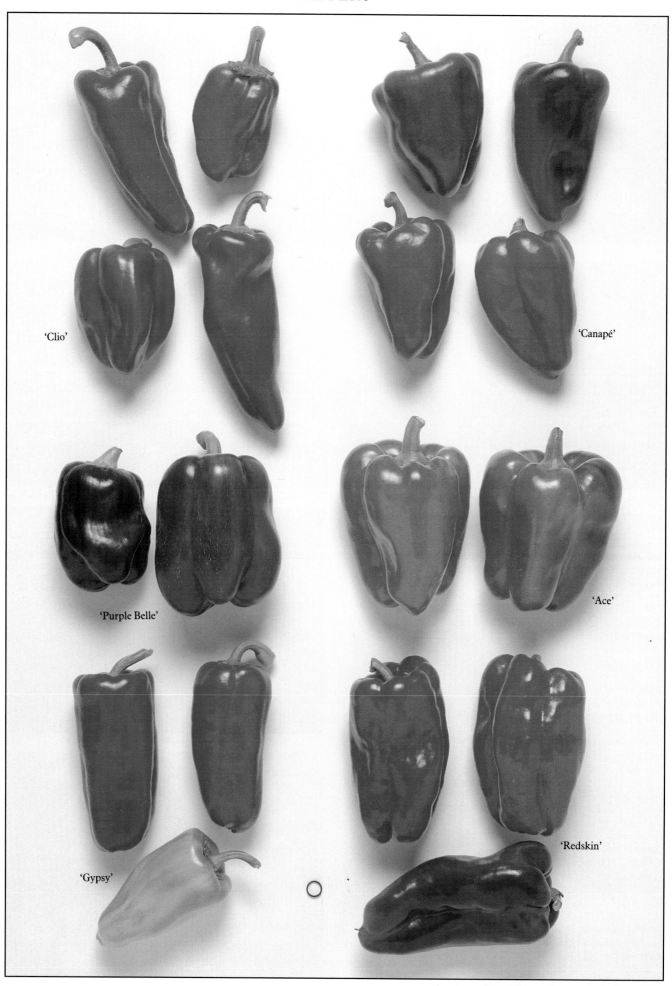

'Clio'

'Canapé'

'Purple Belle'

'Ace'

'Gypsy'

'Redskin'

Specimens from Wisley, photographed 3 September

Bell Pepper 'Big Bertha'

'Ace' An F1 hybrid, raised by Burpee. Fruit 3–4 lobed, large, green, quick-maturing, suitable for growing in a greenhouse in Britain; maturing in about 60 days in North America.

'Big Bertha' An F1 hybrid, this is one of the largest-fruited of the bell peppers, with 3-lobed fruit to 25 cm long, 10 cm across, with deep grooves, soon turning red. Matures in about 70 days in North America. Tolerant of tobacco mosaic virus.

'Canapé' This F1 hybrid variety was bred especially for cool climates, and will fruit outdoors in England in a sheltered garden or in an unheated frame. Fruits 3-lobed, turning red. Good yields, maturing in about 60 days.

'Golden Bell' (or **'Belle'**) An F1 hybrid. Fruits 3- or 4-lobed, large and thick-walled, ripening to orange-yellow, maturing in about 65 days in North America. Bell peppers were developed by the Mexicans in pre-Columbian times, and were early introductions to Europe, having been grown and illustrated by Joachim Camerarius in around 1589.

'Gypsy' An F1 hybrid; this is one of the cubanelle group of peppers, with large, elongated pale yellow fruit, ripening red, up to 10 cm long, and 7 cm wide. The plants are much more prolific than bell peppers, and are said to produce 40 or more fruits per plant in ideal conditions. A very popular variety in North America, maturing in about 65 days.

'Lipstick' An easily grown, high-yielding variety with thick-fleshed, heart-shaped fruit, about 12 cm long, maturing in 53 days in North America.

'Purple Belle' An F1 hybrid. Raised by Burpee. Plant compact. Fruit rather short, about 9 cm long, 4-lobed, almost square, changing from green to purple and red, maturing in about 70 days in North America. Bell peppers are now available in purple, almost black and yellow, and mostly ripen to orange and red. See also pages 168/169.

'Redskin' An F1 hybrid. Plant very compact, to about 37 cm. Fruits green, ripening to red. Suitable for growing in pots.

Cubanelle pepper 'Gypsy' at Wisley

Bell Pepper 'Golden Bell' at Wisley

'Lipstick' peppers, grown and photographed by Leslie Land in Maine

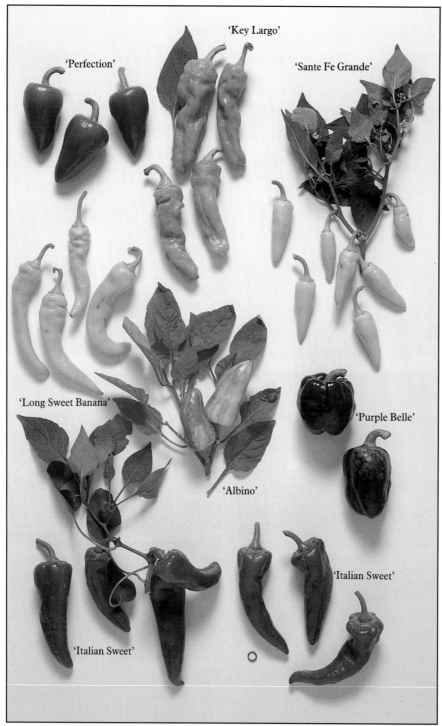

'Perfection'

'Key Largo'

'Sante Fe Grande'

'Long Sweet Banana'

'Albino'

'Purple Belle'

'Italian Sweet'

'Italian Sweet'

Specimens from Anthony Rix in Malawi, photographed 20 December

'Albino' In Malawi

'Albino' These varieties with upright, pointed fruit belong to the 'Fresno' group with larger fruit than the related 'Santa Fe Grande' groups. 'Cascabelle' is an intermediate cultivar with smaller yellow, orange and red fruits. In 'Albino' the fruit ripens from white streaked purple to red, on a very dwarf bush.

'Habanero' This is a variety of *Capsicum chinense*, grown in the Caribbean and in the Yucatan peninsula of Mexico. The fruits ripen golden yellow and are exceptionally hot, about a thousand times hotter than a Jalapeno, it is said.

'Italian Sweet' The fruits are 20 cm long in a good specimen, and about 5 cm across the shoulder, but generally smaller. They ripen red, and are generally sweet, not hot, and are often used in pickled antipasti salads.

'Key Largo' An F1 hybrid, cubanelle type; fruit yellow-green to orange-red, 15–18 cm long, tapering from a wide base, with irregular grooves. A very productive cultivar, with thick sweet flesh and more flavour than the large bell types.

'Santa Fe Grande' The fruits of this pepper are 5–8 cm long, generally held upright, pale yellowish-green when mature, but finally ripen red.

'Long Sweet Banana' These long pale yellow peppers are generally called Sweet Yellow or Banana when they are not hot, and Hungarian Yellow wax, when hot. The hot variety was introduced to the United States from Hungary in the 1930s and the not hot Banana varieties were introduced in 1940 by the Cornelli Seed Co. Both are pale yellowish when mature, ripening to red, about 15 cm long.

'Perfection' A true pimento, with smooth, heart-shaped fruit about 7 cm long, dark green, ripening red, maturing in 65–80 days in North America. The fruits are sweet with strong flavour, and commonly used for canning. This form originated in Spain from early introductions from Mexico, and varieties with similar-shaped fruit were recorded by Clusius from Italy in 1611.

'Purple Belle' An F1 hybrid. Raised by Burpee. Plant compact. Fruit rather short, about 9 cm long, 4-lobed, almost square, changing from green to purple and red, maturing in about 70 days in North America. Bell peppers are now available in purple, almost black and yellow, and mostly ripen to orange and red. Other varieties can be seen on pages 166/167.

'Italian Sweet'

Capsicum chinense 'Habanero'

Banana peppers at Villandry

'Sante Fe Grande'

'Golden Bell' (text p. 167)

'Key Largo'

'Cayenne'

'Hot Gold Spike'

'Serrano'

'Red Chili'

Specimens from Sellindge, Kent, photographed 25 September

Chili pepper plants in early fruit

'Red Chili'

'Hot Gold Spike'

'Apache'

'Apache' This is a modern F1 hybrid pepper of the chili group.

'Cayenne' An ancient cultivar, from pre-Columbian times, first referred to in 1542 in French Guiana. It is now mainly grown in Asia. The pods are long, slender and curved, ripening bright red, and very hot. When dried and powdered this and similar cultivars produce the well-known Cayenne pepper.

'Hot Gold Spike' This yellow-fruited variety is a development of 'Santa Fe Grande', commonly grown in the southwestern United States. It is very hot when mature.

'Jalapeno' This is another Mexican variety, named after the town of Jalapa, and it is still widely grown commercially in Mexico and the southwestern United States. It is commonly pickled or canned, and often smoked but also eaten fresh. The fruits are dark green, ripening to red, and thick-skinned, with a blunt end, about 5 cm long when mature. Taste is usually very hot, especially if the seeds are left in.

'Peter Pepper' This is an old variety, preserved in Texas, often rudely called the penis pepper, because of the folded skin of the tip. There are both red and yellow variants. The fruit is very hot and grown mainly as a curiosity, or for pickling while green.

'Red Chili' This form of hot pepper has large, long fruit of variable hotness, maturing green, at which stage it is commonly eaten, and ripening red. The fruits are generally 10–15 cm long. This variety is often grown for canning in California and New Mexico, and the group of varieties called 'Anaheim' was developed for the canning industry.

'Serrano' This Mexican chili is grown commercially from near sea level to high in the central plateau. It is generally eaten green or canned. It is not difficult to grow, in a greenhouse in cool climates, and produces a prolific crop on tall, much-branched and distinctly hairy plants.

The grotesquely shaped 'Peter Pepper'

'Jalapeno' peppers, grown and photographed by Leslie Land

Lamb's lettuce: wild type at Sellindge

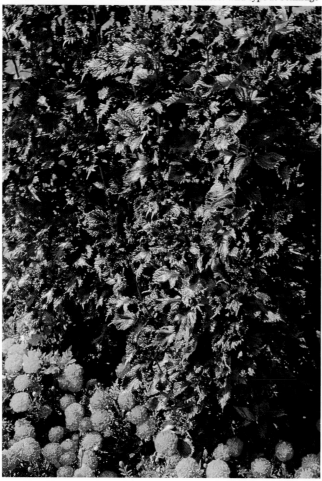

Purple-leaved Perilla

Perilla

Perilla frutescens L. (Britt.) var. *crispa* (Thunb.) Decne (*Labiatae*)
Shiso (Japanese)

Perilla is a very popular herb in Japan, used mainly as a garnish in the same way that parsley is used in Europe. The nettle-like leaves are bright green, reddish or purple. Often, in packaged food, or in a neatly boxed picnic, the elegant perilla leaf turns out to be a clever plastic copy.

Perilla frutescens is a bushy annual, native to southeast Asia, and long grown in China for the oil extracted from its seeds. Var. *crispa*, the variety grown as a herb, differs in its longer calyx and smaller seeds, and in the wrinkled margin of the leaves. The flowers of both are small and whitish. The plant is also used medicinally, and is supposed to kill some of the parasites which are found in raw fish. Perilla needs light slightly acid soil, and a warm position, rather like basil. Seed is generally sown indoors in early spring, and the plants grown singly in pots before being planted out after the weather has warmed up in early summer. It was popular in Victorian times for exotic bedding schemes, often grown under the name *Perilla nankinensis*.

Chinese Artichoke

Stachys affinis Bunge (*Labiatae*)
Crosnes

The Chinese artichoke belongs to the same family as mint, sage and many other herbs, and is closely related to the common woundworts, *Stachys sylvatica*, hedge woundwort, and *S. palustris*, marsh woundwort. The plant looks similar to a rather small marsh woundwort, but the tuberous roots are very different, with their swollen rounded segments, like a deformed specimen of the Tower shell *Turritella*. These tubers are the edible part of the plant, and are usually washed and boiled for about five to ten minutes, before being finished off in butter or eaten when nearly cold in a vinaigrette.

Chinese artichokes are native to China, and were long grown there and in Japan as an exceptionally special vegetable, because of their likeness to jade when freshly dug. They were not introduced to Europe until 1882, when some were sent to the Société d' Acclimatisation in Paris, by the famous student of Chinese botany Dr E. Bretschneider who had found them growing in gardens near Peking. The French name alludes to the town of Crosne, where the plants were first grown in the garden of M. Pailleux, vice-president of the Société.

The tubers should be planted in rich sandy soil in early spring, about 15 cm apart and 7.5 cm deep. They should not be allowed to dry out, and will tolerate partial shade. They are ready for digging in late autumn, when the frost has killed the top growth. Because the tubers are so small, quite a large plantation of them is required for a reasonable crop.

Livingstone Potato

Plectranthus esculentus N.E. Br. syn. *Coleus esculentus* (N.E.Br.)
G. Taylor (*Labiatae*)

This unusual vegetable is described in detail by Dr Herklots in *Vegetables of South-east Asia*, from material he saw in Malawi in 1969. It is used as a vegetable in many parts of Africa from Nigeria and Zimbabwe south to the Transvaal and Natal, but it is not known from Cape Province. The material shown here was obtained by my brother Anthony near Dedza in Malawi, and grown in England.

The tubers are elongated, about the thickness of a man's wrist in a large specimen, with irregular branching. When cooked they have the consistency and taste of a potato. Propagation is by pieces of root with a sprout, planted in late spring or at the beginning of the rainy season. Growth is very fast; the tall stems with softly hairy leaves can reach 1 m or so, and the plant also produces stems trailing to 3 m long, which root and form tubers at the nodes. The flowers are yellow, around 2 cm long. The roots are usually dug after seven months.

The genus *Plectranthus* contains about fifty species, mainly in Africa. Several are grown as greenhouse ornamentals and as ground cover in mild climates. It is closely related to the genus *Coleus*, one species of which, *Coleus parviflorus* Benth., the Sudan or Madagascar potato, also produces edible tubers. This *Coleus* is an important crop in the drier parts of tropical Africa, and is also grown in India, Malaya and Java. The edible tubers are round, brown or black, and produced in bunches at the base of the stems. The plant is grown either from small tubers or from nodal stem cuttings. In cultivation in England, tubers were only formed in autumn.

Lamb's Lettuce or Corn Salad

Valerianella eriocarpa Desv., and *V. locusta* (L.) Laterrade (*Valerianaceae*)
Nüsslisalad (Switzerland), Mache (France)

Lamb's lettuce is a useful salad for use during the winter. In January, when I first went to work in Switzerland, the University canteen served little salad bowls of what looked like dark green daisy leaves; the name, nüsslisalad, described the rather nutty flavour, but I did not at first recognize it as the same species which grows on the brick walls of our vegetable garden in Kent. In this weedy, wild form the leaves are softer and pale green, but have a similar flavour. The plant flowers in early spring, making tight heads of silver-blue flowers on branching stems.

About thirty species of *Valerianella* are native to Europe and Turkey, but the two named above seem to be those usually grown. They can be distinguished by their fruits, smooth in *V. locusta*, hairy and with a persistent unequally-toothed calyx in *V. eriocarpa*, which is a more southern species, commonly grown in Italy. Var. *oleracea* (Schlecht.) Beistr. is a cultivated variety of *V. locusta*, with larger leaves and more corky fruits. Some other species have large fruits ornamented with hooks or curved spines which become burrs.

Lamb's lettuce is now rarely grown in England, but over fifteen varieties are available in the United States, where it is usually called corn salad. If their names mean anything, most seem to have originated in Holland or northern France, though they vary in their cold-hardiness. 'Verte d' Etampes' is unusual with its savoyed leaves.

Cultivation

Lamb's lettuce is a winter crop, and should be sown in July and August or even early September, in rich well-drained soil, for use in late winter and early spring. It will continue to grow in mild spells, and can be harvested at any time. It can be grown in summer, but then the plants are liable to suffer from mildew and drought. The plants of larger varieties should be thinned to 15 cm apart. Either single leaves may be picked, or later the hearts of the plants can be pinched out before they flower.

Fedia cornucopiae (L.) Geartn. (*Valerianaceae*) is closely related to *Valerianella*, but has bright purplish, large flowers, with the tube longer than the lobes. It is common in the Mediterranean region of southern Europe, growing in olive groves and similar open places. It was formerly grown as a vegetable in the same way as corn salad, but I have not heard of it being cultivated in recent years.

Chinese artichokes, *Stachys affinis*

Flowers of Chinese artichoke

Livingstone potato – young shoots

'Little Gem' squash

Pumpkin field in California

Marrow, Pumpkin and Squash

These three groups of vegetables, and several others belong to the genus *Cucurbita* which contains twenty-seven species of vigorous trailing and climbing annuals and perennials, originating in North and South America. Six species were originally important food plants in the pre-Columbian culture of the Americas, which was based on maize, beans and the cucurbits.

The genus is renowned for the large and often curious fruits which are commonly known as gourds, squash, pumpkins, vegetable marrow and courgettes. Although all these names refer to plants within the genus, some, e.g. gourd, may apply to other plants in other families. To add to the confusion many squashes and pumpkins are plants belonging to any of the four species: *C. pepo* L., *C. maxima* Duch. ex. Lam., *C. moschata* (Duch. ex Lam.) Duch, ex Poir, and *C. mixta* Pangalo.

In cultivation these fruit are further classified to some extent according to their season of maturity e.g. summer and winter squash, or their shape e.g. turban gourds, crookneck squash, banana squash, or by other names – hubbards, scallops and acorns. Zucchini (Italian) and courgette (French) are the immature fruits of the vegetable marrow.

Pumpkins can be eaten as a vegetable baked or grilled with butter, used as a pie filling, made into marmalade, or in some kinds eaten raw. They include some of the largest of all vegetables, often weighing 100 kgs. Many winter squash are useful as stock feed, because they can be stored for several months. The seeds of most species can be roasted and eaten, and contain a valuable vegetable oil which can be extracted. Gourds can be grown purely as ornamentals, or scooped out and dried for a great number of uses, e.g. water vessels, drums floats, penis sheaths, snuff boxes etc.

Medicinally some *Cucurbita* have been used as anthelmintics or vermifuges (worm-expellents). A substance called cucurbitine, a carboxypyrrolidine, has been isolated from within the seeds of *C. maxima* in particular.

Cucurbita pepo L.

Vegetable Marrow, Autumn Pumpkin, Summer Squash, Gourd

This was originally native to North America north of Mexico City, but is not now known as a wild species, though related species with small, hard and horribly bitter fruit are still found wild in Mexico and Guatemala. Most of the recognizable types were already developed when they were introduced to Europe in the sixteenth century.

Cucurbita pepo is a vigorous annual with trailing or short upright (in bush cultivars) stems, with long tendrils. The stems are angled; the leaves are broadly triangular and deeply lobed, and both leaves and stems are rough, covered in small prickles. The

Young fruit of summer squash

Summer Crookneck squashes, photographed by Leslie Land in Maine

flowers are yellow, with upright corolla lobes. The fruit stalk is hard, angular and deeply grooved.

Cultivars of *Cucurbita pepo* may be divided in the following groups:

Pumpkins   Rounded or flattened, often ribbed fruits. The larger ones are usually too tasteless for human consumption, and are used as animal feed. Pumpkins of *Cucurbita pepo* are best eaten shortly after harvesting.

Vegetable Marrow, Zucchini or **Courgette**   These have long or round fruits of various colours. The bush kinds do not make long trailing branches, and are therefore more suitable for small gardens or intensive cropping. The young leaves, mature male flowers and very small fruits can also be eaten, the open flowers may be cooked in batter, the young leaves cooked as greens.

Summer Squash   This is a very large group with highly ornamental fruits. The name squash is derived from a North American Indian word meaning food eaten raw. Almost all summer squash are forms of *Cucurbita pepo*, while autumn and winter squashes are forms of *C. maxima*. Summer squash are divided into four groups: Scallop or Custard Squash, Straightneck, Crookneck, and Vegetable Spaghetti.

The variety 'Delicata', sometimes called the Sweet Potato Squash, is distinct. It has compact growth with a high yield of small fruit with a rounded end; the skin is white with green stripes, the flesh bright orange and sweet.

'Pompeon' (pepo)   This is an old variety, with very dark green fruit. In the past the name 'pompeon' was used for any kind of pumpkin or squash, and pepo, the Latin for squash is derived from this word.

'White Vegetable Spaghetti'   Vegetable spaghetti is said to have originated in Manchuria. The original form is a climber, with pale fruit, ripening yellowish.

Yellow Crookneck Squash (pepo)   A popular group of summer squash varieties in North America, generally eaten when the fruits are about 25 cm long. In many varieties the stem is also yellow. In North America the first fruits are ready in around 50 days.

Flowers of 'Burpees Golden' zucchini

Vegetable Spaghetti fruit

Pumpkins and squashes climbing on a fence at Wisley

Cucurbita maxima Duch. ex Lam.

Winter Pumpkin, Autumn and Winter Squash, Gourd

This was originally a native of South America, from Chile, Argentina, Bolivia and Uruguay. It is a vigorous trailing annual, with long tendril-bearing shoots. The stems are soft and round; the leaves nearly orbicular, not pointed nor deeply lobed. The flowers are yellow, with the rounded corolla lobes curving outwards and reflexed. The fruit stalk is somewhat cylindrical, soft and corky, very distinct from that of *Cucurbita pepo*. The fruits are very variable, and include the ornamental gourds with thick, hard shells.

Cultivars of *Cucurbita maxima* may be divided into the following groups:

Pumpkins   These include varieties with some of the largest fruits of the vegetable world, including Arthur Vesey's 'Show King', reputed to weigh 181.44 kg or 400 lbs.
Winter Squash   This is a large group with highly ornamental fruits. The gourds ripen in autumn, creating a curious and colourful display well into winter. Winter squash are very useful as they can usually be stored for long periods in cool, dry places, protected from frost. They include acorn, buttercup, hubbard, turban and banana squashes.

Cucurbita moschata (Duch. ex Lam.) Duch.
ex Poir

Butternut, Winter Squashes and Pumpkins

This is probably the earliest species to have been cultivated. Evidence of its use has been found at Tehuacan, south of Mexico City, from around 3400 BC, and almost as early in Peru. It makes a long trailing or climbing plant (though there are also bush varieties) with large, soft, shallowly-lobed leaves, hard and angular stems, three- or four-branched tendrils and yellow flowers, often with stalked leafy bracts. The fruit stalk is angled and flared where it joins the fruit. The fruits are usually smooth skinned, with orange flesh, and keep well.

There are three main cultivar groups:
Butternut, bottle-shaped with a straight neck, such as 'Butternut Waltham' or 'Ponca'.
Crookneck, with a smooth skin, such as 'Golden Cushaw'.
Kentucky Field or **Large Cheese**, a flattened sphere.
'Early Butternut' is a bush variety.

Cucurbita ficifolia Bouche

Fig-leaved Gourd, Malabar Gourd, Chilicayotl

This is one of the most widely distributed species, ranging from Mexico through central and South America to Chile. Archaeological evidence of this species has been dated at 2000 BC, from Huata Prieta in Peru. In spite of this long history of cultivation there are no distinct cultivars.

The plant is perennial in frost-free climates, with long trailing shoots. The leaves are prickly, and often deeply lobed and fig-like; the flowers yellow to light orange with short, obtuse corolla lobes, and produced only in short days. The fruits are oblong to nearly globular, dark green with white stripes and blotches, with white flesh and black seeds. The stalk is hard, round or slightly angled without cork. There are no named cultivars, but the species is widely grown throughout South America and eastern Asia and India. It has been grown in Europe at least since 1613 when it was illustrated, on the same page as the large, yellow-fruited tomato, in *Hortus Eystettensis*, the garden book of the Bishop of Eichstatt in Germany. (Illustrated on page 192.)

'Delicata', photographed in Maine by Leslie Land (text p. 191)

Flower and fruit of *Cucurbita maxima*

'Pompeon', an ancient variety of squash (text p. 175)

Flower of *Cucurbita maxima*

Upper left: 'Jaune Gros de Paris'　　　Lower left: 'Mavis Sweetener'　　　Centre: 'Hungarian Mammoth'　　　Upper and lower right: 'Etamples'
A selection of ripe pumpkins grown at Wisley

Cucurbita mixta Pangalo

Green Striped Cushaw, Ayote (Mexico)

This species is cultivated mostly in the southern States of America where it is called 'Green Striped Cushaw'; it is very similar to a variety grown by the Pueblo Indians in Arizona in pre-Columbian times, and has large curved fruit, widening towards the apex and striped with dark green. Evidence for the use of this species dates only from AD 1200.

The plant is similar to *C. moschata*, but has a hard swollen corky stalk to the fruit, not flared where it meets the fruit, and no leafy sepals. It thus has some of the characters of *C. maxima*, hence the name *mixta*.

Two cultivars are grown:

'**Tennessee Sweet Potato**' has large pear-shaped fruit, and pale yellow skin with greeenish stripes which fade with age. It is a good keeper, with smooth flesh and a good flavour.
'**Green Striped Cushaw**' has bottle-shaped fruit with a somewhat curved neck and cream-coloured skin with dark green lacy stripes. The flesh is sweet when young, cream-coloured and good for baking.

Cultivation

All the cultivated species of *Cucurbita* are very voracious feeders and require plenty of manure dug into the soil where they will be grown. It is essential that strong supports are positioned prior to planting and that enough space is allocated to them so that nearby plants are not smothered. They will make considerable growth if watered regularly, especially from the time they begin to flower until ripening of the fruits.

Seed should be sown early in May under glass, or alternatively outside *in situ* at the end of May once frost danger has diminished. The seed can be sown individually into 10 cm pots or into a seed tray planted 7.5 cm apart. A peat or other such organic compost is best. Seedlings are ready for planting out two weeks after germination or once the seedlings have developed four to six mature leaves. It is advisable to harden the young plants off for a few days before planting them. Planting distances are governed by the plant's vigour. More vigorous kinds can be spaced 1.2 m apart, less vigorous kinds 1 m apart. The young leaves, male flowers and first baby fruits are all delicious to eat and can be picked within two months of planting out.

'**Crown Prince**' (*maxima*)　The trailing vines produce beautiful grey-blue skinned fruit with a distinct ring near the apex, and very fine-ground orange flesh. A very good keeper and eater, around 5 kg in weight.
'**Etamples**' (syn. 'Rouge vif. d'Etampes') (*maxima*)　An old French variety, since before 1830. Fruit about 9 kg flattened, reddish-orange with knobbly skin. Plant long-trailing. See page 187.
'**Hundred Weight**' (*maxima*)　Fruit large, with yellow skins, rather flattened. Will keep well.
'**Jackpot**' (*maxima*)　A hybrid pumpkin, with mottled fruit weighing 5–7 kg, ripening to orange, maturing in about 100 days. Flesh orange-yellow, plant heavy yielding on compact vines.
'**Jack-be-Little**' (*pepo*)　A very small pumpkin, only 7.5 cm in diameter with sweet flesh, or for use as ornamentals. Fruit mature in around 85 days, and keeps well.
'**Hungarian Mammoth**'(*pepo*)　Skin colour variable, from white to dark green, grey or orange. Seeds edible. Weight up to 378 lbs.
'**Jaune Gros de Paris**' (*maxima*)　Pinkish with a russet skin. Flesh very dense and keeps well. Usually around 45 cm across.
'**Mavis Sweetener**'　A mottled pumpkin, grown at Wisley. We have been unable to find any references to this name.

'Hundred Weight'

Pumpkins for sale in the fall in California

'Jackpot'

'Crown Prince'

'Jack-be-Little'

'Clarita'

'Supremo'

'Table Dainty'

'All Green Bush'

'Burpee Golden'

'Tiger Cross'

'Tender and True'

'Minipak'

Specimens from Wisley, 15 September

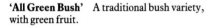

'Minipak'

'White Lebanese' zucchini

'All Green Bush' A traditional bush variety, with green fruit.

'Burpee Golden' (syn. 'Golden Zucchini') A bush variety, maturing in North America in around 54 days. Leaves deeply lobed. 'Gold Rush' is a similar F1 variety.

'Clarita' An F1 hybrid.

'Long Green Trailing Marrow' (syn. 'Long Green Striped') Dark green mottled with pale green and deep yellow. A trailing variety, fruiting in 68 days in North America. The ripe fruits can be stored for use in winter (not shown).

'Minipak' A bush marrow, with small green striped fruits to about 30 cm long, freely produced.

'Supremo' An F1 hybrid.

'Table Dainty' Introduced by Suttons in 1909. Plant trailing. Fruits rather small, best at 15–20 cm long. Flesh white.

'Tender and True' A vegetable marrow, raised by Suttons in 1907. Plant semi-trailing, early maturing; fruit round, 12–15 cm long, and slightly larger in diameter, dark green with some cream blotches and dark green ribs with cream mottling.

'Tiger Cross' An F1 hybrid. Fruit around 28 cm long, 10 cm diameter. Dark green mottled cream. Resistant to cucumber mosaic virus. A bush variety for use either as a marrow or as a courgette when young.

'White Lebanese' An old variety with very pale green fruit, ready in 45–55 days in North America. This variety is widely grown in Europe, the Middle East and Mexico. A modern F1 hybrid called 'Cousa' is similar.

'Burpee Golden' zucchini

Round marrow, 'Tender and True' from Suttons

'Pattipan'

'Little Gem'

'Yellow Bush Scallop'

'Uchiki Kuri'

'Jackpot'

'Banana Squash'

'Golden Hubbard'

Specimens from C.R. Upton, Slindon, Sussex, photographed 15 September

'Green Hubbard' and marrow

'Golden Hubbard' at Harry Hay's

'Pattipan'

'Banana Pink'

'Banana Pink' (*maxima*) Banana squashes originated in Mexico and reached North America in the 1890s. The yellow and pink was separated from the blue, green or grey by H. L. Musser in California. Fruits generally 50 cm long, weighing up to 25 kg.

'Banana Squash' (syn. 'Mexican Banana', 'Plymouth Rock') (*maxima*) This is a spindle-shaped variety of Banana Squash with orange-yellow flesh.

'Little Gem' (*pepo*) These small round squashes are very popular in South Africa, boiled whole and eaten with butter. The plants are slow to mature, in 90–120 days in a warm climate. There is also a miniature 'Golden Hubbard' named 'Little Gem' in N. America.

'Golden Hubbard' (*maxima*) raised by J. J. Harrison of Painsville, Ohio, in around 1895. Fruit matures in around 110 days.

'Green Hubbard' (syn. 'Hubbard') (*maxima*) Introduced to North America in c. 1798 and named by James J. H. Gregory of Marblehead, Mass., in honour of Mrs Elizabeth Hubbard who brought it to his notice. The name 'Green Hubbard' is also used for a pale green variety.

'Jackpot' (*maxima*) A hybrid, with mottled fruit weighing 5–7 kg, ripening to orange, maturing in about 100 days. Flesh orange-yellow. Plants heavy yielding on compact vines.

'Pattipan' (syn. 'White Bush Scallop') (*pepo*) Long grown by the American Indians and noted by the early European immigrants. Formerly called symnels from their cake-like shape. Introduced to Europe in the sixteenth century. Very quick to mature, in around 54 days in North America. Best eaten young.

'Uchiki Kuri' (syn. 'Orange Hokkaido', 'Red Kuri', 'Baby Red Hubbard') (*maxima*) A small Hubbard variety, raised in Japan. A small green variety raised in America in c. 1914, was called 'Kitchenette'. Fruit 2–4.5 kg, with smooth-textured flesh of good flavour, maturing in about 92 days in North America.

'Yellow Bush Scallop' (*pepo*) An old variety, cultivated since 1856. Flesh coarse, pale yellow.

'Turk's Turban'

'Sweet Mamma'

'Buttercup'

'Crown Prince'

'Triamble'

'Butterball'

Specimens C.R. Upton, Slindon, Sussex, photographed 15 September

PUMPKIN AND SQUASH

'Table King'

'Ebony Acorn'

'Golden Acorn'

'Peter Pan'

'Kumikuri'

'Scallopini'

Specimens C.R. Upton, Slindon, Sussex, photographed 15 September

'Butterball' (*maxima*) Raised and introduced by the Agricultural Experiment Station at Durham, New Hampshire, in 1960. Early maturing in around 90 days and adaptable. Flesh medium-orange, thick, dry and sweet.

'Buttercup' (*maxima*) Buttercup was developed for North Dakota and the northern plains. Raised from the variety 'Quality' in 1925, probably crossed with 'Essex Hybrid'. Introduced in 1931. Fruit small, 15–20 cm in diameter, with well-flavoured dry and sweet orange flesh. Matures in 105 days in North America, where it is very popular.

'Crown Prince' (*maxima*) A rather small-fruited variety with a pale greyish skin. Grown by C. R. Upton, Slindon, Sussex. Very fine-grained orange flesh. A very good keeper and eater. Around 5 kg weight. (See also p. 187)

'Ebony Acorn' (syn. 'Table Queen') (*pepo*) An old variety, probably originating from the Arikara tribe in North Dakota. Flesh orange–yellow, quite sweet.

'Golden Acorn' (*pepo*) Derived from Ebony Acorn introduced by the Iowa Seed Co. of Des Moines, Iowa, in 1913. Also known with pale green fruit. Plant trailing. Fruit small, to 15 cm long. Good for keeping.

'Kumikuri' A Japanese pumpkin received from C. R. Upton of Sindon, Sussex. Fruit ripening orange, with rounded ribs.

'Peter Pan' (*pepo*) A semi-bush, hybrid variety with fruit about 10 cm across, maturing in around 52 days in North America.

'Scallopini' (*pepo*) A cross between scallop and zucchini, maturing in about 50 days.

'Sweet Mamma' A hybrid variety with dark, grey-green fruit, maturing in about 85 days. Plants short-trailing. A good keeper.

'Table King' (*pepo*) A bush acorn variety: fruits with thick, golden flesh, maturing in around 75 days in North America.

'Triamble' (*maxima*) An unusual three-cornered pumpkin, with thick skin and sweet, firm orange flesh. A very good keeper. Grown by C. R. Upton, Slindon, Sussex.

'Turk's Turban' (syn. 'French Turban', 'Turk's Cap') (*pepo*) Cultivated in Europe since 1818, firstly in France. This is mainly grown for decoration, but can be cooked and stuffed like a marrow.

'Scallopini'

'Turk's Turban'

'White Cheesequake'

'Queensland Blue'

'Crown Prince'

'Kentucky Field'

'Etamples'

'Gold Nugget'

Specimens C.R. Upton, Slindon, Sussex, photographed 15 September

Pumpkin, 'Etamples' at Villandry

'Crown Prince' (*maxima*) A rather small-fruited variety with a pale greyish skin.

'Etamples' (syn. 'Rouge vif. d'Etampes') (*maxima*) An old French variety, since before 1830. Fruit about 9 kg flattened, reddish-orange with knobbly skin. Plant long-trailing. See page 178.

'Gold Nugget' A bush variety. Fruits 12 cm diameter, 10 cm deep, orange-red, with slightly mottled orange ribs. Weight ½–1½ kg. Raised in 1966 by North Dakota Agricultural Experiment Station, Fargo. Fruit maturing in

85–95 days, a good keeper with deep orange flesh of good flavour, without fibre.

'Kentucky Field' (syn. 'Large Cheese') (*moschata*) Fruit flattened, with pale skin. A good keeper, maturing in around 110 days.

'Queensland Blue' (*maxima*) An Australian variety, introduced to the USA in 1932. Slow to mature. Vines very vigorous to 8 m. Fruits 3–5 kg, c. 22 cm in diameter, bluish-green with orange flesh and good flavour.

'White Cheesequake' An old variety, dating from c. 1824. Flesh orange.

'Etamples'

'Golden Delicious'

'Orangetti'

'Little Boo'

'Triple Treat'

'Rebecca'

'Warted Hubbard'

'Melon Squash'

Specimens from Wisley, photographed 19 October

PUMPKIN AND SQUASH

'Orangetti' on a wayside stall

Two cracked-skin squashes

'Golden Delicious (*maxima*) Selected from hybrids between 'Boston Marrow' and 'Delicious'.   Raised by Gill Bros. Seed Co. of Portland, Oregon, in 1922. Fruit 3.5–4 kg with thick, starchy orange flesh, moderately sweet. Good for baking and a good keeper.

'Little Boo' (*pepo*)   A white-skinned winter squash.

'Melon Squash'   This looks like a variety of *C. pepo*. 'Tahitian Melon Squash' is a *C. moschata* cultivar, which needs a long warm summer to ripen.

'Orangetti' (*pepo*)   An F1 hybrid, vegetable spaghetti, with deep orange skin and orange

flesh. Plant with semi-bush habit. Eat when ripe. Fruit matures in around 85 days.

'Rebecca' (*pepo*)   Quick-maturing, with fruit c. 12 cm across.

'Triple Treat'   A variety with hull-less, edible seeds which can be eaten raw or roasted. Fruit around 25 cm long. This is said to belong to the species *Cucurbita moschata*.

'Warted Hubbard' (*maxima*) (syn. 'Chicago Warted Hubbard')   Developed by Budlong Gardens of Chicago from 'Hubbard Squash', and introduced in 1894. Flesh darker orange than 'Hubbard', orange-yellow, with good keeping qualities. Weight around 5–6 kg.

'Early Butternut'

'Zenith'

'Ponca'

'Sweet Dumpling'

'Delicata'

'Waltham Butternut'

Specimens from Wisley, photographed 19 October

Winter squash, 'Sweet Dumpling' with young fruit

'Delicata' (syn. 'Sweet Potato')   Introduced in 1894 by Peter Henderson & Co. of New York. Fruits small oblong, about 20 cm long, 7.5 cm in diameter. Flesh deep orange-yellow, sweet, of good flavour, and keeps well. Plant strongly climbing, with fruit maturing in around 100 days. A form of *C. pepo*. See page 177.

'Early Butternut' (*moschata*)   A bush variety, quick maturing in around 75 days, with rich orange flesh and good keeping qualities.

'Ponca' (*moschata*)   A Butternut type with a small cavity, and fruits around 30 cm long. Good in cool seasons. Vines compact. Maturing in 85–110 days in North America.

'Sweet Dumpling' (*maxima*)   A small flattened fruit about 10 cm in diameter. Plants climbing. Fruits very sweet, with tender orange flesh, maturing in around 100 days.

'Waltham Butternut' (*moschata*)   Raised by Dr C. E. Young at the Waltham Experimental Station in Massachusetts. Fruits 20–25 cm long with a swollen apex maturing in around 95 days. A good keeper.

'Zenith' (*moschata*)   A hybrid Butternut with thick-necked fruits with a small cavity, maturing in around 88 days. Fruits weigh around 1 kg.

'Sweet Dumpling'

Flowers and young fruit: 'Sweet Dumpling'

Gourd from Ceylon

'Crystal Apple' cucumber
(text p. 196)

Fig-leaved gourd
(text p. 176)

Bottle gourd

Bottle gourd (elongated fruit)

Specimens from Wisley, 10 October

Cucurbita ficifolia in Mexico (text p. 176)

Chayote

Sechium edule (Jacq.) Swartz (*Cucurbitaceae*)
Choko, Christophine, Shu-shu; Chinchayote, Camochayote, Ichintla (the root)

This vigorous climbing gourd originated in southern Mexico and central America, where it was long cultivated by the Aztecs. The name chayote is derived from the Aztec word chayotl. After the Spanish conquest this vegetable became widely grown all over the tropics.

Sechium edule is one of six species of tuberous-rooted perennials. It is known only as a cultivated plant, though primitive varieties may be found naturalized in the wild, and its closest wild relative is *Sechium compositum* from Mexico and Guatemala. The shoots climb vigorously, growing to over 15 m in one season. The leaves are 12–15 cm across, rough in texture, angled or shallowly lobed. The male and female flowers are separate, greenish-white, the small, greenish male flowers in an axillary raceme, the similar female solitary in the same leaf axil. The fruit is variable in shape, commonly pear-shaped, either smooth or covered in soft spines, pale green or nearly white, 6–16 cm long. It contains a single large, flat seed, 4–5 cm long.

The fruit is baked or boiled or, in Chinese dishes, sliced and stir-fried; the tuber may be boiled and then candied or sliced and fried. The succulent young shoots may be cut and eaten like asparagus.

The plant is easily cultivated in warm climates. The whole fruit may be planted, laid on its side, the narrow end protruding a little. The plant will grow very fast in warm, fertile soil. Flowering takes place only with a daylength of a little more than twelve hours. Soil should be sandy and well drained, but rich and fertile, and with ample water in the growing season. The plantation shown here was in very loose soil in a hot area on the north shore of Lake Chapala in central Mexico. In fully tropical areas the plant grows best in the hills.

Bottle Gourd

Lagenaria siceraria (Mol.) Standl. syn. *L. vulgaris* Ser., *L. leucantha* Rusby (*Cucurbitaceae*).
White-flowered Gourd

Although they are originally native to Africa south of the Sahara desert, there is evidence of the cultivation of bottle gourds in South America around 7000 BC. Remains of the hard shells of this plant have been found in Mexico, dating from before 500 BC. As South America is only 1900 miles from Africa at its nearest point, it is possible that the gourds may have floated from one continent to the other. Experiments have shown that gourds floating in seawater will survive for more than 220 days with no loss of seed viability.

Gourds of this species were used by the ancient Egyptians between 3000 and 4000 BC, and numerous fruit shapes have evolved, some of which are 2 m long. Only the immature fruits are edible; they have a powerfully bitter taste, and are best eaten in curries. The gourds are principally grown for their dried shells,

Chayote growing near Lake Chapala, Mexico

Chayote fruit

which have been and still are used in a variety of ways: water bottles, ladles, cups, musical instruments, fish net floats and rafts.

The plants are annuals with ribbed stems climbing to 10 m or more. The tendrils have one long and one short branch. The leaves are cordate, with acute apices. The flowers are solitary in the leaf axils, large, white, fragrant and open in the evening. They are either male or female; the male have very long flower stalks, to 25 cm long on opening; the female flowers are as large, their ovary clothed in glandular hairs.

Snake Gourd

Trichosanthes cucumerina L. syn. *T. anguina* L., *T. colubrina* Jacq. fil.
Serpent Gourd, Chicinda (not illustrated).

The curious cucumber-like fruits of this gourd may grow to 2 m long. They are green, streaked lengthways with white when young, curling and twisting as they grow, and turning bright red when ripe. It is common practice to tie a small rock to the base of the fruits to keep them straight.

The plant is an annual, native to tropical Asia. The fruit is eaten cooked, but only when young. If peeled, then sliced and boiled, it has a strong flavour and is more nutritious than many cucurbits. The flowers are large and white, and the petals are finely cut into a netted fringe; at night they are sweetly and powerfully fragrant.

It will grow outdoors in the warmer parts of the United States and southern Europe, but in cool climates such as Britain needs to be grown in a greenhouse.

Flower of Bottle gourd

'Long Green Ridge' (text p. 196)

'Kyoto' (text p. 196)

Cucumbers

Both cucumbers and melons are members of the genus *Cucumis* L., which consists of about twenty-five species of trailing or climbing annuals, native to Africa and Asia. In addition to cucumbers and melons, two other members of the genus are commonly cultivated: The West Indian gherkin or bur cucumber, *Cucumis anguria* L., was probably derived from the African *Cucumis longipes* Hook. fil. It is extensively grown in the West Indies as a vegetable, and the almost spherical fruits are used for pickles. It is also cultivated in Texas and Florida. The African horned cucumber, *Cucumis metuliferus* E. H. Meyer ex Schrad., is an annual with rough hairy stems. The fruits are oblong with thick spines, reddish when ripe.

Cucumber

Cucumis sativus L. (*Cucurbitaceae*)
Gherkin

The cucumber was probably cultivated in India around 3000 years ago. It appears to have been unknown to the ancient Egyptians, though grown by the Greeks and spread to the west in early Classical times. Its original wild home is believed to be in the mountains of northern India, where there is a very similar wild species, *Cucumis hardwickii* Royle, which is fully interfertile with the cultivated cucumber. It has small bitter fruit with stiff spines. Nearly all other species of *Cucumis*, including the melon, *Cucumis melo*, are native to Africa.

In India two forms are grown. One is a green-fruited form whose fruits reach 45 cm long, with white stripes running longitudinally. The second form is shorter and near white, becoming rusty-red at maturity. Another distinct form is called 'Crystal Apple', an oval slightly bristly variety with fruit white when ripe. It was introduced in 1933 by the seedsmen Arthur Yates & Co. of Sydney.

Most varieties grown in Europe and North America have green skins, and some of the hardier varieties still have warts or soft spines. Male and female flowers are distinct, though produced on the same plant, but some modern varieties have fruit which develop parthenocarpically, i.e. without fertilization.

Cucumbers are usually eaten raw as salad vegetables or made into pickles, but they are excellent lightly cooked, and in the eastern Mediterranean are often mixed with yoghurt. They are largely made up of water, and contain very little nutrition.

Cultivation

The highest yields of fruit in temperate climates are produced from plants grown under glass. Seed should be sown in November or December, and the young plants put in a raised bed or growbag in January or early February. A minimum temperature of 15°C is needed for satisfactory growth, and so in unheated greenhouses planting should be left until April or May. The climbing shoots should be trained on vertical wires, and the apical shoot pinched out to encourage side shoots. The female flowers are usually solitary in the leaf axils; the male flowers in clusters. Cucumbers require a very rich soil, with plenty of well-rotted manure and compost; the plants also need plenty of water, and should never dry out.

Ridge cucumbers are hardier kinds, usually grown outside, planted on ridges. The shoots can be left to trail on the ground, or trained on horizontal wires. Many of the ridge varieties have only short stems, with crowded leaves. When picked very small, cucumbers are called gherkins, a word derived ultimately from the Greek for water melon.

In both greenhouse and ridge varieties it is important that the fruits are picked as soon as they are of edible size, so that further flowers and fruits are produced.

'Crystal Apple' (text p. 196)

'Bush Crop' (text p. 196)

'Telegraph Improved' and 'Kyoto' in the greenhouse (text p. 196)

'Long Green Ridge' (text p. 196)

A trailing outdoor

CUCUMBER

'Diana'

'Chinese Long Green'

'Athene' An F1 hybrid. An all female, greenhouse type, with large, dark green fruit.

'Beit Alpha Ellam' An outdoor, gherkin type; fruits around 12.5 cm long, 5 cm in diameter, suitable for outdoor culture in NE U.S.A.

'Burpless Tasty Green' An F1 hybrid. An indoor or outdoor type; not bitter. Best used at around 25 cm long.

'Bush Crop' A short-growing, ridge or outdoor type, with slightly prickly fruit. The internodes are reduced in length, giving extra heavy crops. Very good for growing in pots or growbags in a confined space. (Shown on p. 195.)

'Chinese Long Green' A hardy, outdoor type, with long fruit to 50 cm long. The plant is a robust climber.

'Conda' An F1 hybrid. Listed by Unwins. A small variety, used for pickling. (Not shown.)

'Crystal Apple' (syn. 'Lemon Cucumber') Fruits whitish, almost round, turning yellow when ripe, and edible even at that stage. (Shown on p. 195.)

'Diana' A greenhouse type; plants all female; fruits about 34 cm long. An F1 hybrid.

'Kyoto' Suitable for outdoors or in the greenhouse. A strongly climbing variety, with narrow fruit to 60 cm long. (Shown on pp. 194–195.)

'Long Green Ridge' (syn. 'Long Prickly') Fruits dark green, slightly prickly. A heavy cropper. (Shown on pp. 194–195.)

'Surprise' A smooth-skinned cucumber, suitable for growing outdoors in S. Britain. Photographed at Wisley.

'Telegraph Improved' Suitable both for greenhouse and outdoors in a sheltered place. The fruits are long and slender, dark green and not bitter if the male flowers are removed to prevent pollination. (Shown on p. 195.)

'Beit Alpha Ellam', photographed by Leslie Land in Maine

gherkin 195

Greenhouse cucumber, 'Athene', growing outdoors

'Surprise'

'Telegraph Improved'

'Kyoto'   'Burpless Tasty Green'

'Bush Champion'

Specimens from Sellindge, Kent, 1 August

Cyclanthera brachystachya

Bitter Cucumber

Momordica charantia L. (*Cucurbitaceae*)
Bitter Gourd, Karella, Balsam Pear

This vigorous climbing gourd has long been cultivated in Asia for
its curious fruits. They are commonly eaten throughout Asia when
very young, but are extremely bitter and do not appeal to Western
palates. In India and Ceylon they are popular when added to
curries. They have, in addition, some medicinal value as they
contain a substance similar in effect to insulin. The young shoots
are also eaten especially, according to Dr Herklots, in the
Philippines.

The fruits are very colourful when ripe – bright orange-yellow –
and when the valves open the crimson-red seeds are exposed. The
genus *Momordica* contains about forty-five species, native to Asia
and Africa. *M. charantia* is a native of tropical Asia, where it has
been cultivated for many centuries. It has been known in Europe
at least since the late seventeenth century, when it was illustrated
by Rheede tot Draakstein, the Dutch governor of the Malabar
coast, in his *Hortus Indicus Malabaricus*, a treatise on garden plants
from what is now Kerala.

The plant is a slender annual, climbing to 3–4 m, with simple
tendrils arising from the leaf axils. The leaves are long-stalked,
cordate, with five to nine deep, rounded lobes. Male and female
flowers are separate, long-stalked, yellow, with five nearly
separate petals, and are vanilla scented in the morning. The fruits
are pendant, and vary in length from 10 to 25 cm, according to
variety. The long variety is preferred by the Chinese; the short by
Indians. The seeds are brown or white, covered in a scarlet aril.
The pulp is sweet when ripe.

Two related species are also cultivated. *Momordica
cochinchinensis* (Lour.) Spreng., the spiny bitter cucumber, has
three or five-lobed leaves and straw-yellow male flowers, the inner
three petals with a blackish-purple spot at the base. The fruits are
ovate, about 12 cm long, covered with small conical spines. They
are orange or red when ripe, but are usually eaten green.

The bitter apple, *Momordica balsamina* L., is closely related to
M. charantia, and is a native of eastern Asia. The flowers are
smaller, the fruit is ellipsoid, with the surface covered in
protuberances or almost smooth, splitting into three when ripe.

Cultivation

The bitter cucumber and its relatives are easily cultivated. The
seed should be sown under glass in spring and the seedlings
planted out after danger of frost is past, in well-manured soil. In
cool climates the plants need a greenhouse culture similar to that
of cucumbers; in hot climates the seed may be sown directly where
the plant is to grow.

Korila

Cyclanthera pedata (L.) Schrad. (*Cucurbitaceae*)
Caygua (Haiti), Achoccha (Peru)

This climbing gourd is native to central and South America, and is
also reported by Dr Herklots to be cultivated in Taiwan and
Nepal. The plant sprawls or climbs to about 3 m, by branched
tendrils. The leaves are like those of a Japanese maple, deeply cut
into five lobes, with the basal lobes each divided into three again.
The flowers are small and greenish-yellow, the male in racemes,
the female solitary. The fruits are ovoid, pale green and flattened,
and hollow for much of their length. They may be smooth or
covered in soft spines, and open explosively, ejecting the black
seeds, which are 10 mm long and rectangular with a projection at
one end. The thick flesh of the fruit is eaten raw or cooked and
tastes like cucumber.

Wax gourd

Bitter cucumber in Malawi

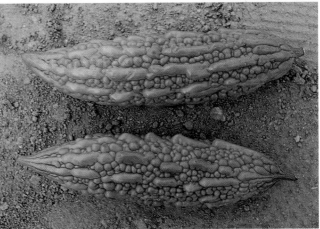

Bitter cucumber

Cyclanthera brachystachya (Ser.) Cogn. is similar with five-lobed leaves and curved, softly spiny fruit which explodes when ripe. Both species require a long, cool, wet summer to grow and then fruit in autumn and winter.

Wax Gourd

Benincasa hispida (Thunb.) Cogn. (*Cucurbitaceae*)
Ash Pumpkin, Chinese Preserving Melon, Tung Kwa, Mo Kwa, Cham Kwa, Chinese Fuzzy Gourd

This large gourd is a native of Java, and possibly also Japan, but has been cultivated in China for several millennia. Now it is widely grown throughout eastern Asia, and may be found on sale in Chinese shops in Soho. The fruit are cylindrical, 90–150 cm long, and can weigh up to 14 kg (30 lb). The leaves are shallowly lobed, the male flowers are 10–15 cm across, yellow, with almost separate petals, on a long stalk; the female are on a short stalk, and smaller. The plant is an annual and a very robust climber when given support; otherwise it can be grown trailing on the ground, like a pumpkin.

Dr Herklots mentions four varieties; in two, called fa kwa, the fruits are covered with fine white silky hairs when young and are waxy white when mature. They are eaten fresh. In another, called mo kwa or tsit kwa, the fruits are slightly waisted, hairy when

Spiny bitter cucumber in Kashmir

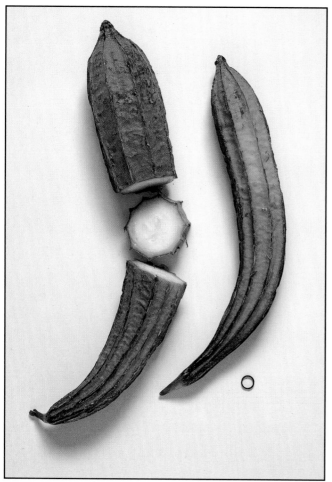

Young angled loofahs

Smooth loofah

young but not waxy, and eaten when young, like a marrow. In the most important variety, called cham kwa because the fruit is shaped like a pillow, the huge fruits are also green when mature, and keep for up to a year. They are often used as part of a mixed, sweet pickle, or may be stuffed with meat and vegetables and steamed.

Cultivation

Seed of Wax Gourd is generally sown in the warm, wet season and requires very rich, well-manured ground and ample water. It also needs a very strong framework if it is to be grown as a climber. It is often, therefore, planted near water, with the framework of bamboos placed over the water to save valuable growing space. Fruit is ready in the tropics in about sixty days, in the warm states of North America in around eighty-five days.

Smooth Loofah

Luffa aegyptiaca Mill. (*Cucurbitaceae*)

It is this loofah which is used in the bath as a scraping sponge for the back, especially in Turkish baths in Turkey. It is probably native to India, but was named by Philip Miller, of the Chelsea Physic Garden, from plants grown in Egypt. The young fruit is edible, though not much valued, and does not have the ridges

characteristic of the angled loofah. The flowers are yellow, about 10 cm across.

Commercial loofahs are collected when ripe, the seeds shaken out and the fruit retted in water to remove the skin and the remains of pulp. The fibrous skeleton is then dried and often bleached in hydrogen peroxide. As well as for the bath, dried loofahs are used as filters to extract oil from water and as stuffing in saddles and cushions. The black seeds are rich in a colourless and tasteless but edible oil.

Angled Loofah

Luffa acutangula (L.) Roxb. (*Cucurbitaceae*)
Sze kwa

This is a fast-growing annual which is found wild in India, and is now cultivated in much of Asia for its fruit which are from 60–270 cm long, with about ten raised ridges from the narrow base to the slightly wider apex. The leaves are shallowly five-lobed, the flowers yellow, about 5 cm across.

The fruits are edible when young, but when mature are very bitter and purgative. They are normally sliced across and boiled, and are valued for their unusual cross-section and crisp texture. The seed should be sown early in the wet season, and the vines trained on a trellis. Both the angled and smooth loofah need greenhouse cultivation in England.

Smooth loofahs and pink aubergines on Dal Lake, Kashmir

Angled loofahs in Malawi

Lake gardens in Kashmir

Young plant of *Lactuca serriola*

Wild lettuce, Lactuca serriola in France

Lactuca virosa

Lettuces on Mull

Lettuce

Lactuca sativa L. (*Compositae*)

Lettuces in their various forms are the most important salad crops, easily available at any time of year since the development of varieties which can be grown under glass in winter. The heavy, crisp Iceberg lettuces are more popular in America, and were developed to survive transport from California to the markets in the east. Looser, softer cabbage lettuces are more popular in northern Europe. Cos lettuces, at their best in spring, are much grown in the eastern Mediterranean. In China the Celtuce, a variety with swollen crisp fleshy stalks, is widely grown for use sliced and stir-fried.

Lactuca serriola

Lactuca canadensis in Connecticut

Origin

All lettuces were developed from the wild species *Lactuca serriola* L. found wild in clearings in woods, rocky slopes and waste places from Asia and North Africa to northern Europe. It is a winter annual, germinating in autumn, and forming rosettes of leaves which become very conspicuous on roadsides when they begin to flower in late summer, the stems reaching 2 m in height. The leaves are often spiny and usually held in a vertical position; they are either obovate and entire, or deeply lobed. The small flowers are pale yellow, and the seeds greyish-green. *Lactuca virosa* L. is similar, but has leaves which are held flat, and blackish seeds. It has been used in the breeding of some varieties, such as 'Vanguard'. Another wild species, *Lactuca saligna*, is an altogether slenderer plant with narrow leaves.

Some closely related wild species are found in the mountains of Turkey, Iran and the south Caucasus, and other wild lettuces are native to woods and plains in North America, including *Lactuca canadensis*, sometimes called wild opium.

Lactuca indica L. is a perennial, a native of China and grown there and in Indonesia for its lanceolate stem leaves which are usually cooked, but may be eaten as a salad.

History

Lettuces were grown by the Romans, but are thought to have been cultivated first by the ancient Egyptians in around 4500 BC. Wall paintings in some Egyptian tombs are thought to represent a narrowly pointed form of Cos lettuce, though there are suggestions that the plant was first cultivated for the edible oil in its seeds, rather than as a salad. The wild species is horribly bitter even when young, and the selection of less bitter forms would have been one of the first actions of the early cultivators of the crop as a salad. Bitterness is associated with the production of latex, the milky juice still found in the cultivated varieties when they bolt.

Lettuce as a food plant was probably introduced to Britain by the Romans, who favoured the plant after it was said to have cured the Emperor Augustus. Their varieties needed blanching to make them less bitter. The earliest post-Roman mention in Britain is in Gerard's *Herball* in 1597. He mentions eight varieties. Seeds were taken to America by the early settlers. Lettuces with firm hearts are only known with certainty from the sixteenth century onwards. Modern breeding has concentrated on resistance to disease and bolting in the common types, and on more fancy leaf shapes and colours such as red and curled. As readers of Beatrix Potter will know, lettuces are soporific. This property has been recognized since ancient times, and is mentioned by Hippocrates, who was born in Cos in 456 BC. The bitter latex was often used as a substitute for opium or laudanum. Dr A. Duncan of Edinburgh studied the effects of lettuce juice, which he called 'lactucarium', and in 1809 published a paper entitled 'An account of a method of preparing a soporific medicine from the inspissated white juice of the common garden lettuce'.

Lettuces, rhubarb, chard and roses at Villandry

Cultivation

Lettuce requires a rich but well-drained soil, kept continually moist during the growing season. Premature drying out causes the lettuces to go to seed early, before they have developed their full size. The ideal soil is one in which manure or compost has been incorporated the previous autumn, but failing that the plants can be watered with a nitrogen-rich fertilizer.

Seed requires cool conditions to germinate, and may become dormant above 20°C. Early spring and autumn crops are best sown in boxes indoors and then planted out at a spacing suited to the variety, but late spring and summer crops are best sown in position and then thinned. This is probably because they produce deeper root systems and so are more tolerant of drought.

Pests and diseases

Apart from the usual danger of slugs and snails, lettuces are particularly attacked by aphids and by cutworms. The lettuce root aphid (*Pemphigus bursarius*) is the worst danger. The fat pale brown aphids crowd around the tap root and the plant grows poorly, goes yellowish and collapses in dry warm weather. The aphid is spread by ants, and often infects weeds such as sow thistles (*Sonchus* spp.), several ornamental daisies and perennial vegetables like globe artichokes. It is said to survive the winter on poplars, where it breeds in the young leaf stalks before flying to the lettuces and other hosts in July. The worst attacks therefore are in July, August and September.

Other aphids affect the leaves, and the main danger is that they can carry virus diseases. Modern breeding has produced varieties resistant to root aphid, and where root aphid has proved to be a problem, the varieties 'Avoncrisp' and 'Avondefiance', or the aphis-tolerant variety 'Debbie' can be grown. Some strains of the wild species *Lactuca virosa* have provided breeders with a useful source of resistance to these aphids.

Cutworms, which are the caterpillars of various moths, can also be a nuisance. They eat into the root of the lettuce at ground level, and before they have been detected, the plant collapses, and the caterpillar has moved on. They are best controlled by going out with a torch at night and searching around the base of the plants. The cutworms are brownish or greenish, fat and juicy-looking and about two centimetres long. A fierce watering in early June will also kill the young caterpillars, before they have been able to do any damage.

Leatherjackets, the larvae of the daddy-long-legs or cranefly, are also sometimes troublesome; they eat the roots but seldom kill the plants outright.

Various mildews may also infect lettuces. The worst is grey mould or *Botrytis* which affects plants outdoors in exceptionally wet and humid weather, and in winter lettuce grown under glass. Better air circulation and avoiding wetting the leaves of plants under glass will make this mould rare. Downy mildew, which affects the leaves, can also be a problem especially in the autumn; again 'Avoncrisp' and 'Avondefiance' and 'Debbie' show some resistance. Spraying with fungicide is not usually worthwhile.

'Bunyard's Matchless'   A very old variety of lettuce.
'Misticanza' (sometimes called Mesclun, or Saldist)   A mixture of salads which are sown thickly and eaten young, the leaves being cut and the plants encouraged to resprout. It may contain all or most of the following: lettuce, endive, chicory, dandelion, chervil, rocket, mustard and even Buck's Horn Plantain.

Ancient variety, 'Tom Thumb' (text p. 206)

Winter sun in the model vegetable garden at Wisley

'Little Gem' Cos (text p. 211)

Misticanza at Ryton

Lettuce root aphid

Ancient lettuce, 'Bunyard's Matchless', at Ryton

LETTUCE

'Crescendo'

'Capella'

'Pia'

Specimens from NIAB, Cambridge, 10 July

'Continuity'

'Capella'   A dark green butterhead.

'Cindy'   Raised by Nickerson-Zwaan BV. A large butterhead, with heads about 30 cm across, pale green, not bitter, held well above the soil. Plant maturing in around 57 days in North America.

'Clarion'   A disease-resistant butterhead, for summer use, between June and October. Leaves thick, of good dark green colour. Resistant to downy mildew.

'Continuity' (syn. 'Brune Continuité', 'Bronze Beauty', 'Crisp as Ice', 'Hartford Bronzehead')   A crisp butterhead, with a small tight sweet heart, good for growing in summer, as it is tolerant of heat. Leaves wavy, often reddish; seeds black. Maturing in 65–70 days in North America.

'Crescendo'   A butterhead from Yates.

'Cynthia'   A greenhouse variety, suitable for sowing in mid-October, planting out in mid-November and harvesting from February to early April. If basal moulds become troublesome, it is a help to plant out on ridges so that damp air cannot lie around the base of the plant.

'Dandie'   A greenhouse variety, suitable for growing in heated glass. Upright growth. Sow in August to November for harvest in November–April.

'Debbie'   Raised by Nickerson-Zwaan BV. 22.5 cm high 30 cm across. Compact head firm. A modern variety suitable for growing in unheated polytunnels or frames.

'Magnet'   A pale green butterhead, used for forcing.

'Merveille de Quatre Saisons' (syn. 'Besson Rouge', 'Red Besson')   An old variety listed by Vilmorin-Andrieux in 1880. Leaves dark reddish-brown, one of the darkest of the butterheads. Popular in France and South America.

'Pia'   A pale yellowish-green butterhead.

'Tom Thumb' (syn. 'Tennis Ball')   An old variety, introduced in around 1860. Plant matures in 65 days, with a white, crisp centre. Suitable for sowing in spring; slow to bolt in summer. See p. 205.

'Valdor'   A winter lettuce for cold greenhouse culture, with good resistance to botrytis. Also suitable for sowing outdoors in September for harvest in spring.

'Dandie'

'Cindy'

'Merveille de Quatre Saisons'

'Debbie'

'Magnet'

'Valdor'

'Clarion'

'Cynthia'

'Red Head'

'Red Salad Bowl'

'Sioux'

'Royal Red'

'Antina'

Specimens from NIAB, Cambridge, 10 July

'Red Salad Bowl'

'Red Cos' (text p. 211)   'Merveille de Quatre Saisons' (text p. 206)

'**Antina**'   A French variety; crisphead-type lettuce, plant 23 cm high, 29 cm across; head slightly soft. Leaves medium green with bluish and reddish edge. A good variety which is slow to bolt.

'**Red Head**'   Leaves crumpled and frilled, with a yellowish heart. Tolerant of heat, maturing in 50 days in North America.

'**Red Salad Bowl**' (syn. 'Stuuwelpeter Gelber Krauser')   A red-pigmented loose leaf lettuce, developed in 1988 from Oak Leaf.

'**Royal Red**'   Leaves with a savoyed edge.

'**Sioux**'   A red-tinged crisphead.

Red lettuces at Dry Gulch organic farm, California

'Pavane'

'Little Gem'

'Bubbles'

'Romance'

'Red Cos'

'Lobjoits Green' Cos

Specimens from NIAB, Cambridge, 28 September

'Bubbles' Raised by Dr P. R. Dawson of Tozers of Cobham, Surrey. Plant 18 cm high, 25 cm across, compact. Leaves medium green blistered, heads fairly firm like 'Little Gem' but with blistered leaves, and sweeter flavour. Suitable for early crops.

'Cosmic' A Cos lettuce from Tozers.

'Little Gem' (syn. 'Sucrine', 'Sugar Cos') A small, compact semi-cos, leaves crumpled. Plant 17 cm high, 20 cm across with a firm, sweet heart. An old variety illustrated by Vilmorin-Andrieux in 1880 under the name 'Romaine Leboeuf'. In North America this matures in around 70 days; in England, if sown under glass in early March, it matures in late May.

'Lobjoits Green' Cos Plant 32 cm high, 32 cm wide; upright or slightly spreading, medium green. Heart crisp and sweet, and tolerant of heat. Seeds white.

'Marvel' A cos with crumpled leaves at Wisley.

'Pavane' A little Gem type, Latin small semi-cos from Sluis en Groot.

'Red Cos' (syn. 'Rouge d'Hiver', 'Red Winter', 'Red Roman') An old cos or romaine lettuce with red leaves, tolerant of both heat and cold. Best grown quickly with ample water.

'Romance' Raised by Sluis & Groot. A large lettuce; plant around 30 cm high, 33 cm across, fairly compact; leaves medium green, surface blistered. Large, firm well-folded hearts, with a tendency to spiral. Plants mature in 75 days in North America.

'Winter Density' Raised by Messrs Tozer's of Cobham. Plant around 24 cm high, 26 cm across. Close to 'Little Gem'. A semi-cos type, but larger, darker and slower to mature. Heart with a rounded top and well-blanched centre. Seeds white. Resistant to cold, and slow to bolt.

'Winter Density' and 'Red Cos'

'Cosmic'

'Marvel'

'Winter Density'

'Wallop'

'Pablo'

'Pennlake'

'Crestana'

'Saladin'

'Malika'

Specimens from NIAB, Cambridge, photographed 28 September

'Crestana' A thick-leaved Batavian raised by BSL/SEG.

'Crispino' A small to medium crisphead, raised by Royal Sluis Ltd. Leaves frilled, best in mid-July to August.

'Ithaca Great Lakes' A modern iceberg-type lettuce, with glossy, slightly frilled leaves. Resistant to tip-burn. Slow to bolt.

'Malika' A crisphead producing dense, fast growing, small to medium-sized heads. Said to be tolerant of mosaic virus, for harvest in June and in autumn.

'Marmer' Raised by Bruinsma Selectiebedrijven BVA. Plant 17 cm high, 30 cm across. Compact. Leaves medium green, crumpled; heads firm. Suitable for greenhouse and cold-frame cultivation. Maturing in around 75 days.

'Pablo' raised by Royal Sluis Ltd. A reddish crisphead with outer leaves heavily pigmented.

'Pennlake' (Great Lakes × Imperial 847) A crisphead, raised by Nickerson-Zwaan. Plant fast growing, medium-sized, seeds white. Maturing in around 88 days.

'Premier Great Lakes' (crisphead) August 1987 (sown 11 June) 30 cm high, 47 cm across. Leaves blistered, head firm. Great Lakes types were introduced by Michigan Agricultural Experimental Station in 1941. 'Premier Great Lakes' is a quicker maturing variety 7–10 days earlier than the general type. Very resistant to heat and tip-burn.

'Saladin' A dark green, large crisphead; good shape and suitable with large hearts for Iceberg lettuce in late June to early October. Plants slow to develop but resistant to tip-burn.

'Wallop' Raised by Leslie Watts in New Zealand. An unusual variety. Cross between crisphead and cos; upright bunched centre leaves of good texture and flavour.

'Webb's Wonderful' (syn. 'New York') (crisphead) The original Webb's Wonderful is said to have been introduced by Clarence Webb to North America in 1890. It was a development of 'Batavia Chou de Naples', an old variety listed by Vilmorin in 1856. By further development in North America, The Imperial, Great Lakes and New York groups of varieties were developed. Today Webb's is used as a general term for a crisphead lettuce.

'Marmer'

'Crispino'

'Pablo' at NIAB, Cambridge

'Premier Great Lakes'

'Ithaca Great Lakes'

'Webb's Wonderful'

Mixed lettuces at Sellindge

'Carioka'   'Merveille de Quatre Saisons'

'Aida'

'Waldemann's Green'

'Goya'

'Green Ice'

Specimens from NIAB, Cambridge, 28 September

'El Toro'

'Green Ice'

'Goya'

'Aida'   A green Batavian with good heart.

'Blonde à Bord Rouge' (syn. 'Iceberg', 'Cool & Crisp', 'Brittle Ice', 'Batavia Blonde', 'Batavia à Bord Rouge')   A very old crisphead variety, mentioned by Vilmorin in 1771. Reddish on the leaf edge, especially in dry or cold weather, with some bitterness. Seeds white. The original of the 'Iceberg' introduced to America by Burpees in 1894.

'Carioka'   A red Batavian introduced by Clause (UK) Ltd.

'El Toro'   A new crisphead lettuce, with a good, sweet heart. It is both quick to mature, and stands well without bolting. It also appears to tolerate both wet and hot, dry conditions. Matures in around 75 days in North America.

Various lettuces at Joy Larkcom's

'Till'

'Frisée de Beauregard' (syn. 'Batavia de Beauregard', 'Reine des Glaces', 'Summerwunder')   An old variety illustrated by Vilmorin in 1883. Seeds black, leaves dark green, wavy and indented. Crisp, slow to bolt, so valuable for summer use.

'Goya'   A new Dutch variety, raised by Royal Sluis Ltd. A very red loose-leaf variety, semi-cos, with no heart.

'Green Ice'   A Batavian semi-cos leaf lettuce; leaves dark green, savoyed with crisped margins. Resistant to powdery mildew, with a good shelf life and a long season of cutting, from 45 days onwards in North America.

'Merveille de Quatre Saisons' (syn. 'Besson Rouge', 'Red Besson')   An old variety, listed by Vilmorin-Andrieux in 1880. Seeds black. Leaves dark reddish-brown, one of the darkest of the butterheads. Popular in France and South America.

'Till'   A variety like a tight-headed 'Oak Leaf'.

'Waldemann's Green' (syn. 'Walderman's Dark Green, Grand Rapids' MI)   An American variety, raised by Asgrow Seed Co. International. 'Salad Bowl' type with fairly firm-textured, green, slightly wrinkled leaves.

'Frisée de Beauregard'

'Blonde à Bord Rouge'

'Salad Bowl'

'Red Salad Bowl'

'Lollo Rosso'

'Royal Oak Leaf'

'Lollo Verde'

Specimens from NIAB, Cambridge, 28 September

'Salad Bowl' (centre) and 'Red Sails' (right) at Wisley

'Royal Oak Leaf'

'Lollo Rosso'

'Lollo Rosso' Leaf margins finely frilled and heavily tinged with red. Can be cut through the summer.

'Lollo Verde' (syn. 'Lollo Bionda') A pale green version of 'Lollo Rosso'. It is better to cut out only individual leaves, not the whole head.

'Oak Leaf' (syn. 'A coupé à feuille de Chêne,

Blonde à graine noire') First listed by Vilmorin in 1771 under the name 'Laitue épinard'; 3 main groups: pale green, brown, dark green. 'Salad Bowl' is a development of this type which bolts less readily, and 'Royal Oak Leaf' is a modern selection, with darker green leaves.

'Red Sails' A Batavian loose leaf with

crinkled, deep bronze-red leaves. Slow to bolt; a popular variety in North America. 45 days.

'Red Salad Bowl' A red-pigmented loose leaf, developed from 'Oak Leaf' in 1988. Plant slow to bolt, with a pale self-blanching centre.

'Salad Bowl' Similar to 'Oak Leaf' but much slower (c. 1 month) to bolt. Seeds black.

Trimmed stems of celtuce for sale in a village in Yunnan

Celtuce in the market in Chengdu

Two varieties of celtuce in a garden in Chengdu

Celtuce

Lactuca sativa var. *augustana* Irish ex Bremer, syn. var. asparagina Bailey
Asparagus Lettuce, Chinese Stem Lettuce, Woo Chu, Woh Sun.

Celtuce was developed in China, and introduced from there into Europe where it was listed by Vilmorin-Andrieux in 1885. It was probably introduced to France by missionary botanists who worked in China. Celtuce was introduced to the United States from western China in 1938, and seed sold by the Burpee Seed Company in 1942. White, wrinkled, cleft-leaved, purple-leaved and red-leaved, as well as rounded-leaved and pointed-leaved varieties are mentioned by Dr Herklots as being grown in northern China. Most of the seed offered in Europe and North America seems to belong to one variety, with soft, rounded leaves.

It is usually grown as a winter crop in warm climates, but will grow well in the same conditions as ordinary lettuce when planted in spring, or in late summer for harvesting in autumn. The plants are left in the ground until the swollen stem has reached about 30 cm long. They are then peeled and thinly sliced before being stir-fried. The hearts may also be eaten like small cos lettuces.

Narrow-leaved celtuce at Ryton

Endives with pots for blanching

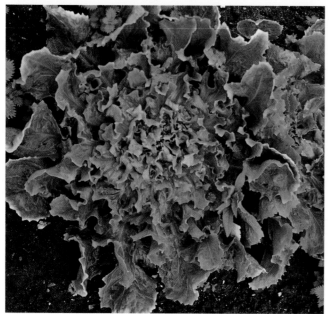

Batavian green endives

Chicory

Cichorium intybus L. (*Compositae*)

Endive

Cichorium endivia L.
Scarole

These two vegetables are closely related to one another; endive differs from chicory mainly in being annual rather than perennial. The leaves of chicory are often hairy, those of endive always hairless. Both have a long tradition as a salad plant, especially in the Mediterranean region, and many different forms are cultivated.

In French the names of chicory and endive are reversed; endive is the name for the forced shoots of *Cichorium intybus*, while chicorée frisée is the cut-leaved form of *C. endivia*, and Scarole the name for broad-leaved Batavian endive.

Cichorium belongs to the family *Compositae*, and within it the tribe *Lactuceae*, which includes also the vegetables lettuce, scorzonera, salsify and dandelion.

Both chicory and endive were grown as salads by the Greeks and the Romans, and are mentioned by Aristophanes (in *The Frogs*), as well as by Horace and Pliny, and there is evidence that endive was grown even earlier in ancient Egypt, whence it became the bitter herbs used at the Passover.

Perennial chicory is common as a native plant in Europe and western Asia, and is often naturalized in North America, where the beautiful blue flowers are a conspicuous feature of roadsides near New York. The origin of annual endive is uncertain. Some authorities suggest that it is a native of northern China, others that it originated in the eastern Mediterranean as a hybrid between chicory and the wild annual species *C. pumilum* Jacq., a native of Turkey and western Syria. A third theory is that it is a cultivated subspecies of *C. pumilum*, which is then named *C. endivia* subsp. *divaricatum* (Schousboe) P.D. Sell, subspecies *endivia* being the cultivated endive.

The roasted roots of chicory have been widely used as an adulterant of and a substitute for coffee. John Lindley, writing in the nineteenth century, records that the roasted chicory was itself adulterated with 'carrot, mangold-wurzel, oak-bark, tan, mahogany saw dust, baked horse liver and Venetian red'!

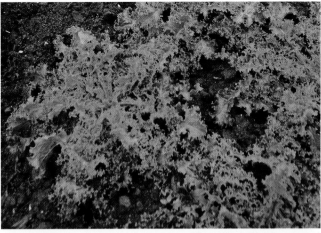

'Green Curled' endive (p. 223)

Cultivation

Chicories are grown in two distinct ways. Witloof chicory for forcing indoors in winter is a crop adapted to conditions in northern Europe and the northeastern United States. The object is to use a long cool growing season to produce a large root for forcing. Seed is sown, in late May or early June, in the open ground in deep soil which may be chalky or sandy. It is important to keep the plants well watered, so that none flower the first year, and well fertilized so that they build up a strong root system. The plants can be thinned to 15 cm apart. The plants are dug, a few at a time, from late autumn onwards and forced in the dark; they are ready in about three weeks if forced indoors. The roots should be trimmed to about 20 cm, and the tops cut off 2 cm above the root. Do not be tempted to leave more on top, as that only produces a more untidy chicon. The ideal root is one which is about 5 cm across at its thickest. The roots are forced by planting them in moist peat, usually in a large plastic pot, and keeping them warm and totally dark. Any light getting through to the leaves causes them to become bitter. The plants may also be blanched in the open by covering them, after the leaves have been trimmed, with about 20 cm of sand or peat. They should be picked before they reach the light.

The variety 'Barbe de Capucin', widely grown in the past in France, was nearest to the wild form. The small plants with lobed leaves were forced in bunches in a warm, dark place such as a cellar. The leaves were thin and delicate, eaten at about 25 cm.

Another variety, the Italian 'Radichetta', has wide stalks which are cooked like asparagus. This is available from several sources in America, but rare in Europe.

Sugar loaf chicories and endive are grown in a similar way to lettuce. They are generally sown either in early spring for an early summer crop, or after midsummer for an autumn crop. They take two to three months to mature. In cold climates the heads can be cut before the onset of hard frost, and stored in a cool place. Alternatively they can be left in the ground and protected from frost. They do, however, have a tendency to go rotten in wet weather, so they should not be kept in a closed frame. Sugar loaf chicories need no blanching, and the red-leaved radicchio varieties can be either cut directly from the garden or forced as described for witloof.

Endives often need blanching. The leaves can be tied up so that the hearts are kept dark, or the whole plant can be covered with a large plastic pot or clay pot as used for forcing seakale. Alternatively the plants can be lifted, brought under cover and blanched in a cold place. No heat is needed, and care should be taken that the plants are dry when covered, or they will be affected by a slimy brown rot. In mild and Mediterranean climates the plants can be sown in autumn and overwintered outside for harvesting in early spring.

Flowers of endive

Flowers of chicory, with mint

Spring leaves of 'Red Treviso' at Sellindge (text p. 225)

'Red Treviso' forced in the dark (text p. 225)

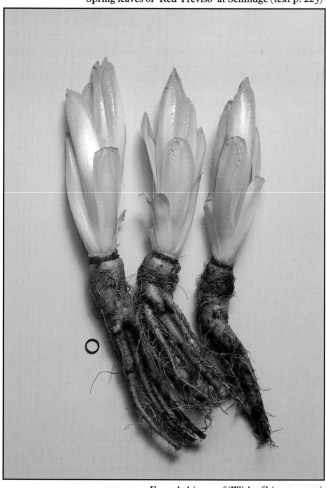

Forced chicons of 'Witloof' (text p. 225)

'Green Curled' (syn. 'Moss Curled', 'Chicoreé Frisée') A variety of endive. Leaves finely crisped and cut. The leaves are often tied or the plant covered with a dark pot to blanch the centre and make it less bitter. 'Pancalière' (syn. 'Riccia di Pancalieri') is a variety with particularly finely dissected leaves available from Clause, Bretigny-sur-Orge, France and from Suffolk Herbs.). 'Fine Maraichaire' is a dwarf, finely crisped variety, about 20 cm across, said to be rather tender.

'Sottomarina a palla precoce' A very decorative red and white speckled round-hearted radicchio, from the village of Sottomarina near Chioggia.

'Sugarloaf' (syn. 'Pan di Zucchero', 'Pain de Sucre') The hearts are somewhat self-blanching, plants large and cabbage-like, not, or only slightly, bitter. This is best sown in June or July and used in autumn or through the winter if protected by frames or cloches. 'Crystal Head' is a good selection of this type.

'Variegata di Castelfranco' Heads round, variegated in winter. From Chioggia on the southern corner of the Venetian lagoon.

'Variegata di Chioggia' Heads round, variegated in winter. From Chioggia on the southern corner of the Venetian lagoon.
   These decorative radicchios are beautifully displayed in the vegetable markets of Venice in early spring.

Chicory, 'Sugarloaf'

Endive, 'Green Curled'

'Variegata di Chioggia'

'Variegata di Castelfranco'

'Sottomarina a palla precoce'

'Snowflake'

'Coquette'

'Alouette'

'Red Verona'

'Red Treviso'

Specimens from Sellindge, 21 March

'Grumolo Verde'

'Alouette' at Wisley

'Alouette' A variety of radicchio, available from Thompson & Morgan, forming a good red heart, with white ribs, with good flavour, crisp and tender. Sow in mid-May for harvest in autumn and winter.

'Coquette' A variety of curled endive which stands very well through the winter from a later summer sowing.

'Grumolo Verde' Plant with a small, dark green rosette of leaves formed in winter; leaves more upright in summer. Summer leaves can be used singly and the rosettes will overwinter, and can be used in spring.

'Red Treviso' (syn. 'Rossa di Treviso') A red-leaved form of 'Witloof', which is pale pink when blanched, and produces a rather looser head. Dark purple leaves in winter.

'Red Verona' (syn. 'Rossa di Verona') A red-leaved radicchio with large, tight round hearts; leaves with rather narrow white midrib and veins. A hardy, tight-heading radicchio for winter salads or lightly cooked. Sometimes called also 'a palla', like a ball.

'Scarola Verde A Cuore Pieno' (syn. 'Full heart Italian Broadleaved') A large plant with slightly curled leaves, The hearts are normally blanched by tying the other leaves over them, or by covering with a pot. For use in early summer, or after overwintering from a September sowing, in spring. Very close to 'Batavian Green' syn. 'Batavian Broad-leaved'.

'Snowflake' (syn. 'Winter Fare') An easily grown variety of the Sugarloaf type with very thin leaves. Best planted in June and July and grown in rich, moist conditions for harvest in autumn and winter.

'Witloof' (syn. Belgian, 'Brussel Witloof') This is nearest to the wild form. The plants have rather upright, dark green lobed leaves, and are used as a winter vegetable when blanched, as described above under cultivation. A well-grown root is short and thick, and produces the fattest chicons. 'Crispa', 'Normato' and 'Witloof Zoom F1' are relatively recent varieties which produce compact white chicons without earthing up. (See page 222.)

'Red Verona', grown in warmth not forming a proper heart

'Scarola Verde A Cuore Pieno'

'Coquette'

'Green Globe'

Globe artichokes at Wisley

'Purple Roscoff'

At Villandry

Globe Artichoke

Cynara cardunculus L. (*Compositae*)

Globe artichokes are unusual amongst vegetables in that it is the immature flowers that are eaten. When very young nearly the whole flower is soft enough to eat. When older, only the fleshy bases of the bracts (strictly phyllaries), and the choke (the thickened receptable) are soft enough. The very young flower stalks and leaves are also edible.

The globe artichoke belongs to the same part of the family *Compositae* as the thistle, and the more primitive varieties have prickly phyllaries and slightly prickly leaves. The plant is a perennial; the flowers, when they are open, are like huge thistles, and make handsome dried flowers.

Globe artichokes are not known as wild plants, but are closely related to the cardoon (see p. 228), and to *Cynara syriaca* Boiss. from the eastern Mediterranean area, and probably developed from one or other of these. They were grown by the Greeks and the Romans who imported them from North Africa. In England it was always considered an aristocratic vegetable, and was grown at least from the sixteenth century when it was a favourite of Henry VIII, possibly because it was considered an aphrodisiac. Head gardeners took great pains to produce a continuous supply throughout the summer.

Modern varieties aim to produce a large succulent flower without spines on the phyllaries. Seed-raised plants are usually variably spiny, so it is worth buying offsets of a good form if they can be found. 'Green Globe Improved' is a seed selection with a reduced number of spiny seedlings. 'Violetta', a purple-budded Italian variety, has elongated heads, suitable for pickling when very young. 'Purple Roscoff' is a similar variety from Brittany, with purple-tinted phyllaries.

Young plants of artichokes lined out in a Scottish kitchen garden

Cultivation

Artichokes are easily grown in warm, light soils in northern Europe, but often die in winter in heavy soils and cold localities. In hot areas they will tolerate heavier soils and some midday shade. The great artichoke-growing areas of France (in Brittany, near Treguier, where it has been grown since 1508) and Italy (on the coastal plain near Brindisi) have light soils and a very mild winter climate. The plants grow best in a warm, sheltered bed, in rich well-drained soil. Young plants or cuttings made of side shoots are planted in spring, around 1 m apart and in a double row. They grow quickly, and should be given a dose of nitrogen-rich fertilizer when they are growing well. Some will have small flowers in their first autumn, but these should be picked young to encourage the plants to form side shoots. Established plants should be protected from hard frost by putting a good layer of dry straw round them and their root area. They should then be mulched with good soil and fertilizer in early spring. The old plants may need replacing after about three years, with young, more vigorous ones.

Pests and diseases

I have found lettuce root aphid a serious pest of artichokes, severely weakening the young plants. If this is found in the garden, and it also affects lettuces and sow-thistles, a careful watch must be kept on the tops of the artichoke roots, and any infected plants drenched with an aphicide. If the weather is exceptionally cold and wet, and the air stagnant, the flowers may rot, but otherwise they are usually pest- and disease-free.

Young cardoons ready for blanching

Cardoon

Cynara cardunculus L. (*Compositae*)
Other names: Cardon (French).

This is like a giant artichoke with smaller, prickly flower heads. It is grown for the fleshy leaf bases formed by the basal rosette of huge leaves, which are tied up and blanched. They can be eaten raw or cooked, like celery. The dried flowers can be used as a substitute for rennet, and in parts of France are used for La Caillebotte à la Chardonette, a soft curd cheese.

Cardoon is found wild in southern Europe from Crete and Sicily westwards to Spain and Portugal, and in North Africa. It grows in stony places and in dry grassy places on clay soils. The plants in cultivation reach at least 2 m in height, the leaves over 1 m long. A little cartoon in Mme Vilmorin's *The Vegetable Garden*, published in English in 1885, shows a rotund Frenchman needing a stepladder to put the final tie on the leaves of his cardons. A few cultivated varieties are available in America from specialist seedsmen, and in France and Italy. 'Italian Dwarf' is a small variety; 'Plein Blanc Énorme' presumably the opposite.

Cultivation

Cardoons are usually raised from seed, which is generally sold as an ornamental. The plant is certainly one of the handsomest for the back of a large border. Seed should be started indoors in sandy soil in early spring and planted out, at least 60 cm apart, when all danger of frost is past. Two or three seeds are best sown in each pot, and the strongest plant left to grow on. In dry areas the plants may be put in a shallow trench. The plants need full sun, and the same type of soil as artichokes, though they are tougher and easier to grow. They need ample water, and a thorough watering with liquid fertilizer every week. When the young leaves have reached a good size they should be tied together, making sure they are quite dry, and wrapped round with newspaper and black polythene. Blanching takes about two to three weeks.

Cabbage Thistle (*Cirsium oleraceum* (L.) Scop.) is a true thistle, which was formerly cultivated and the young shoots eaten. It is a native of most of Europe, as far north as Normandy and Belgium, growing in moist woods and wet meadows, and is very common in the foothills of the Alps. It is not native to the British Isles, but is naturalized in Ireland, presumably having been cultivated in the past. It is easily recognized by the almost spineless leaves and the heads of pale yellow flowers, surrounded by yellowish-green bract-like leaves.

Cardoons in flower

Cardoons blanched with brown card

Cabbage Thistle, flower head and leaves

Burdock leaves

Burdock flowering

Scorzonera, 'Black Giant Russian'

Salsify, 'Mammoth Sandwich Island'

Specimens from Wisley, 27 September

Dandelion

Taraxacum officinale L. (*Compositae*)
Pissenlit

In the British Isles the dandelion is familiar as a weed of lawns, and as a conspicuous feature of damp meadows and grassy roadsides. In France, however, it is a popular spring vegetable, and various cultivars have been selected, and are grown in gardens and blanched like endive to make them more tender and less bitter. They usually have broader leaves than the wild species and these blanched leaves can also be cooked and eaten like spinach. Young unblanched leaves are edible, but bitter, though they can be used to add flavour to a tasteless winter lettuce. There were also varieties with almost moss-like leaves, shown in Vilmorin's vegetable garden in the nineteenth century.

Wild dandelions are found almost throughout the world. Most have an unusual breeding system in which the seeds form without fertilization (apomixis). This, and their great variability have led to numerous microspecies evolving; over 1,200 have been named in Europe, mainly in the northwest. All come true from seed, so any selected plant is easily stabilized in cultivation. So far the dandelion has not been the subject of much breeding effort, but could no doubt be improved as have the closely related chicory and lettuce.

Scolymus hispanicus L., Tagarnina in Spanish, is a spiny-stemmed biennial or perennial, rather like a yellow-flowered thistle or chicory. It is now seldom cultivated, but was grown for its edible leaf stalks and midribs. The young leaves are in a rosette, deeply divided, with few spines. It is native of dry, stony places in southern Europe from Portugal to Turkey and southern Russia, flowering in late summer.

Burdock

Arctium lappa L. (*Compositae*)
Gobo (Japanese)

Burdock is a common wild plant of grassy places and open woods throughout Europe, but is seldom eaten, though it was used medicinally in the past. In Japan, however, it is a popular vegetable, and Dr Herklots records that it is also grown in Taiwan and Hawaii, especially by overseas Japanese. The plant is a biennial, making in the first year a rosette of large, rounded long-stalked leaves, with a tap root which may be 120 cm long, 2.5 cm in diameter, though usually about half that. In the second year the flowering stem grows up to 2 m or more tall, much branched, with numerous flowers. The young shoots and leaves are also edible.

In Japan the roots are often sold pickled with pieces about 15 cm long in a sweet brown sauce. The roots may also be eaten boiled until soft, or raw if very young. They need soaking for an hour or two before cooking to remove any bitterness which may be present.

It is surprising that burdock does not seem to be native of Japan, though it is now found wild in Hokkaido. It is a native of Europe eastwards to the Caucasus, and was introduced to Japan from China where it had long been used in medicine. The Japanese have selected cultivars with better roots and smaller leaves which take up less room. Several closely related species grow wild in Europe, and are naturalized in North America, but I am not certain which is the one usually cultivated in Japan. It does seem to be *Arctium lappa* with large, glabrous flower heads which is naturalized in Hokkaido. Other species are often taller, with smaller, cottony flower heads.

Scorzonera (centre); salsify (at sides)

A dandelion in the vegetable garden

Cultivation

Burdock seed should be sown in early spring or in autumn. As long a growing season as possible is necessary to get roots of a good size. The soil should be very deep, finely textured, and not recently manured so that the roots do not fork. The spring sowing may be made indoors, and the seedlings planted out when very young. The autumn sowing should be made no earlier than September, so that the plants are small (Joy Larkcom says with roots less than 3 mm in diameter) at the onset of winter. Any larger and the plants flower the following year. Small plants will grow all through the second year, and be a good size by autumn. The usual Japanese variety is called 'Takinogawa Long'.

Salsify

Tragopogon porrifolius L. (*Compositae*)
Oyster plant or vegetable oyster

Scorzonera

Scorzonera hispanica L. (*Compositae*)

Salsify and scorzonera are closely related both botanically and in the way they are grown and used. Both are members of the daisy family (*Compositae*), closely related to chicory, lettuce and dandelion. In both salsify and scorzonera the long soft tap roots are commonly eaten, but the young shoots and flower buds are also excellent, cooked like asparagus.

Salsify has a white root, narrow grassy leaves and purple flowers. It is biennial, and similar to yellow-flowered Goatsbeard or Jack-go-to-Bed-at-Noon, *Tragopogon pratensis* L., which is common on grassy roadsides throughout Europe and much of North America, and is also said to be edible in the same ways as salsify. True salsify is probably native only to the Mediterranean area, growing in dry grassy meadows, but has long been cultivated and is now naturalized in other areas of Europe and in much of North America.

Scorzonera has a black-skinned root, broader, lanceolate leaves and yellow flowers. It is perennial, so if the roots are rather small after their first year, they may be left in the ground and grown on for a second season. Scorzonera is native to southern Europe from Portugal to southern Russia and Siberia, growing in dry fields and open woods.

Salsify was probably first cultivated in Italy in the early sixteenth century and in England in the late seventeenth. It appears in the garden list of John Tradescant the Younger in 1656, but it is not clear whether he was growing it as a vegetable or as an ornamental. Tradescant also grew scorzonera, though that seems to have been introduced earlier, around 1560. Scorzonera was also grown in Spain at an early date, hence its Latin name. Neither has received much attention from breeders, and there are few named varieties in cultivation. 'Mammoth Sandwich Island' is the commonest variety of salsify, while 'Black Giant Russian' is the commonest scorzonera. Other varieties do not appear to be much improvement on these.

Cultivation

Both salsify and scorzonera are easy to grow, but slow to produce roots of a good size. Seed should be sown in early spring, and the plants thinned to 10 cm apart. The soil should be of fine texture and not recently manured, or the roots will tend to be forked. On heavy or stony soils it may be worth filling a narrow trench about 30 cm deep wth finely sieved sandy soil, so that the roots grow straight to begin with before forking. The roots should be ready for harvest from October onwards, and should be scrubbed gently to remove the earth, then boiled and skimmed as you would a hard-boiled egg, under the cold tap. The young flowering shoots appear the following spring, and can be left until the buds are showing. If the crop proves useless for roots, because so many of them are forked, then all the remaining plants can be kept for their shoots and buds.

Garland Chrysanthemum

Chrysanthemum coronarium L. (*Compositae*)
Thong Wo (Chinese, Cantonese), Chop Suey greens, shun giku.

This is a native of the Mediterranean region, growing in open places often in large quantity, with other annuals. It is commonly cultivated in both China and Japan, and the young shoots about 10 cm long are used as a vegetable, usually stir-fried, As far as I know, this species is not eaten in its native area, and how it came to be such a popular vegetable in the east is not recorded. Varieties are grown both with broad-lobed leaves and deeply dissected, narrower leaves (see page 45). Cultivation is as for any hardy annual, and successive sowings produce crops in as little as thirty days. It also has the advantage that it will grow through the winter, as it would do naturally in its native Mediterranean.

Flowers of chrysanthemum

A field of Jerusalem artichokes outside Vienna

Jerusalem Artichoke

Helianthus tuberosus L. (*Compositae*)
Topinambour

Jerusalem artichokes are grown for their fleshy, tuberous rhizomes, which are similar to knobbly potatoes. The name Jerusalem is often assumed to be a corruption of girasole, the Italian for sunflower, and these artichokes do belong to the same genus as the common sunflower *Helianthus annuus*, but Salaman pointed out that the name Jerusalem for the artichoke is earlier than girasole, and suggested that Jerusalem was a corruption of Terneuzen, the place in Holland from which artichokes were first introduced to England in 1617. The Jerusalem artichoke is a native of North America, from Ontario and Saskatoon, south to Georgia, Tennessee and Arkansas, growing in damp places on good soils. It is therefore completely frost hardy, unlike the potato, and can be left in the ground the whole year. The tubers contain the sugar inulin instead of the starches and sucrose sugars found in most tubers, so they are good for diabetics. The plants have tall, stiff stems which, in some varieties, produce small yellow sunflowers in late summer.

Jerusalem artichokes were cultivated by the American Indians before the sixteenth century, though they mostly relied on collecting tubers from wild plants. Early introductions to Europe had tubers larger than the wild types, so they were probably of already domesticated varieties or selections from the wild. Propagation from tubers is so easy that any selection is easy to keep in cultivation indefinitely. Modern cultivars have aimed to select a less knobbly tuber which is easier to peel. 'Fuseau', a French variety, is one of the best of the traditional ones. 'Dwarf Sunray' is a free-flowering, small variety with stems 150–210 cm.

The usual one has stems to 250–300 cm and never flowers. 'Golden Nugget' has carrot-like tubers. 'Stampede' is a quick-maturing, early-flowering variety with large tubers, available in America. There is also a red-skinned variety called 'Smooth Garnet'.

Cultivation

Jerusalem artichokes are easily grown, and in fact can become a nuisance if they are not dug regularly. Plant the tubers in spring in fine, sandy soil. Big ones can be cut up so that one or two eyes are left on each part. They grow equally well in heavy or lumpy soil, but are then even more knobbly and uneven. The tubers are ready for harvesting after frost has killed off the tops, or about a month after flowering has finished.

Yacon

Polymnia sonchifolia Griseb. syn. *P. edulis* Wedd. (*Compositae*)
(Not illustrated.)

The Yacon is a tall leafy plant with yellow daisy flowers. The leaf blades are hastate, with a winged petiole. It produces large, dahlia-like tubers, which can be eaten raw and taste like a sweetish water chestnut. Like Jerusalem artichokes, their sugar is inulin, not sucrose. Their flavour is said to improve after the tubers have been exposed to the sun (Herklots). Yacon is native of Peru, and was eaten by the Incas and is now being grown experimentally in New Zealand. Other species of *Polymnia*, e.g. the leafcup, *P. canadensis* L., are found in woods on limestone in North America, but they do not have tuberous roots.

'Fuseau'

Old garden variety

Jerusalem artichoke tubers

Old garden variety, non-flowering

Annual sunflowers at Sellindge

Jerusalem artichoke, early flowering form

A village near Mount Ararat in 1965

'Martha Washington'

'Connover's Colossal'

Asparagus

Asparagus officinalis L. (*Liliaceae-Asparagaceae*)

Asparagus is the most delicious of all vegetables, and one of the easiest to grow, provided that it is planted in full sun and well-drained soil.

Asparagus is a large genus with about 300 species found in Asia and Africa. Most are tough climbers, but their fleshy young stems are edible. *Asparagus acutifolius* L. is collected and eaten in Spain and Turkey. The closely related genus *Smilax* also has edible young stems, and great bunches of the hop-like curling shoots of *S. aspera* L. can be seen for sale in Greece and Turkey, collected from the maquis.

Asparagus officinalis L. is found wild all over Europe, northwest Africa and Asia east to Iran. Its native range is uncertain, since it has been cultivated at least since Greek times. It grows in sandy places, in dry meadows, on limestone cliffs and volcanic hillsides. We found great quantities of young shoots in May when camping on the lower slopes of Mount Ararat, and they made an excellent breakfast combined with scrambled eggs. The shoots were at most 1 cm in diameter.

In the British Isles wild asparagus is commonest in sandy places by the sea. It has probably escaped from cultivation in most of these sites, as the red fruits are eaten and dispersed by birds. There is, however, a native subspecies, subsp. *prostratus* (Dumort) Corb., found on cliff tops in the Lizard peninsula and in South Wales, on sand dunes in southeastern Ireland, and on the western coasts of Europe from Germany to Spain. It has more or less prostrate stems, rigid leaves (strictly cladodes) 5–10 mm long (10–25 mm in subsp. *officinalis*), larger male flowers with a reddish base, and smaller fruit usually with only two seeds; it is a tetraploid, whereas the wild plants of subsp. *officinalis* and most cultivars are diploid.

Asparagus is first mentioned as a vegetable by the Greeks, but it may not have been cultivated then, only collected from the wild. Pliny the elder, however, writing in about AD 77 mentions elaborate methods used by the Romans for the production of huge, blanched stems; the centre of its cultivation was then in the neighbourhood of Ravenna. Later it was widely grown near Venice where the richness of that city in the sixteenth century made it such a profitable crop that it displaced the growing of corn and flax.

Modern varieties do not vary much. Male and female flowers are on separate plants, and male plants are supposed to produce better stalks, called 'spears', as they do not use up energy making fruits. Nineteenth-century varieties included 'Connover's Colossal' which is still available, the 'Argenteuil' and 'Sutton's Giant'. Modern varieties include F1 hybrids, aiming to produce a uniform and vigorous crop from seed, polyploids, and early selections especially for use in southern California. Others varieties are particularly tolerant of disease and adverse conditions. The variety 'Giant Mammoth' in particular is said to tolerate heavy soil. 'Lucullus', 'Saxon' and 'Franklin' are all-male varieties.

Cultivation

Asparagus is easily cultivated if it is provided with the right soil conditions. A well-made bed will last in good condition for about twenty years. The plant is a perennial with a large crown; its fleshy roots spread out in all directions and do not penetrate deeply, but put out small feeding roots. The soil beneath the plants should be very well drained, so there is no chance that the fleshy roots will rot. There should be ample feeding in the surface layer above the

Asparagus beds at Sandling Park   'Lucullus'

plants to encourage the production of thick, succulent spears.

Asparagus seed is sown in early spring, either indoors or in a seed bed outdoors, and the young plants are grown on carefully for the first year. The soil should be very sandy and well drained, rich and with a fine tilth. It is also possible, though more expensive, to buy young plants. Seed should be soaked for two days before sowing.

On well-drained sandy soils the plants can be set out in a shallow trench, on a slight ridge, and good sandy soil mixed with bonfire earth – which we call 'denture'! – can be placed over them to a depth of 8 cm. March is the best time for planting.

On heavy, cold or wet soils it is worth making a raised bed. Cultivate the surface of the soil, and incorporate much old rubble, grit and bonfire soil. On top of this, and above the level of the surrounding soil, place a layer of very sandy, gritty soil; a load of sandy aggregate from a seaside quarry is ideal, as it probably contains a proportion of shell. This aggregate, mixed with leafmould, peat or fine compost and bonfire soil is the planting mixture; if acid sand is used, lime should be added. There should be about 15 cm of mixture below the young plants and 5 cm above to begin with; more should be added around the plants as they grow. A top dressing of fertilizer containing nitrogen and potash, but little phosphate, is recommended after planting. A mulch of sharp grit is helpful, as it retains water and discourages slugs. It may be necessary to edge the raised bed with bricks or stones to retain the soil.

The crowns should be planted at least 30–45 cm apart, in single rows, with the same distance between the rows. Two rows would fit in a bed 1–1.5 m wide; narrow beds such as this are easier to keep weeded, and easier to pick. The first cutting should be possible when the plants are three years old, but this should be for no more than six weeks. Established beds are generally cut for eight weeks, from May until mid-June. Then the stalks, called fern, are allowed to grow up. They may need support against wind when they get tall.

When the bed is established it should be top dressed with fertilizer in early spring, and it may also be mulched in winter with old manure. The crowns should, in any case, have a good (15 cm) layer of soil on them. Salt is traditionally applied in May to September, a good white sprinkling over the beds. Some recent research indicates that salt is not necessary, others say it increases yield. It probably discourages most weeds and the slugs which are the worst pest.

If this seems an awful lot of hard labour, bear in mind that you need only make a new bed every twenty years or so!

Pests and diseases

Apart from being eaten by slugs, which damage the young spears when they are still underground, the fern is often attacked by asparagus beetle; small black and yellow beetles can be caught on the fern; they drop if touched and can be caught on a piece of paper. The grubs are small, greyish, and look like bird's messes. They can be picked off or sprayed with an insecticide such as derris.

Late frosts can spoil the early crop, and set the growth back several weeks. A delicate polypropylene net, sold as horticultural fleece, can protect against c. 5°C of frost. Violet root rot can kill the plants, and any which show signs of this should be burnt and all the surrounding soil removed as the fungus survives for years in the soil.

'Saxon'

Arrowhead (*Sagittaria*)

Water chestnut (*Eleocharis*)

Specimens bought in London, December

Taro leaves

Lily bulbs

Lilium lancifolium Thunb., syn. *Lilium tigrinum* Ker-Gawl; *Lilium brownii* var. *australe* (Stapf) Stearn and *Lilium davidii* Duchartre (*Liliaceae*)
Paak hop (Chinese)

Lily bulbs are commonly eaten in both China and Japan, and are sometimes seen grown for this purpose, though they may also be collected from the wild. The two species usually eaten are the common tiger lily and the white-flowered trumpet lily, *Lilium brownii*, and in western China, *L. davidii*.

The tiger lily is an ancient cultivated species, possibly originally a hybrid between two species found in northern Japan and northeast China, *Lilium leichtlinii* and *L. maculatum*. The commonly cultivated clone is triploid and sterile, but produces numerous stem bulbils by which it can be propagated. It is also very tolerant of virus infection which kills or seriously weakens most lily species. Although it had been grown for food in China for over a thousand years, the first plants to be introduced to Europe were grown as ornamentals; it was brought to England from the Far Tee nursery in Canton by William Kerr in 1804. Nowadays it is commonly seen in gardens in Scotland where the cool summer climate is suitable for it.

Lilium brownii is common throughout southern China, either wild or as an escape from cultivation, and may be seen growing in Hong Kong along the path round the Peak. It has never grown well in cultivation in England, probably because it is a tender, subtropical species, and needs greenhouse treatment. It also produces numerous stem bulbils.

Both species grow best in a loose, well-drained compost. In heavy soils they are best grown in pots, and the best tiger lilies I have seen were planted in a large tub, standing in the shady, sheltered corner of two buildings. The bulbs are better kept dry in winter, either by raising them and storing them in peat or sand, or by covering the pot. Any fertile, well-drained soil is suitable, and the bulbs should be planted with at least 10 cm of loose soil above them, and good drainage below.

Mature bulbs are harvested in the autumn or winter, and eaten boiled or used as a thickening for soups. They are slightly sweet and E. H. Wilson reported that they are reminiscent of parsnips in flavour.

Giant Taro and related tubers

Alocasia macrorrhiza (L.) Schott (*Araceae*)
(Not illustrated.)

This species originated in Ceylon, and requires similar conditions to taro, but is larger with stiffer, more upright leaves; Giant Swamp Taro *Cyrtosperma chamissonis* (Schott) Merr. from Indonesia, which can tolerate brackish water, is an important food plant in some areas, especially on coral atolls, such as the Gilbert Islands. The tubers can take several years to grow, and reach a huge size.

Tannia or yautia, which cover several *Xanthosoma* species, are natives of South America and the Caribbean, but now grown in West Africa also, where they are called New Cocoyam. More recently their cultivation has spread to southeast Asia, and they are important crops in New Caledonia. The leaves of tannia are sharply pointed, sagittate at the base, in contrast to the more rounded peltate leaves of taro. Both leaves and side tubers are eaten, but the main tubers are usually left in the ground. Nut Eddoe is a name for one of these in the West Indies.

Another giant edible aroid is *Amorphophallus campanulatus* var. *hortensis* (see introduction p. 8) known as the elephant foot yam. It has a large rounded tuber which may weigh 10 kgs or more. This puts up a single huge, much-divided leaf, and at times a short but massive, smelly flower. I was given some pieces of a tuber to eat in the hills in south India and they were brownish-grey in colour and tasted like a coarse and nutty potato.

Lilies and garlic near Dali in Yunnan   Arrowhead at Dali

Taro

Colocasia esculenta (L.) Schott (*Araceae*)
Dasheen

This is a very important root vegetable throughout the wet
tropics, and small amounts are imported into temperate countries
for use by immigrants, to remind them of home. *Colocasia
esculenta* is a very ancient crop, and is not now known in the wild.
It has been estimated that it originated between 4000 and 7000
years ago, probably in wet parts of India which now grow rice.
Primitive man would soon have selected wild forms which lacked
the poisonous calcium oxalate, and were easy to propagate by
offsets. Ancient rice terraces may have been originally made for
taro cultivation, as it requires the same conditions as rice,
particularly submerged and very warm in summer, tolerant of
drought but not frost in winter. Taro tubers are similar to those of
a potato, but usually more slimy. Even the selected cultivated
forms contain some calcium oxalate crystals, so cooking must be
thorough enough to destroy them. The leaves can also be eaten,
and are commonly used in soups. In Hawaii, the young shoots are
sometimes blanched before boiling.

The plants are easily grown in very warm and wet conditions,
and their bold leaves look fine on the edge of a pool. Propagation is
by planting side tubers or preferably by cutting off the top of an
existing large tuber with its shoot, and planting that.

Arrowhead

Sagittaria sinensis Sims, syn. *S. trifolia* L. var. *edulis* (Sieb.) Ohwi
(*Alismataceae*)
Tzi Koo (Chinese)

Edible arrowhead is a Chinese species, cultivated in China and
Japan for its starchy corms which, like those of Water Chestnut
(*Eleocharis*), are produced in the mud on the ends of long stolons.
These enable the plants to survive the cool dry winter season, and
then grow very quickly when the monsoon comes in summer.

Arrowhead has arrowhead-shaped leaf blades and three-
petalled, white flowers. The European species *S. sagittifolia* L. is
not generally eaten, but the North American species *S. latifolia* L.
is called wapato or duck potato, and was eaten by the Indians. The
corms are planted in spring in rich, wet ground and grown in
about 15 cm deep water. They are harvested in the dry in autumn.
They should be peeled, cut up and cooked until tender. They are
generally eaten on Chinese New Year's Eve, sliced and fried with
meat and hoi sin sauce.

Water Chestnut

Eleocharis dulcis (Burmann fil.) Trin. ex. Henschel. syn. *Scirpus
tuberosus* Rox. (*Cyperaceae*)
Ma Tai (Chinese)

Water chestnut is commonly grown in southern China and in
southeast Asia, needing the same conditions as rice: good soil and
shallow water combined with high temperatures of 30–35°C are
needed for a good crop. The plant makes a tuft of smooth and
straight, cylindrical leaves, like those of our familiar wild
Eleocharis palustris, which are tubular and about 60 cm tall. The
rhizome sends out numerous runners ending in dark brown corms
about 4 cm across, which are edible either raw or cooked. They
are nutty, sweet and crunchy. The corms are planted in spring in a
paddy field, and the soil is then flooded to a depth of about 10 cm.
In autumn the field is drained and the corms dug and stored cool
and dry through the winter.

Joy Larkcom reports that the *Elecocharis* is now more widely
grown than the traditional *Trapa*, and in warm areas can be raised
in a child's paddling pool.

Taro

Specimens bought in London, December

Ginger and other vegetables in the Chinese Agricultural Mission farm in Malawi

Greater Galangal

Languas galanga (L.) Stuntz. (*Zingiberaceae*)
Siamese Ginger, False Galangal

Greater galangal is a spice used in the same way as ginger, which it resembles, except that the rhizome is thinner and the young shoots and leaf bases are bright pink. The fruits may also be used as a substitute for cardamoms, the rhizome as a yellow dye. Galangal has a very long history of cultivation in southeast Asia, particularly in Malaysia and southern China, and it has been imported to Europe since the time of Marco Polo. It is both cultivated and found wild in clearings in the jungle. The roots are used in curries and in satay sauce.

True cardamoms are the seeds of *Ellateria cardamomum*, native of the Cardamom hills in southwestern India. They are still found there in the wild, and cultivated in the hot, wet, leech-infested forests, the plants forming large clumps of ginger-like leaves.

Bamboo Shoots

Dendrocalamus and *Phyllostachys* species (*Graminae*)

All species of bamboo produce edible shoots, and many different species are utilized in China. The bases of the plants are earthed up in winter with mud and manure, and the young shoots cut in spring, as soon as they begin to emerge from the piled-up soil. They are generally cut when about 15 cm long, but some species are left till they are longer. If left too long they become tough; if they are exposed to light they become bitter. After cleaning off the leaf sheaths the young shoots need boiling for about half an hour, or longer, to remove the bitterness but retain the crisp texture.

The large tropical species are the ones generally cultivated for food, but smaller temperate species are edible and often collected from the wild in the mountains of western China.

Turmeric

Curcuma domestica Valeton (*Zingiberaceae*)
Yellow Ginger

Turmeric is another ginger-like plant, used dried and ground to flavour curry and as a yellow dye for wool, cotton and silk. The rhizomes are similar to those of ginger, but smaller and bright orange-yellow inside and require the same conditions as ginger. *Curcuma xanthorhiza* Roxb., also grown in Malaya, is a much larger plant with a thicker, yellow rhizome.

Bamboo shoots in a market in China

Ginger

Zingiber officinale Roscoe (*Zingiberaceae*)

Ginger is commonly grown throughout the tropics, but is thought to have originated in southeast Asia or India, where it has long been cultivated. It had reached Europe by classical times, but was always a rare imported spice. It was one of the first eastern spices to be taken to the West Indies, and by 1547 it was being exported from Jamaica to Spain.

Ginger requires shade, and warm, moist but well-drained soil. It may be planted in ridges like potatoes, but the best ginger roots are grown by planting the tubers at the bottom of a deep trench on well-drained soils. As the shoots emerge they are earthed up with loose, rich soil mixed with manure or compost. This method produces a large crop of very soft, mild-flavoured ginger, from the stems rather than from the roots, suitable for preserving in sugar or slicing with garlic to form the base of many Chinese dishes. Fresh ginger is often sprouting when bought, and can be planted in a large pot in the greenhouse. In temperate areas the tuberous rhizomes are best planted in the spring, so they have the warmest possible growing season.

Greater Yam

Dioscorea alata L. (*Dioscoreaceae*)

Although there are about 600 species of the genus *Dioscorea* found throughout the tropics, most are poisonous because they contain the alkaloid dioscorine. About ten species are regularly cultivated, mainly because they have large tubers, and varieties of them, with less poison, have been selected in cultivation. *Dioscorea alata* is the most widely cultivated and is now found throughout the tropics. In the West Indies alone more than sixteen distinct cultivars are grown. The variety shown here, which was bought in London, is probably one of these; the flesh is pure white, and very pleasant and floury when baked in the oven.

The greater yam is not known as a wild plant, but it certainly originated in eastern Asia. It is widely grown in India, Malaya, Thailand and China and about a thousand years ago spread to east Africa, arriving in the West Indies in around 1500. Other species such as the cush-cush, *Dioscorea trifida* L. with 3-lobed leaves, are native to central America. There is one European species, *D. balcanica* Kosanin, which is native to southern Yugoslavia and Albania. Black Bryony, *Tamus communis* L., is the only species of the yam family found in England. It has characteristic tall climbing stems and shiny leaves, and is conspicuous for its bunches of bright red berries left in the hedges after the stems have died down. The young shoots can be eaten like asparagus, but the tuber is very mucilaginous and it and the fruits have medicinal properties.

The tubers of the greater yam are produced in bunches and are commonly white or deep red, and have been recorded up to 62 kg in weight, sometimes penetrating two metres deep into the ground. Propagation is usually by slicing off the top of a tuber, and planting that in the ground after it has sprouted. Good, fertile soil is required. The plant produces tall climbing shoots with long pointed leaves, which often have bulbils in their axils.

Another species, the Chinese yam, *Dioscorea opposita* L. syn. *D. batatas* Dcne., is a cultivated form of the species *Dioscorea japonica*, which is native to the mountains of China and Japan, northwards to Honshu. It was introduced to France in 1846 at the time of the potato blight, but is now seldom cultivated. The tubers are often elongated and club-shaped; the stems can climb to 3 m, and have edible bulbils in the leaf axils; the leaves usually opposite and broadly heart-shaped.

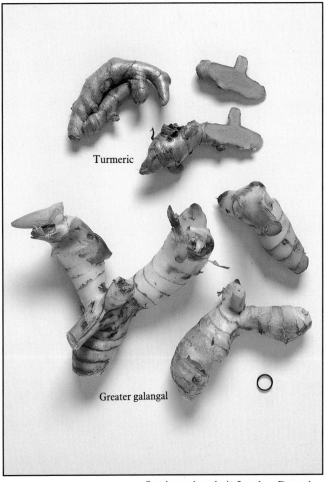

Turmeric

Greater galangal

Specimens bought in London, December

Ginger showing deep planting

239

The kitchen garden at Goodnestone, Kent

Egyptian onion at Wisley

Allium pskemense at Harry Hay's

A trug of shallots, 'Hâtive de Niort'

Onion

Allium cepa L. (*Alliaceae*)
Shallot

Onions and shallots are both forms of *Allium cepa* and are closely related to leeks, chives, garlic and Chinese chives. All these belong to the genus *Allium* and have the characteristic onion smell, caused by alkyl sulphides. The onion is a cultivated vegetable of great antiquity and is not known as a wild plant. It was certainly cultivated by the Egyptians in around 3200 BC, but must have been domesticated earlier, as it is thought to be derived from some species now found wild in the mountains of Central Asia. These have small bulbs and long hollow stems, often with a swelling near the middle. The wild species most similar to the onion are: *Allium oschaninii* O. Fedtsch. from the Pamir-Alai; *Allium praemixtum* Vved. from the Tien Shan and the Pamir Alai; *Allium vavilovii* Pop. & Vved. from the Kopet Dag in Turkmenia, named after the great Russian expert on the origin of cultivated plants; *Allium pskemense* B. Fedtsch., from the Pamir Alai; and *A. galanthum* Kar. & Kir. from the Dsungarian Ala Tau and the easternmost Tien Shan, extending into Chinese Sinkiang. Although all these are closely related diploid species, they cannot be used in onion breeding, because though they can be crossed with the onion, the resulting hybrids are highly sterile.

Onions were commonly grown in Europe in the Middle Ages, and modern varieties have been developed from old ones. The main objects have been to breed resistance to common pests and diseases which affect onions when grown on a large scale. Different bulb shapes and skin colours have remained the most visible differences between varieties, and hotness of taste and sweetness also vary. F1 hybrid seed, which produces vigorous plants of uniform size and shape, is now often planted commercially and is available to amateur gardeners. It is produced by crossing two inbred varieties, one of which has been specially bred to be male-sterile.

Onions may have brown, yellow, white, red or purple skins and may be globe-shaped, flattened globe or spindle-shaped. Those which are grown as annuals for harvesting in late autumn and storing over winter may be either raised from seed, or planted as sets which are small seedling bulbs about 1 cm across. Another group are planted as seed in late summer, usually August, and allowed to stand outside through the winter, before being ready for harvest in midsummer. They are often called 'Japanese onions' as the modern cultivars originated in Japan, and are usually yellow-skinned, but in the nineteenth century autumn-sown Mediterranean varieties such as 'Tripoli' and 'Blood Red' were recommended. Another group of varieties such as 'Barletta' or 'White Pearl' are sown thickly and harvested small for use as pickling onions.

Shallots are like small onions which grow as a bunch of bulbs, and are used when only a small quantity of onion is needed. Many are old varieties, and the Greeks and Romans considered that they originated in Ascalon in Palestine. It is from this that the name scallions originated. Shallots differ in colour as much as onions and in the number and size of bulbs produced. The 'Grey Shallot' or 'echalote grise' is the most highly regarded in France. 'Beltsville Bunching' and 'Delta Giant' are crosses with *Allium fistulosum*.

Egyptian or tree onions produce a head of up to sixteen small onions instead of flowers; sometimes a second umbel grows out of the first, and a few flowers often appear as well.

The potato onion, an old variety, produces several bulbs within the main bulb and bulbils around the base of the mother bulb, and these are planted for the next crop.

Cultivation

Onions do best in a sunny open position, and in well-drained, sandy and limy soil. The soil should not be freshly manured with organic manures, as this is likely to encourage bulb rots, and the place where onions are planted should be moved each year, to prevent a build-up of fungal spores. Inorganic fertilizers such as bonfire soil or soot, and balanced fertilizers such as Growmore

'Torpedo' or 'Red Italian' onion

Pickling onion, 'Paris Silverskin' at Wisley

with as much potash and phosphate as nitrogen are suitable to be used either before planting or as a top dressing around growing bulbs.

Sets, the young bulbs grown especially for planting, should be planted where conditions are less than ideal for onions, or where pests have proved a problem. Small heat-treated sets are less likely to bolt, that is flower in the first year, than are large sets. March or early April, after hard frost has passed, is the normal time to plant, and they are usually planted 5 cm apart in rows 25 cm apart. Wider spacing produces fewer, larger onions. The small bulbs should be planted without firming, so that the tips are just visible. If the soil is wet or heavy, it is worth putting a large handful of coarse sand under each set. It is important to keep the young plants weeded, and free from shading by other vegetables.

Seed should be planted in a fine, warm seed-bed in April, or earlier if a warm position is available. It should be sown thinly in drills about 2 cm deep, and thinned when the seedlings are established to 4 cm apart for smaller onions, or up to 10 cm apart for large ones. Seed may also be sown indoors in February in soil blocks or small pots and planted out in early April after being hardened off. Germination is best at 10–15°C.

Japanese overwintering onions should be sown in August, in the north at the beginning of the month, further south towards the end. The exact timing is important, so that the young plants are old enough to survive the winter, but small enough that they do not go to seed the following summer. The plants overwinter as small bulbs, about ten plants per 30 cm of row, and are thinned in spring to 5 cm apart. They are ready for picking in June and July, earlier than onions grown from sets or seed. A well-drained soil is essential, and a dressing with nitrochalk in January helps prevent disease and produce good growth early in the spring.

Onions which are grown for pickling should be sown in March and April, aiming to grow about thirty plants in a 30 cm square; about fifty seeds will be needed to achieve this density. Harvest is usually in August.

Shallots are planted as sets, ideally about 2 cm in diameter. They are planted in early spring, from January in mild areas and in a warm position. They should be spaced about 15 cm apart, with 20 cm between the rows. The remains of the old stem should only just reach the surface. Weeding is important, especially at an early stage of growth. The bulbs should be harvested in late July and August, and be well dried before being stored. They keep better than ordinary onions, and are often a more useful size for cooking.

Pests and diseases

Onion Fly
The onion fly is like a small, blackish, narrow-bodied house fly, which lays its eggs in the bulbs of young onions. The yellowish maggots eat the bulbs and the leaves soon go yellow and die. Several generations may occur in a single season, and infect larger bulbs as well. Infestations are worse in hot weather and on dry soils.

There are various methods of control. Parsley sown with the onions is said to keep onion fly away, and it is also beneficial to plant onions in a soil previously used for umbellifers such as celery. Once the maggots are present they may be attacked with soot, or with a soil insecticide applied as granules to the soil. As soon as there is any sign that the fly may be there, dig up wilted plants or those with yellow leaves and burn them, with the maggots, and make sure that no maggots are left in the soil.

Small black slugs can also cause damage, especially on rich, moist soils, as they graze off the young roots of the bulbs below the ground.

Fungal diseases
Various soil fungi attack onions, causing rotting of the bulbs, and mildew on the leaves. Onion mildew is worst in damp, humid areas, and can be controlled by dusting with soot or lime sulphur, or a modern fungicide such as thiram. Bulb rots are caused by *Botrytis*, *Fusarium* and *Sclerotium*, all common diseases of bulbs. They can be controlled by spraying with benomyl, or by using seed treated with thiram and benomyl or a recommended fungicide. Well-drained soil makes these diseases less likely, and they are worse in warm, humid weather. All bulbs should be carefully checked for signs of disease before they are stored.

From left: Shallot, 'Hâtive de Niort', 'First Early' (from sets), 'Express Yellow', 'Buffalo' (text on p. 245); 'Senshyu Semi-Globe Yellow' (text p. 247)

Japanese salad onion, 'Hikari' (text p. 245)

White onions in France

Onions drying

'Hikari Bunching' at spring onion stage (text p. 245)

From left: 'Reliance'; 'Ailsa Craig'; 'The Kelsae'; 'Mammoth Red' (text p. 245)

'Crossbow'

'Red Baron'

'Bounty'

'Marion'

'Rijnsburger Jumbo'

'Hygro'

'Carmen'

'Marcel'

'Mercato'

Winter onions for keeping: specimens from NIAB, Cambridge, 20 November

From left: Marshall's 'Autumn Gold'; Marshall's 'Giant Fen Globe'; 'Rocardo'; right: 'Turbo'

'**Ailsa Craig**'   A large variety, suitable for showing if sown indoors in January, and grown on in good conditions. (Shown p. 243.)

'**Bounty**'

'**Buffalo**'   An F₁ hybrid variety for sowing in August, and harvesting in mid summer. Usually a very high-yielding variety, with rather flat bulbs. (Shown p. 243.)

'**Carmen**'   Blood-red scales, pink flesh; a good storer. A Spanish cross.

'**Crossbow**'

'**Express Yellow**'   A Japanese variety for sowing in August and harvesting in midsummer. Bulbs semi-flat. Yields moderate. (Shown p. 243.)

'**First Early**'   (Shown p. 243.)

'**Hâtive de Niort**'   A good traditional shallot, producing 3 or 4 bulbs from each one planted.

'**Hikari Bunching**'   A *fistulosum* cultivar used for spring onions. (Shown p. 243.)

'**Hygro**'   A Rijnsburger type, F₁ hybrid, usually grown from seed sown in spring. Bulbs globe-shaped, with mild flavour.

'**Mammoth Red**'   A large red show onion, from W. Robinson & Sons. (Shown p. 243.)

'**Marcel**' and '**Marion**'   These are new varieties, suitable for storage.

'**Marshall's Autumn Gold**'   Usually planted by sets. Skins pale golden. Bulbs rather flat, of good size, and good for keeping.

'**Marshalls Giant Fen Globe**' syn. 'Fen Globe'   Maincrop, usually planted by sets. Bulbs globe-shaped. Good keeper.

'**Mercato**'   An F₁ hybrid.

'**Paris Silverskin**'   (pickling onion) Usually sown thickly and harvested very small. (Shown p. 242.)

'**Red Baron**' (T & M) Dark red scales, red flesh. A Southport Red Globe hybrid.

'**Reliance**'   syn. 'Oakey'

'**Rijnsburger**'   Maincrop; bulbs round with yellow skin. A good keeper.

'**Rocardo**'   A slightly flattened, red-skinned variety, usually planted from sets. A good keeper.

'**Sturon**'   Open pollinated. Early Maincrop, usually planted by sets. Bulbs rather flat. (Shown p. 245.)

'**Turbo**'   Open pollinated. Maincrop, usually planted by sets. Bulbs rather flat. Said to keep better than the very similar 'Sturon'.

'Sturon' (from sets)

Young plants of 'Mammoth Red'

'Albion'

'Staro'

'Kurenai Red'

'Rosso di Firenze'

'The Kelsae'

Specimens from Wisley, 1 November

'Torpedo'

'The Kelsae' at Wisley

'Albion' An F$_1$ hybrid onion, with perfect globe-shaped white bulb of good size, raised from seed. (Shown p. 246.)

'Kurenai Red' A flattened sphere, with a red skin. (Shown p. 246.)

'Robusta' A Rijnsburger selection, with high yields, good quality and storage. (Shown p. 247.)

'Rosso di Firenze' A red-skinned variety, shaped like a spinning top, wide in the middle and tapering to top and bottom. (Shown p. 246.)

'Senshyu Semi-Globe Yellow' A Japanese variety for sowing in autumn, and harvesting in midsummer. Skins deep yellow. (Shown p. 243.)

'Staro' A small, spherical white onion.

'The Kelsae' A large, show onion; bulbs globe-shaped, with a mild flavour, but do not store well.

'Torpedo' syn. 'Red Italian' A spindle-shaped onion, sweet and mild flavoured, but short keeping.

'Robusta'

Young plants of 'Kurenai Red'

247

'White Lisbon'
'Savel'
'Ishiko Straight Leaf'
'White Flash'
'Hikari Bunching'

'Yoshima'
'Guardsman'
'White Knight'
'WW Bunching'
'Winter Over'

Specimens from NIAB, Cambridge, photographed 10 May

Flowering Welsh onions

'Ishikura'

Spring onions and celtuce in a market near Dali

Spring onions in China

Welsh onions and other vegetables in the Chinese Agricultural Mission, Malawi

Spring or Bunching onions

Allium cepa L.

Spring onions are small specimens of common onion, with a long neck and a small bulb, used raw in salads or in Chinese cooking. 'White Lisbon' is the variety most commonly grown. (The Chinese and Japanese usually use *Allium fistulosum*, often called the Welsh onion, described below).

Spring onions are sown in July in the north to September in the south, to give crops from March to May, and may also be sown from March to June for summer crops. Some protection will be required by the overwintering crop in cold areas. Seed should be sown so that there are about thirty plants in 30 cm square, or about 6 mm apart in rows. The plants should grow fast, so water will be needed in dry weather.

Welsh Onion

Allium fistulosum L.
Japanese Bunching Onion, Chinese Small Onion, Scallions (a name also used for Shallots)

This is like large and very coarse chives, with hollow evergreen leaves and almost no bulb at the base, forming large perennial clumps. It is widely used in Chinese and Japanese cooking as a flavouring in fried vegetables, and may also be used raw as a winter substitute for chives.

Allium fistulosum has been grown in China since prehistoric times, and is thought to have been domesticated in western China from *Allium altaicum* Pallas, a similar wild species found in easternmost Kazakstan and northwestern China. It is not clear how this onion came to be associated with Wales, since it reached western Europe from Russia in the early seventeenth century, but it may be derived from the German *welsche* meaning foreign.

Allium fistulosum has been hybridized with *Allium cepa*, but the hybrids are sterile. One such hybrid is 'Louisiana Evergreen', with the shallot 'Louisiana Pearl' as the other parent. Numerous varieties have long been cultivated in China and Japan, some of which are now available in Europe and America. Most are grown as annuals, although some are perennial and can be propagated by side shoots. 'Ishikura' has a long white stem, and bluish-green leaves. 'He Ski Ko' is an evergreen perennial and very hardy variety. There are several red-skinned varieties including one called 'Santa Claus'!

Welsh onions are grown in the same way as spring onions, described above. Soils should be well drained but moist in the growing season. The modern varieties are self-blanching, but the stem portion may be increased by earthing up with 20 cm or so of soil.

All may be sown in August and harvested in April and May, or planted at monthly intervals from March onwards.

'Guardsman' A hybrid between *cepa* and *fistulosum*, which stands well without becoming strong-flavoured or bulbing.
'Hikari Bunching' A *fistulosum* cultivar, slight bulbing, with good resistance to *Botrytis*.
'Ishiko Straight Leaf' A *fistulosum* cultivar, no bulbing, with good resistance to *Botrytis*.
'Ishikura' A *fistulosum* cultivar, slight bulbing, bluish leaves.
'Savel' A *fistulosum* cultivar, no bulbing; Botrytis-resistant.
'White Flash' A *cepa-fistulosum* hybrid, slight bulbing, good for overwintering.
'White Knight' A *cepa* cultivar, bulbier than most; dark green leaves.
'White Lisbon' A *cepa* cultivar, some bulbing, and quite hardy.
'Winter Over' syn. 'White Lisbon Winter Hardy' A *cepa* cultivar, the hardiest of all the varieties. Rather bulby, with dark green leaves, susceptible to botrytis.
'Winter White Bunching' A *cepa* cultivar, slightly bulbier than average, moderately hardy.
'Yoshima' A *fistulosum* cultivar, bulbier than most.

Garden chives

Chinese chives in the market in Chengdu

Wild chives in Finland

Blanched Chinese chives

Chives

Allium schoenoprasum L.

The slender, hollow leaves of chives are generally used as a flavouring for salads, and may be used fresh or dried. The plant is a perennial, forming tufts of narrow bulbs. The leaves die down in winter.

Chives are found as wild plants in the mountains of Europe, from England and Ireland eastwards to Siberia and Japan with a variety, var. *laurentianum* Fernald, found from Alaska and Washington to Newfoundland. They usually grow in damp meadows on limestone, by streams and on lake shores.

Chives are easy to grow in a cool place in moist, well-drained soil. Clumps may be divided and replanted in spring, or new plants raised from seed. They must not be allowed to become too dry and I have lost the plants in a hot summer by neglecting to water them until too late.

There are several varieties in cultivation, differing in the colour of the flowers, from lilac to flesh pink, and in the diameter of the leaves. Larger forms, with leaves to 50 cm tall, sometimes called *Allium montanum* Schrank or *Allium sibiricum* L., are probably tetraploids, and are found on high mountains and in the Arctic.

Chinese Chives

Allium tuberosum Rottler ex Sprengel
Nira, Kau, Tsoi

This species is commonly grown in China for its flat leaves, which are about 6 mm wide. It is probably a native of China and the eastern Himalayas, and possibly also of Japan. The plants are

A field of chives near Dali, Yunnan

perennial and form dense clumps, with flowering stems about
45 cm tall and umbels of white flowers with pointed petals. A very
similar species, *Allium ramosum* L., a native of Siberia, has flowers
which do not open flat, and petals with a reddish line outside.
Both have been confused under the name *Allium odorum* L.

In China, Chinese chives are used as a vegetable rather than as
flavouring and the leaves are blanched so they look like pale straw.
Light is excluded either by large tiles propped up along the rows
with the gaps sealed, or by having mats suspended on either side
of the plants. A good seakale-forcing pot would be equally
effective. The young flowering shoots are also eaten, but Herklots
reports that they are not blanched.

Cultivation is easy. They may be raised from seed sown in the
spring or by division of the plants. They need good, rich moist
soil. The green leaves may be used in place of ordinary chives, or
the leaves may be blanched in the summer.

Chinese chives showing flat leaves

Rakkyo

Allium chinense G. Don

Rakkyo is grown in China and Japan for its bulbs, which are like
small shallots. It is a native of the mountains of central and eastern
China. The plant is perennial, forming dense clumps of narrow
bulbs. The leaves are hollow, three- or five-angled and bright
green, and are usually three to a bulb. The leaves die down in
early summer, and the inflorescence and new leaves appear in
early autumn. The flowering stem is solid, and has a flattened
umbel of fifteen to twenty purplish flowers. Plants are usually
grown from small bulbs, which are planted out in August or
September, and harvested the following May. They may also be
left for a second year of growth. Light sandy soil and ample
fertilizer are recommended.

Flowering Chinese chives

Garlic harvest in Green Gulch Farm, Muir Beach, California

Garlic

Garlic

Allium sativum L.

In this species the bulb is used for its distinctive and strong
flavour. It is also said to have numerous beneficial medicinal uses,
derived from its natural antibiotic and antibacterial properties. It
is a basic ingredient of nearly all Chinese cooking, and of much of
the cooking of southern and central Europe as well.

Garlic is not known as a wild plant, and is probably derived
from *Allium longicuspis* Regel, a native of central Asia, found in
the Tien Shan, the Pamir-Alai and the Kopet Dag. Garlic has been
grown since the first Egyptian dynasty in around 3200 BC, and
from early times in India and China.

Garlic is now propagated entirely vegetatively and does not set
fertile seed. The numerous varieties must either be very ancient,
or have arisen by mutation and been preserved in cultivation. One
such is the Rocambole or serpent garlic, var. *ophioscordon* (Link)
Doll, in which the flowering stem is coiled when young. Others
have bulbs of different size and shape, skin colour of white, pink
or purple, and various numbers of bulbils or flowers on the
inflorescence.

Garlic is generally planted in spring, in climates with a cold
winter, or autumn in Mediterranean climates. Single cloves are set
firmly in the ground, in sandy soil in a warm position. These often
make single solid bulbs called 'rounds' in the first year, and if kept
overwinter and planted next spring, will form a large, multicloved
bulb. Garlic should be harvested in late July or August and dried
in the sun before storing. In southeast Asia, Dr Herklots records
that garlic is often harvested when immature, and that the leaves
and stem are used as well as the bulb. I have seen what I believe to
be the blanched flowering stems of garlic sold in the markets in
Chengdu and unblanched stems are sold in the west as Suan Tai.

Field of garlic near Ili in Sinjiang, central Asia

Flowering leeks

Leek

Allium porrum L.

The leek is commonly grown for its thickened and overlapping leaf bases, which are generally white. Leeks are harvested from autumn to spring, and generally flower and go to seed in their second summer.

The leek is derived from *Allium ampeloprasum* L., a common and very variable wild species found in southern Europe from Portugal and North Africa eastwards to Turkey, Iran and the Pamir Alai, growing in uncultivated ground, pine forest, cliffs and sandy shores. The usual form has flowering stems to 2 m tall, and numerous yellowish bulbils around the parent bulb. The flowers are white, pink or dark red. Two forms which have bulbils instead of flowers are found wild in western Europe. Var. *babingtonii* (Borrer) Syme has a few flowers in the umbel and bulbils 8–15 mm long. It is found in western Ireland from Clare to Donegal, and in the Scilly Isles, and Cornwall in southwest England, growing on rocky promontories and sandy places usually on offshore islands. It is often associated with early Christian sites and may have been cultivated by the monks as a substitute for garlic.

Var. *bulbiferum* Syme is rather similar, but has smaller bulbils, 6–8 mm long. It is found on Guernsey and in western France. W. T. Strean has pointed out that these varieties probably owe their survival to their bulbils which are a great advantage for a Mediterranean plant which may be unable to set seed in the cooler and wetter summers of northern Europe.

One form of *Allium ampeloprasum* is commonly cultivated in the eastern Mediterranean, and was grown in England in around 1650 by John Tradescant the Younger. This is the great-headed garlic, a hexaploid, which forms large, garlic-like bulbs and numerous bulbils, both around the bulb and among the leaf bases. It forms large heads of flowers but sets few seeds. Kurrat is an ancient variety of leek cultivated in Egypt and the Near East. It is

genetically closer to the common cultivated leek, but is grown for its leaves rather than its stem.

Numerous varieties of leek are now grown, but they differ mainly in the colour of their leaves, their hardiness and in the degree of bulbing at the stem base. Those with blue or purplish-green leaves tend to be hardier, and should stand outside in all but the hardest winters. Commercially grown leeks aim to be about 25 cm long and less than 2 cm in diameter, but the giant pot leeks, which are a speciality of northern England, are grown to be as fat as possible by using much nitrogenous fertilizer over a long growing season.

Cultivation

Leeks like a rich but well-drained soil, with ample nitrogen and organic matter, in an open position. Very good leeks are grown commercially on the peaty fen soils of eastern England. Seed can be sown indoors in gentle heat c. 7°C, in January or February, and the plants grown on before planting out in May. Late varieties can be sown in a seed-bed outside from March onwards, when the soil has warmed up. When the young leeks are about 20 cm tall they are planted out into their final positions, and this may be done any time from June to August; for instance they may be planted in ground from where the new potatoes have just been dug. Extra nitrogen is beneficial at planting time, either from a granular fertilizer or from a watering of manure solution. After planting, watering is important until the plants are well established. Traditionally, leeks are planted at the bottom of holes about 15 cm deep, made with a dibber. They are then merely watered in. Alternatively, they may be planted in the bottom of a v-shaped trench, and gradually earthed up during the growing season. Blanching may also be done using brown paper collars or tubes of black polythene. These methods give a longer white area at the base than if the plants are set on the level and not blanched.

Plants should be spaced between 15 cm apart in rows, or up to 30 cm apart in blocks. Wider spacings give larger leeks.

Diseases and pests

Rust is probably the most serious disease which affects leeks. Orange patches of spores appear on the leaf surfaces; in some seasons the disease is serious, in others it does not appear at all. It is not easily controlled, so any infected plants should be burned before next season's leeks are planted out. Some varieties are more susceptible than others.

Stem and bulb eelworm which affect onions also affect leeks. Leaves become swollen and distorted, and the bulbs finally rot. Again there is no simple cure, so any infected plants should be burned.

Leeks at Villandry

'Alita'

'Rustic'

'Elina'

'Verina'

'Longa'

Specimens from NIAB, Prickwillow, photographed 10 November

'Bleu Solaise'

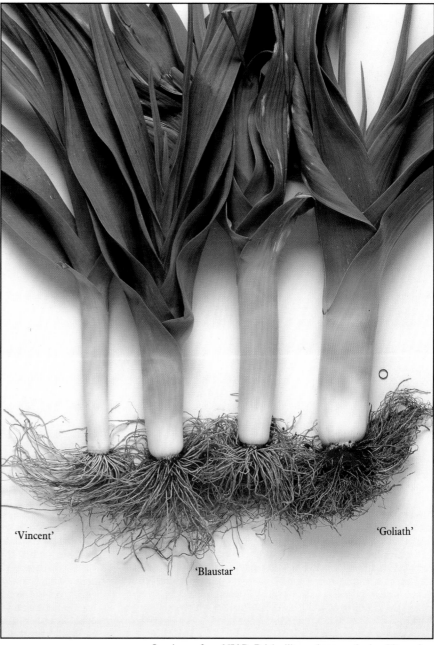

'Vincent'   'Blaustar'   'Goliath'

Specimens from NIAB, Prickwillow, photographed 10 November

'Alita'   Franz Zomer group; ready from September to December; stems naturally about 22 cm long, slightly bulbous at the base. Quite resistant to rust.

'Blaustar'   Blauwgroene Winter group; ready from April to May. Stem naturally about 17 cm long. Hardy, leaves dark green, bluish in winter. Rather susceptible to rust. Can grow very large.

'Bleu Solaise' syn. 'Blue Solaize'   An old French variety, cold-resistant, with leaves blue-green in winter, and standing until spring.

'Elina'   Swiss Giant group; ready from September to December. Stem naturally about 20 cm long of very even diameter. Average susceptibility to rust. Leaves upright.

'Goliath'   Autumn Mammoth group; ready from September and stands well until April. Stem naturally about 20 cm long. Average susceptibility to rust. Can reach a large size.

'Longa'   Bulgaarse Reuzen group; early maturing in September–October. Stem naturally very long, about 40 cm. Leaves light green. Susceptible to rust, and not very hardy.

'Mammoth Pot'   These are fat leeks, grown for their thick stems, for use in winter. 'Musselburgh' is a traditional variety for producing this type of leek, by gross feeding and wide spacing, ready from November onwards.

'Rustic'   A new variety, from Interzaden UK Ltd. A short-stemmed blue-green variety with leaves that turn purple in winter.

'Verina'   Blauwgroene Herfst group; ready from September to December. Stem naturally about 20 cm long. Leaves dark green erect. Very resistant to rust.

'Vincent'   Giant Winter group; ready in April and May. Stem naturally about 16 cm long. Leaves dark green. Very susceptible to rust. Frost-hardy.

'Mammoth Pot'

Leeks in Malawi

White-grained corn for sale in La Paz, Bolivia,
photographed by Sam Phillips

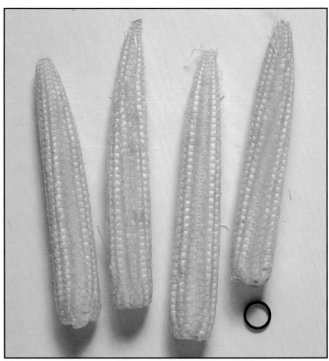

Baby corn: young cobs for eating whole

Sweetcorn

Zea mays L. (*Graminae*)
Indian Corn, Baby Maize

Sweetcorn is a variety of maize which has a grain that contains
more sugar than starch. Maize itself is a very important crop, as
important as wheat and rice, though most of the huge crop grown
in the North American corn belt is for consumption by livestock
rather than directly by humans. In parts of Africa and in much of
Central and South America maize is the staple human diet, either
in the form of porridge or as tortillas. Popcorn is a distinct variety
which has grains containing particles of starch which explode on
heating.

History

Maize originated in pre-historic times in Mexico, but is not now
known as a wild plant. Its nearest wild relative is the teosinte, *Zea
mexicana*, which is found in the mountains of Mexico and

Young maize in China

Guatemala, generally as a weed of open ground where it often
hybridizes with cultivated maize. A second wild related genus is
Tripsacum, of which there are several species. There are three
main theories which attempt to account for the evolution of
cultivated maize: firstly that maize, teosinte and *Tripsacum* are
derived from a common ancestor; secondly that teosinte was the
ancestor of maize, with contributions from *Tripsacum*; or thirdly,
maize is the ancestor of teosinte, with *Tripsacum* as the other parent.

What is certainly true is that maize and teosinte are very closely
related, and that there was introgression between teosinte and the
early cultivated forms of maize in central America. The earliest
archaeological records of *Zea* are from the area of Mexico city,
where pollen has been found in deposits dating from 60,000 to
80,000 years ago, before the area was inhabited by man. This
could be either maize or teosinte, as their pollen is similar. The
earliest, very small and primitive cobs were found in the Tehuacan
caves (see also beans p. 90), dating from around 3500 BC. The
earliest finds in Peru are from the dry coastal zone and date from
1000 BC, and the first whole cobs from this area, dating from
500 BC, show that Andean varieties were already distinct from
Mexican. It did not become a staple crop in North America until
after AD 800.

These early small-grained forms are thought to have been eaten
as popcorn. The early maize growers in South America who first
discovered sweetcorn, valued it as a source of sugar, and as a
means of getting a higher alcohol content into their local beer.
Sweetcorns have been developed, especially in North America, for
use as vegetables, and have been bred to produce good crops
further and further north. Modern American sweetcorns are
divided into groups according to colour of the grain – yellow,
white, blue or variously coloured; and amount of sugar – sugary,
ultra sweet (also called supersweet, extra-sweet or shrunken, from
the appearance of the seed) and sugary enhanced (derived from a
sugary-floury cross).

The quickest-maturing yellow varieties for northern gardens
include 'Early Arctic' (60 days), 'Early Sunglow', a modern
hybrid (63 days) and 'Polarvee' (52–55 days). The traditional
variety 'Golden Bantam', dating from 1902, is rated 78–83 days.
'Seneca Chief', a popular modern hybrid variety, is rated 82–86
days. Popular white-seeded varieties include the early 'Stardust'
(66 days) which can be planted early in spring, and 'Platinum

This red-stemmed variety of maize is commonly grown in the mountains of central Mexico where cultivated maize originated

A mixed group of yellow-seeded, white-seeded and mixed cob types or 'Peaches and Cream'

Lady' (75–85 days). 'Silver Queen' (94 days) is a late-maturing hybrid of good flavour.

Bi-coloured sweetcorns are now very popular. They have a mixture of yellow and white grains. 'Butter and Sugar' and 'Honey and Cream' are both extra sweet, ready in about 80 days. 'Peaches and Cream', especially recommended in Canada, is an early-maturing hybrid, ready in 62–78 days.

Supersweet or extra-sweet varieties include 'How Sweet It Is' (87 days), and 'Sugar Buns' (65–72 days). Many of the supersweet varieties should be isolated from non-sweet varieties of corn, as the sweetness of the endosperm is affected by the pollen they receive.

There are also numerous odd varieties which can be grown for special uses: 'Blue Tortilla' is used for grinding into blue flour; 'Black Popcorn' pops white. 'Baby Asian' and 'Baby Corn' are used very young and the ears are eaten whole. They should be harvested within five days of the appearance of the silks (the styles of the female flowers).

The number of days to maturity given above are calculated for a hot North American summer. Early varieties grown in southern England take much longer to mature. Recommended varieties include 'Kelvedon Sweetheart' 118 days, 'Earlibelle' 123 days (rated 71 days in USA), 'Seneca Star' 123 days (67 days in USA). 'Earliking' (?63–66 days in USA) was good in trials at Wisley. Dates of maturity given for other varieties differ by about the same amount, taking between 50 and 56 days longer to mature in England! The supersweet varieties are now starting to be available in Britain; 'Candle', one of the earliest of the supersweets available in Britain, matures in around 122 days.

Cultivation

For cultivation in northern Europe, seed is planted singly in pots in April in a greenhouse, and the plants put out after hardening off in late May, after all danger of frost is past. These young plants grow on faster if planted out in a frame to give them extra heat. Seed may be sown directly outside in mid-May, but in this case it is better if the soil has been heated by a cloche or sheet of polythene, and the seeded areas are still protected until the leaves emerge. Soil should be well drained and may be slightly acid. It should be fertile, with a good dressing of balanced fertilizer applied before planting.

Young plants should be spaced 35 cm apart in blocks to assist fertilization. They should be earthed up when they are about 30 cm high, to support them against wind and encourage the formation of extra feeding roots. Watering is beneficial when the plants are flowering, improving the quality of the cobs. Diseases are rarely serious in Europe, but there may be outbreaks of smut in which the cobs become grotesquely swollen and blackish-grey with spores. Mice love the newly planted seeds, especially the supersweets, and once they have discovered them will soon clear an area or a group of pots. Birds such as sparrows also find the ripening cobs if they are opened and the grains are left in view.

In America and southern Europe corn is always sown direct into the ground, after the soil temperature has reached 60°F. The seeds are sown in blocks, 2.5 cm deep, and about 15 cm apart, the rows 1 m apart to ensure good pollination. Short-growing varieties may be planted closer. Sowings may be made until July, or until about 80 days before the first expected frost.

A maize field in Malawi, underplanted with beans

A male ear of maize, with one branch abnormally producing grains

The horrible effects of corn smut

'Kelvedon Glory'

'Sugar Chap'

Specimens from Sellindge, photographed 28 August

'Pioneer'

'Dynasty'

'Mellogold'

Sweetcorn planted in a frame, with the top glass removed when the plants grow up

'Pilot'

'Strawberry Popcorn'

'Dynasty'   An F₁ hybrid, ready in around 120 days. Needs ample water at early stages of growth. 16–18 rows of grains.

'Kelvedon Glory'   An F₁ hybrid, ready in around 120 days from sowing in eastern England. Cobs of medium length, 15–18 cm, well-filled.

'Mellogold'   Raised by Rogers Bros. in 1952.

Ready in around 82 days in North America. 14 rows of grains.

'Pilot'   An F₁ hybrid, ready in around 116 days from sowing in eastern England. Moderately filled cobs c. 18 cm long, with 14 rows of grains, 3 per plant. Raised by Rogers Bros. in USA.

'Pioneer'   An F₁ hybrid, ready in around 125 days from sowing in eastern England. High

yield of medium length, poorly filled cobs with 16–18 rows of grains.

'Strawberry Popcorn'   An ornamental variety with short cobs on a plant about 120 cm tall. Must be sown indoors in March in cool climates and planted out in May. The seeds can be used for popcorn.

'Sugar Chap'   An F₁ hybrid, early mid-season (c . 125 days) supersweet.

White Supersweet 'Snowbelle' at NIAB, Cambridge

'Oracle'

'Topnotch'

Male flowers of maize

'Honeydew'

'Sunrise'

'Earlibelle' An F₁ hybrid, ready in around 123 days from sowing in eastern England, 71 days in North America; cobs 16–20 cm long, well-filled, with 16–18 rows of grains. Raised by E. A. Kerr.

'Earlivee' Ready in about 120 days from sowing in eastern England, 63–66 days in North America. (Not illustrated.)

'Eclipse' Raised by Tozer's. Midseason, with around 18 rows of grains.

'Gold Crest' Ready in 67 days in North America. Cobs with 12–14 rows. Raised by Ferry Morse Co. in 1956.

'Green Midget' A variety with short cobs.

'Honeydew' Ready in around 125 days from sowing in eastern England. Long cobs with 14 rows of grains.

'Indian Dawn' Ready in around 125 days from sowing in eastern England. Cobs short, but well-filled, with 14 rows of grains.

'Kelvedon Sweetheart' An F₁ hybrid, ready in around 118 days from sowing in eastern England. Cobs long and well filled, longer than other early varieties. Similar to the American variety 'Earliking'.

'Mellogold' see p. 260.

'Miracle' Ready in around 130 days from sowing in eastern England. Sugary-enhanced, with 16–18 rows of grains.

'Oracle' Ready in around 125 days. Medium to long moderately filled cobs, with 14 rows of grains. Supersweet.

'Snowbelle' A recent white-seeded supersweet variety. Early-maturing, ready in 78 days in North America. 14–16 rows on 20 cm (8 in) cobs.

'Sugar Daddy' This variety seems to have become unavailable since we photographed it!

'Sunrise' Ready in around 116 days from sowing in eastern England. Cobs short, and moderately filled.

'Topnotch' Ready in around 125 days from sowing in eastern England; moderate to well-filled cobs with 14 rows of grains. Supersweet.

'Kelvedon Sweetheart'

'Sugar Daddy'

'Gold Crest'

'Earlivee'

'Mellogold'

'Indian Dawn'

'Miracle'

'Eclipse'

'Green Midget'

'Earlibelle'

Specimens from Wisley, photographed 5 September

Further Reading and most important sources

The Complete Vegetable Gardener's Sourcebook, Duane Newcomb and Karen Newcomb, Prentice Hall Press 1989.

The English Vegetable Garden, written by experts, Country Life c.1912.

Evolution of Crop Plants, N. W. Simmonds (ed.), Longman 1976.

The Gardener's Dictionary, Phillip Miller from 1724, the 9th ed. revised by Thomas Martyn 1797–1804.

The History and Social Significance of the Potato, R. N. Salaman, with a new introduction by J. G. Hawkes, Cambridge University Press 1985.

The Kitchen Garden, David C. Stuart, Robert Hale 1984.

Oriental Vegetables, Joy Larkcom, John Murray 1991.

Peppers, the Domesticated Capsicums, Jean Andrews, University of Texas Press, Austin 1984.

The Potato: Evolution, Biodiversity and Genetic Resources, J. G. Hawkes, Bellhaven Press 1990.

Potato Varieties, photographed by Gifford C. Gates, Potato Marketing Board and National Institute of Agricultural Botany 1981.

The Vegetable Garden, Mme Vilmorin-Andrieux, ed. William Robinson, 1885.

The Vegetable Garden Displayed, Joy Larkcom, Royal Horticultural Society, 1990.

Vegetable Varieties for the Gardener, National Institute of Agricultural Botany 1987.

The Vegetables of Southeast Asia, G. A. C. Herklots, George Allen and Unwin 1972.

Numerous fascinating articles on vegetables and their history may be found in the journal *Economic Botany*.

Index

The common English names and the botanical names of the plants indexed by their text entry, Latin names in italics.

INDEX

INDEX

INDEX